Cunningham 1980

# New Movements in
# Religious Education

# NEW MOVEMENTS IN RELIGIOUS EDUCATION

Edited by
**NINIAN SMART**
**& DONALD HORDER**

## Temple Smith · London

First published in 1975 by
Maurice Temple Smith Ltd
37 Great Russell Street, London WC1

Paperback edition 1978

© Copyright 1975 Colin Alves, Michael C. Brown, C. Edwin Cox,
Julian Frost, Brian E. Gates, Peter Gedge, Jean Holm, Donald
Horder, John M. Hull, Kenneth E. Hyde, O. Raymond Johnston,
Patrick Miller, David Naylor, Richard M. Rummery, Eric J. Sharpe,
R. Ninian Smart, Peter Woodward

ISBN 0 85117 1443

Printed in Great Britain by
Billing & Sons Ltd, Guildford and London

# Contents

## ASPECTS AND ATTITUDES

# Editors' Preface

This is an exciting time to bring together in one volume the many strands of thought and experience which have transformed the concept of religious education in schools during the past decade. What Dr H.F. Matthews described in 1966 as a Revolution in *Religious Education* was only half the story. He has since added a second volume (Matthews 1966 and 1971) and the process is still continuing. The first movement resulted from research based on the insights of sociology and developmental psychology, and reflected too the ferment in Christian theology. The second movement was more radical, bringing to bear questions raised by philosophy, history and curriculum theory. Almost every aspect of the curriculum was affected by these movements, but their effect on a subject which had long resisted change was very dramatic. Change was welcomed because the kind of religious education prescribed by the 1944 Education Act clearly was not succeeding, and the ever-increasing pluralism of British society demanded a fresh approach. The writers of this volume have all been deeply involved in these changes, in school, college or university. Some, in fact, have helped to bring the changes about.

One result of this revolution is that R E teachers are learning to think more as educators, and less as catechists or evangelists. In countries with a long Christian tradition, it is right and proper that a sympathetic study of Christianity should form a large part of the programme, but it does not follow that at this point the school is acting as an agent of the Christian Church: it has its own concern and starting-point, in the concept of education itself. The school cannot be tied to one religious tradition alone without surrendering its own distinctive existence as a centre for open independent enquiry. Though it may wish to help pupils understand more fully their own convictions, and the implications of these beliefs, it also seeks impartially to promote understanding of alternative beliefs and the ability to appreciate and be fair to the religious — and non-religious — convictions of others.

Religious education, however, is not just something that goes on in school; it is a process going on all the time. Many forces are at work, the influence of the home, the mass media, the peer group, and society at large. Some of these forces are more powerful than the school, yet the school has its own special part to play which cannot be delegated to others. Its business is to promote open enquiry into those 'realms of meaning' which are the concern of religion, and to show how these are related to the rest of human knowledge with which education is concerned.

One important practical result of the new-style RE is worth noticing. By forming the habit of approaching other people's religious views fairly and sympathetically one is better able to be patient and objective when discussing other points of disagreement. Religious prejudices tend to be the deepest. When one has learnt to overcome these, it is easier to be patient with those who differ on less important matters. In other words, the 'open' approach to religious education can, in practice, help to promote maturity in personal relationships.

Some readers may think it strange that this book contains no chapter on 'the daily act of worship' prescribed by the 1944 Act. Apart from limitations of space, there were four main reasons why we decided on this omission. The first was that, owing to the restraint imposed by this statutory requirement, the situation is still very confused; more research is needed. The second was that one of our contributors has now written an excellent book on the subject (Hull 1975). The third was that, in a multi-belief society like Britain, an 'act of worship' seems out of place in a publicly maintained school. The fourth was that, in our view, the School Assembly, which has developed from the older custom, is best regarded as an activity of the school as a whole rather than as a part of religious education — the subject of this book.

We hope the book will be of great value to serving teachers and to teachers-in-training in University Departments, Colleges of Education and Polytechnics, as well as to all others who are concerned about this aspect of education and wish to understand the movements that are taking place.

Lancaster 1975

## References

H.F. Matthews (1966) *Revolution in Religious Education* REP
                  (1971) *The New Religious Education* REP
J.M. Hull (1975) *School Worship: an Obituary* SCM Press

# THE APPROACH

# 1 What is religion?

NINIAN SMART

Often it does not matter whether we can define a term. Meaning lies in use rather than a formal translation.

But in the case of religion the definitional problems have intellectual, pedagogical and social (not to say legal) consequences. Thus in the field of religious education, we need to come to an intellectual understanding of what religion is and what the main dimensions of belief, feeling and practice are — so that in the light of this understanding a cogent educational plan can be evolved. Then, at the pedagogical level, we need to understand what elements in human (and in particular young people's) experience are relevant to the religious quest. At the social and legal level: what are the bounds of religious education? How does it engage with other areas, such as moral education?

For these reasons the definition of religion has import.

Of course we should at the outset be clear as to whether we are talking about religion or religions. Perhaps there is no such thing as religion in general — all that we meet are particular religions. However, there are religious sentiments and there are experiences, such as dying, which broadly have a religious significance, so we should not too easily dismiss the concept of religion in general. To this we shall return, but in the meantime it would be best to try to come to a clear view of what *a* religion is, in the traditional and conventional sense. Then we can move on to think about quasi-religions or movements (like Maoism) of a somewhat religious sort even if they purport to reject religion. After that we can, as I have indicated, explore the meaning of religion in general. It will be seen that this procedure is relevant to the distinction sometimes made between explicit and implicit religion (Schools Council 1971).

As for a religion — let us look first at Christianity and then at Buddhism, a good contrast of styles and content. One cannot expect a single core of content in the religions, as has been demonstrated many times in attempts at unity. The demonstration partly springs from the facts of variety, of faith and practice; but it also springs from the fate of unificatory ideologies, such as those of neo-Vedanta. That fate is stated simply. If I claim that all religions really do point to the same truth and I actually specify that truth, as in neo-Vedanta, then surely many traditionalists will reject my description of their faith. Thus many Christians will not recognise the core of their faith as being mystical and non-dualist. On the contrary they may stress the Calvinist distance between heaven and earth. So the unifying doctrine will not command agreement and it will itself become an element in a different religion. The late Aldous Huxley and the Archbishop of Canterbury belonged essentially to different faiths even if the former had in his own mind an ecumenical understanding of Christianity. So then the search for a common core is not fruitful. This does not mean that there are not considerable affinities and overlaps between elements in different religions. Of course there are. But overlaps do not help enough to form the basis of a content-related definition.

So what is to be done? Some throw up their hands and say religion is indefinable. But there is another path — and that is to seek certain common *formal* characteristics of religion. I shall illustrate it by reference to the two religions mentioned above.

I have used this approach in one or two places by invoking a six-dimensional account of religions (Smart 1968). Briefly, this is as follows. First, typically a religion has a system of *doctrines*. Thus in Christianity the Trinity doctrine tries to formalise the implications of revelation. In Buddhism the non-soul doctrine exhibits beliefs concerning the structure of human (and indeed animal and other) existence. Naturally doctrines are not simply metaphysical in aim, but relate in a complex way to practice. Interestingly on one important doctrinal matter, the existence of a creator, Buddhism and Christianity are at odds: another illustration of the difficulties of the common core. Second, religions have *myths*. This is the mythic dimension. I hope it scarcely needs reaffirmation that the word 'myth' is not used in a crude sense (as a story or idea which is false) but more technically as a story of significance somehow depicting, whether in historical event or in imaginative projection, the relation between the transcendent and the human and worldly realm. In Christianity the story of the passion and resurrection of Christ is a central myth. In Buddhism, the story of the Enlightenment of the Buddha and his temptation by Mara, etcetera, is a core myth; of course in the case of the Buddha the transcendent element is not divine, it is rather that extra-mundane state represented by nirvana as the goal and expressed by Dharma (the Buddhist way or teaching) as the message and meaning of what lies in the transactions between here and there. Thirdly, as far as belief is concerned, every religion has a set of social and ethical norms, what I call the *ethical* dimension. In Christianity the central value is love; another is humility (in line with the imitation of Christ and awe before God). In Buddhism, compassion to all living beings is vital, as also a peaceful detached attitude to the normal values of this world. The differing models of Christ, who was crucified, and the Buddha, who died of a digestive complaint at the age of eighty, dictate these norms to a great extent — always remembering the Jewish heritage of Christianity and the early Indian yogic heritage of Buddhism. Doctrines, myths, values — these are the three dimensions relating directly to belief.

On the more practical and existential side: first, a religion involves *ritual*, such as worship. In Christianity, the sacraments are at the heart of the ritual, though other activities such as the singing of hymns can be important also. In Buddhism (save in the Tantra and certain aspects of Mahayana) sacraments are not of the essence. Nevertheless the Sangha (the monastic order) depends upon rituals of initiation, preaching of the Dharma and so forth. First then in the realm of practice and fourth in the total list, there is the ritual dimension of religion. Next, we have to recognize that ritual and other external forms of religion are there at least in part to express and to evoke feelings and *experiences*. Also, experience can spring indirectly and spontaneously upon the religious man — consider Paul on the Damascus Road, the Buddha under the Bo Tree. The love of God in Christianity is inculcated through arousing sentiments via hymns and sacraments; other means are used to induce

serenity and detachment among Buddhists. In addition to the
ritual and experiential dimensions of religion, every religion is
institutionalised, often through a separate organisation or set
of organisations such as the churches in Christianity and the
Sangha in Buddhism. A religion thus has a *social* dimension.

With regard to religions which are coterminous with some
group such as a tribe, there is no strict differentiation out of
religious from non-religious institutions. But similarly even in
'world' religions we may detect what may be called the
superimposition of the religious upon what otherwise would
be the secular. Thus, for example, though marriage can exist
as a 'secular' social institution, in Christian societies and in
Christian thinking it is seen as a sacrament. The concept of
sacrament is superimposed upon the 'secular' situation.

The six-dimensional analysis can be used to see how far
some ideologies may have a religious meaning.

If we consider Maoism, we note that it has a set of
doctrines: it has a mythic dimension (the Russian Revolution, the Long March, The triumph of Mao and so forth); it
has a strong ethical dimension – a new anti-Confucian
puritanism; it has a ritual dimension – rather, the use of the
Little Red Book, etcetera; some experiential aspects –
conversion-experience being important; and of course the
Communist Party and cadres as the institutional transmitter
of the teachings and correct practice. Though Marxism does
not, like orthodox religions, have an other-worldly transcendent reference, and perhaps has some of the dimensions
more weakly than traditional religions, it has a sufficient
resemblance to make it profitable to make comparisons.
Further, since an ideology such as Maoism rivals traditional
religions, the study of religions needs to take it into account.

I conclude from this that the concept of a religion is
non-finite in the sense that, surrounding religions proper, are
certain secular systems of belief which somewhat resemble
them. Thus the study of religion needs to take account of
these ideologies.

There is another lesson to be learned from the six-
dimensional approach, namely that we need to give a rich
account of a religion if we are to bring out its nature. It is not
enough to recount doctrines as though they were meaningful
in themselves outside the context of ritual (worship),

experience and so on. This does not mean that religious education involves direct worship, for the ritual presupposes particular belief and this cannot be counted on or demanded in a plural society. But it does mean that religious education has to explore ways in which the reality of worship and religious sentiments can be conveyed effectively.

The study of religions then in principle is plural and dimensional; and it is non-finite in going beyond the traditional religions to the ideologies and systems which resemble and challenge the religions.

What, now, of the notion of *religion* as distinguished from that of *a religion*?

Here we can perhaps begin by asking what a religious question is. Here we do not mean a question concerning a religion, such as 'Why do Muslims go on pilgrimages to Mecca?' or 'Why do Sinhalese Buddhists lay flowers before the Buddha image in the temple?' Rather we mean a question of human existence to which the religions supply answers. Thus 'Why do men suffer?' 'Why does anything exist at all?' 'What lies beyond death?' — these questions would seem to be religious questions rather than simply questions concerning religion. Indeed in an important sense they do not immediately concern the religions. They spring from problems of human existence and meaning.

Here a word about the meaning of 'meaning' may be useful. When we use the expression in some such phrase as 'the meaning of life' we are not thinking of 'meaning' in the ordinary sense, as applied to words. Rather, we are looking to matters of *value* or *purpose*. If I say that my job is meaningless to me, I mean it has lost its savour, its importance — it no longer seems worthwhile. In other words, the questions of human meaning are essentially to do with value — with its conservation and enhancement. This is why sometimes men are hostile to certain philosophies which in a sense devalue values — such as emotivism, namely the theory that all 'statements' of value, such as 'Stealing is wrong', are all essentially expressions of emotion, amounting to 'Boo to stealing!' So, then, the idea that values are objective — guaranteed somehow either by God or by the structure of the universe or in Buddhist terms by the Dharma — this notion is one which reaffirms the meaningfulness of existence, just as also the historical dialectic in Marxism has a similar effect.

To put the matter crudely, the questions about ultimate meaning that can be regarded as religious are to do with *values*.

'Ultimate': what does this term, which I have so easily and obscurely slipped into the discussion, signify? After all, we may recall Tillich's talk of ultimate concern and the like. For him religion is what concerns man ultimately. Incidentally the formula shows that he is only secondarily concerned with religions and ideologies. Man is an abstraction, likewise ultimate concern. One can understand the drive of his thinking, but he did tend to underestimate the diversity of men and their actual concerns. How then can we understand the inner core of Tillich's idea? I suspect that the word 'ultimate' is not quite right. What he was after was the thought that some of our concerns — our questions about meaning and therefore about value — are deeper and more towards the limits of life than many everyday value-questions.

Let me illustrate. I happen to be concerned about the way universities operate. But this is, though fairly important to me, of less 'ultimate' (that is, deep) concern than the problem presented to me existentially by the death of our youngest child. 'Problem' is of course too weak a word. Death, then, especially when particularised, is a deep concern, or presents religious questions, even if not in a traditional way. After all, I could Stoically hold that death must be accepted just as it is — in modern terms this Stoicism turns out to be J.P. Sartre's existentialism. Incidentally, there is a reason why there is an amplification of the existential impact of death. Apart from the particular sorrow, there is the more general reflection that death threatens values. That is, since much of life seems to get its value from ongoing projects and institutions, death represents a question mark over that value. Hence the grim horror and hopelessness of *On the Beach*. If death claims us, then does it not thereby claim the long-term purposes in which we cooperate with our fellow men?

So then we can reckon some questions about value to be sufficiently 'deep' and serious to warrant their being called religious, even if they are not posed in explicitly religious terms. But since the degree of value is not absolute, but a matter (to be obvious) of degree, it follows that all value-questions have some degree of religious significance. It is only that the more highly charged ones have such an amount of 'ultimacy' that their religious significance becomes obvious.

In brief, Tillich and others have been wrong in supposing that ultimacy is absolute – rather it is a matter of degree of depth.

However, it would be very foolish to think that all value-questions are *ipso facto* religious. Even if such questions are a matter of degree, it does not at all follow that the degree of degree is unimportant. Whether I should have cheese or fruit for the final course of lunch is a value-question, but not deep. It is true that one might consider the choice important (after all, austerity in food is significant in a number of varieties of religious practice). Even so, considered in itself from the 'secular' point of view, the choice is not all that vital. Hence it is a choice which would not normally be included within the ambit of religious 'ultimacy'. In brief then, the *implicit* questions regarding religion and the implicit outreaches of experience arise from those value-questions (therefore related to human life) which are the most important – not just at the limit of ultimacy, whatever that is, but near there, for the truly important questions of value also can raise religious problems and therefore gain religious answers.

Let us expand a little on this point. It is fairly fashionable in these later days to look on life as a series of *questions* or *problems*. That is indeed right from more than one point of view. We live in a plural society where folk, even very young folk, have to make up their own minds, in a context where people generally think, whether in Parliament or in school and whether teaching or learning, that religion is a 'private' matter – a matter for individual choice. Given the previous analysis, all this means that though all value-questions have in principle a religious aspect, in fact it is more practical to see the deeper value-questions as religious. Individual choice is now, in our society and in our world, implicit in the very idea of religious education, so the study of some of these deeper questions will be part of RE.

We can sum up the argument hitherto as follows. Firstly it is important to recognise that a large part of our concern with religion is to do with religions. In other words, religions represent facts and feelings and for this reason represent also the elements of answers to living questions implicit in life. Since ideologies also have a similar role, and have a dimensional analogy to religions, the exploration of religions passes over into the exploration of ideologies. When it comes to considering *religion* (as distinct, at least in conception, from the religions) we are here dealing with 'ultimate' value-questions related to the meaning of human life. And to understand a religion we need to have some grasp of its relationship to these values and meanings.

Since I have on the 'implicit' side stressed the connection between religion, meaning and values, it might be useful to spell out something of the logical relationship between religion and morality — and also in view of what I have said about ideologies, between religion and politics.

First then, morals.

The connection is hard to grasp because morality is both inside and outside religion. It is inside because the ethical is one of the dimensions of religion. After all 'Love thy neighbour as thyself' is one of the two great commandments. But it is outside religion in as much as moral beliefs can be articulated and justified without a necessary appeal to a religious belief-system. It might be argued that *some* ideology or other would be presupposed, but even this is doubtful, for one can have a 'common-sense' morality — perhaps utilitarianism counts as this — which accounts at least for a wide range of moral rules.

We must then move to the question as to what difference it makes if morality is within religion. How does a religious (or indeed ideological) morality differ from a secular or common-sense one? Mainly, I suggest, in the way a religious morality perceives morality itself as being not *just* morality, but also as something religious. This may seem obvious, but it needs further explanation.

That explanation is to do with what may be called *superimposition*. For example, if I wash up, I may regard this service to my family as a way of praising God. It is not that washing up can only be justified in terms of God's command-

ment to me: the reason for doing it has its own common-
sense' justification, for it rests upon respect for persons and
in particular those persons who are bound closely to me by
family ties. But as a Christian, though I recognise this
obligation, I may see my actions as being in continuity with
my Sunday worship. I am (to use the phrase of Brother
Lawrence) involved in the practice of the presence of God.
This, then, is what I mean by superimposition. Loving action
is seen as worship too (though other men might not see it so).
This is the 'superimposition' of religion on morality – though
this is not to say that there is some kind of historical
sequence here. So there is a kind of congruence between
moral questions and those which we have called 'implicit'. In
both cases the questions do not demand religious answers –
in the conventional sense of 'religion' – but they can do so.
Just as the approach to death can evoke thoughts of Christian
or Buddhist survival (different indeed as they are), so too the
approach to moral values – whether to do with killing,
abortion, streaking or whatever – can raise the issue of
whether a religious backing to morality is necessary. But that
presupposition of superimposition is only one (though a
major) part of the story of the relationship between religion
and morality (see Chapter 4).

Similar remarks apply to politics. There again some of the
deeper 'implicit' problems of value and meaning arise. It is of
course absurd here in such a brief compass to say anything
about the various ways in which political institutions in
different countries may operate. But it follows from what has
been said about morals that likewise the political aspect of
human life should in principle attract a superimposed
interpretation. But more particularly we need to consider the
role of political ideologies – as analogous to traditional
religions. If a secular society is also pluralist, partly because
in a secular society there is no immediate cohesion between
people and ideology or religion – if then a secular society is
pluralist, then by contrast totalitarian societies, such as China
and Russia, are not really secular. They may claim to be
anti-religious but they are committed societies analogous to
the Scotland of John Knox or the medieval situation of the
Papacy. In brief the ideological bosses are in their own way
Popes – and they are certainly not attuned to the plural

world of certain Western societies. The democratic theory of such open countries, by the way, is that pluralism is in line with the long search for spiritual truth. So it may turn out in a curious sort of way that my theory of plural politics is in conflict with the ideological stance. But this is only to say that the sort of exploration of religion which logic and pluralism dictate cannot occur in China or Russia. This is a penalty that these countries pay in their search for cohesion.

In brief, then, I have tried to outline what religious and religion mean. The consequences for religious education are fairly clear: it must concern itself both with religions and with values — and both in a plural, not a dogmatic, way.

### References

Schools Council (1971) Working Paper 36 *Religious Education in Secondary Schools* Evans/Methuen.

N. Smart (1968) *Secular Education and the logic of Religion* Faber.

# 2 Why Religious Education?

COLIN ALVES

To define, or describe, religion in one short chapter was a difficult enough task even for someone of Professor Smart's calibre to undertake. To give an adequate answer to the question 'Why religious education in schools?' in the same amount of space is well nigh impossible. The trouble is that any answer to this question is entirely dependent on answers given to two other wide-ranging questions. Only when one has decided what sort of meanings can be given to the phrase 'religious education' can one give a satisfactory justification of religious education within a school context. And one cannot decide on the possible meanings of 'religious education' until one has looked at some of the reasons which have been given for embarking on any form of education at all.

In the hope of being simple and reasonably brief, though at the risk of being superficial, one could say that different views of education spring from different views of the relationship between the individual and the society into which he has been born. If this relationship is seen entirely from the perspective of society, then the task of education will be defined as 'the preparation of the pupil to take his place in society'. This could be seen in purely economic terms (training him to do the job which will best contribute to the material prosperity of society) or in psycho-social terms (conditioning him to fit the role which society has allocated to him). Science fiction from as long ago as Zamyatin's *We* and Huxley's *Brave New World* has pointed up the horrors which could result from the consistent application of this view of education. Not many writers on education would therefore defend such a position. Nevertheless it is a position held, possibly unconsciously, by many employers and administrators, and indeed by many 'men in the street'.

A more liberal view, but one which still starts from the perspective of society, would speak not in terms of 'preparing the pupil for his place in society' but in terms of 'passing on to the pupil his social and cultural heritage'. The experience of men over the centuries is felt to be too valuable to be ignored or lightly dismissed, and so the task of the educator is held to be the 'enculturisation' of each new generation, for the sake of each individual in the new generation as well as for the sake of society as a whole.

When one turns to those who approach the problem by placing their emphasis primarily on the individual, one finds that such an emphasis in fact springs from two quite distinct views about the individual's relationship with society. One view seems simply to exclude society from its considerations: each individual child is believed to contain within himself the seed of his own potential personality; the task of the educator is to help that seed to grow and develop along the lines of the child's own innate individuality. Society, in the sense of the joint experiences and intentions of other people, is virtually irrelevant. The only meaning that the word 'society' can have is as a way of referring to all the other individuals who are similarly developing each into his own full potential, and as such can have no common demands or restrictions to place on any other individual.

The other view which emphasises the individual rather than society, however, sees society not as irrelevant, but as implacably opposed to the developing individual. Society has developed certain structures and institutions which, it is claimed, actively inhibit the fulfilment of most people's potentialities as individuals. Therefore 'education for fulfilment' must be centred on ways of defeating society's inhibiting effects. Education therefore becomes 'a subversive activity' as far as its stance towards society is concerned.

Yet not all approaches which start with the individual dismiss or denounce society so completely as this. There are those who see the task of education as being to help each individual understand society and its cultural heritage, and by using the intellectual equipment which society has itself developed, subject society to critical judgment and then by altering its structures and institutions try to bring about a better society, a better cultural inheritance for the *next* generation to work on in a similar fashion.

Can one usefully apply this analysis, however over-simplified it may be, to the specific area of *religious* education? Obviously there are not many adults who would claim that society will be economically more prosperous as the direct result of the religious education of its children, particularly if the vocational-training aspect of the argument is taken to its logical conclusion. This would mean, of course, that religious education (that is, training in religion) was appropriate for prospective clergy, but for no one else. Absurd as this view may seem, it is certainly one which has often been found among pupils who have been infected by the apparent emphasis their school, or their families, have placed on vocational training. This view of the purpose of education is then applied negatively to religious education. This way of looking at the subject was typified by the girl who once confronted me with 'Why should I have to do RE? I don't want to be a nun! I don't like the uniform!'

Widespread though this view may be among pupils and some parents, it is not likely to be put forward as a serious description, let alone justification, of religious education by those responsible for providing it. However, another version of the 'preparation for his place in society' argument is very frequently brought forward as the *raison d'être* of the subject, by teachers and parents alike. This is the version which claims that religious education is an effective regulator of children's behaviour, and acts as a channel through which the moral demands of society can be conveyed to the child. The fact that the Old Testament contains the Ten Command-ments, and the New Testament contains certain apostolic exhortations to socially acceptable behaviour, makes the Bible appear, in the eyes of many, good material for classroom instruction in 'right living'. At its most banal this view of the subject is exemplified by the headmistress who summoned her RE specialist every time there was an outbreak of writing on the lavatory walls and demanded to know what the RE department was going to do about it. But even at its most sophisticated, this behavioural justification for religious education is too closely tied to one particular view of education to provide a *raison d'être* which would command universal acceptance. Moreover, it fails completely to do justice to the nature of religion. If society wants moral education, then let it call for moral education, and not pervert the nature of another (even if allied) subject in order to achieve its purposes. (More will be said on this issue in Chapter 4.)

When we move to the view that education should enable pupils to enter into their cultural heritage, and apply this view to religious education, then we find ourselves with a variety of propositions which would command considerable support. Very many people would agree with the claim made as long ago as 1938, but still frequently quoted:

> No boy or girl can be counted as properly educated unless he or she has been made aware of the fact of the existence of a religious interpretation of life (Spens Report, 1938 p.208).

This particular form of proposition, however, would not get far enough for some people. They would feel that 'enculturisation' means more than simply making pupils 'aware of the fact' that religious belief has played a part in the past development of our national culture (and indeed of human cultures generally). They would call for some means whereby the rising generation could be persuaded that they need to *enter into* this heritage, to adopt the religious beliefs of their forefathers and pass them on to their children in turn. Two sorts of reason would be given for this plea. One is a basically social one: if our society is to survive in the form in which it has maintained itself in the past, then it needs to use the same building materials as were used in the past. The standards, ideals and perspectives embedded in the Christian gospel need to be maintained, otherwise the whole structure (not just the minutiae of moral behaviour) will collapse around us. Therefore the pupils must be *taught* the gospel, so that they may come to accept the gospel.

The other reason offered in support of such a demand is the simple assertion that pupils must be taught the Christian gospel because the gospel is true, and without knowledge of the gospel our children would totally misunderstand the nature and circumstances of their own existence. It is not merely that the gospel happens to have provided the perspectives around which our society has been structured and therefore to neglect the gospel means to change the character of those structures. Rather is it the case, so this argument would claim, that a society based on the gospel is a society based on truth, so that neglect of the gospel leads not merely to an alteration of structures, but to a collapse of the only workable structures, the only structures which reflect the realities of human existence.

Both forms of this understanding of religious education as 'enculturisation' (both the 'cultural heritage' version and the theologically dogmatic version) are of course to be found, with due variations, in relation to each of the major religions of the world. The same concern is expressed in Jewish schools. As one headmaster put it, 'Unless the boys are established in the faith of their fathers our community will disappear.' Similarly the truth claims made for the gospel by Christians are also made by Jews for the Torah and by Muslims for the Qur'an. The significance of this fact becomes apparent as a particular society like Britain finds itself being shaped by the inclusion of groups from other cultures. The problem then arises, if 'enculturisation' is seen as the aim of religious education, as to which 'culture', which of the competing claims to truth, shall be taught.

But quite apart from these practical problems thrown up by a multi-cultural society, the 'enculturisation' view of religious education is open to much more fundamental objections, particularly when expressed in its theologically dogmatic version. The point at issue is the nature of truth and the validity of different types of truth-claims. What may be fervently held to be true by the religious believer cannot be 'taught' to others in the same way that empirical facts can be taught, because the tests for the validity of truth-claims in the realm of belief are different from empirical tests for validity. Therefore, as Paul Hirst has maintained on many an occasion (see, for example, Hirst 1972, p.8), any teaching of the claims of religion must be accompanied by clear teaching as to the philosophical status of such claims. In other words, any 'passing on of our religious heritage' can only be undertaken in such a way as to invite consideration and evaluation of the heritage, not mere acceptance. This, in fact, is much closer to the last of the views about education identified above, and so can hardly count as 'enculturisation' at all.

We will return to this viewpoint in a moment, but first we need to look briefly at views of religious education derived from a primary emphasis on the individual rather than on society. Certainly the 'growth' school is widely represented within the area of RE, although its heyday there is probably past. For adherents of this view, the task of the religious educator is to facilitate the natural spiritual development of each individual child, by providing wide opportunities for rich spiritual experience, in the fields of the arts, of personal relations and of the numinous (both in contacts with 'nature' and through more formalised acts of worship). Although traditional religious forms and formularies are not often seen as being actually antagonistic to the child's spiritual development, they are frequently dismissed as of no real relevance, and certainly the *study* of traditional systems and institutions would not figure largely in religious education conceived of in these terms.

But it is precisely such study of religion which is the distinctive feature of the final viewpoint we have identified. Religion here becomes the subject matter of study by the pupil and is no longer necessarily the motivating force behind the activity of the teacher. It could provide such motivation, but that would be a largely incidental circumstance. The essential factor in this approach is that the pupil is invited to try to understand the religious heritage (or heritages, if the word can be used in the plural) of his society (or of mankind in general) and, having understood, to assess the significance and value of this heritage for the future of mankind, or at least for his own future development as an individual.

In setting out this analysis of different positions in the way I have done, it will have been increasingly obvious that my own sympathies lie with this last viewpoint, both in the field of educational aims generally, and in the specific field of religious education. My prime emphasis would be on the personal development of the individual, rather than on his 'enculturisation', though I would claim that in the process of individual development the past experiences of mankind cannot be ignored, and the belief systems which have been developed in the past, the 'vehicles of vision' of other times and of other places, all merit careful study if one's own beliefs, symbols and aspirations are to be both effectual and realistic. Sometimes an advocate of this type of religious education will speak as if the individual pupil remains devoid of beliefs, symbols and aspirations of his own until such time as he has studied those of other men, but this is simply not how human beings operate. There is no such thing as a total absence of beliefs. Therefore part of the task of religious education must be to help the pupil examine his own existing beliefs so that he can properly understand these, as well as the beliefs of others. He will need to examine the probable sources of his beliefs, and he will also need to establish the validity of such beliefs, both his own and those held by other people. Only then can he claim to be in any way 'educated' in the area of religion.

But surely, some will say, this is a very personal task, virtually a private task? It may be something people need to do, and they may need some sort of help in order to do it properly, but this help is not something which should be expected of a school; it is not for a school to intrude into such personal matters. Even the study of other religions is bound to have repercussions on the pupils' own beliefs to some extent, so the school should avoid *all* treatment of religion — let that be left to the churches, or to one's family or friends, or to one's own private reading. In any case, the schools are busy enough with all the other things they have got to teach, basic things such as literacy and numeracy as well as desirable subjects like environmental studies, home economics and so on.

It is when one is faced with arguments such as these that the question with which we started emerges at last in its full completeness — Why religious education *in schools*?

The answer to this question surely springs out of the need for religion and education each to provide a context for the other. Religion, to be understood and appreciated properly, needs to be set in a full educational context; and the educational process, in order to be complete, needs to take account of the phenomenon of religion with all its claims about human nature and human destiny.

Those who teach in Sunday School, or who are engaged in church work among adolescents, know how difficult it has become to confine their teaching to 'strictly religious' matters. A whole range of social and scientific material has to be tackled in order to make sense of the religious material, otherwise the latter becomes divorced from everyday life, and pupils develop the 'dual frame of reference' so graphically described by Ronald Goldman (Goldman 1964, p.242). But it is not only that 'religious learning' will remain isolated (and therefore ineffective) unless it is deliberately incorporated into the general pattern of learning. There is also the need to ensure that religious thinking is open to the same educational checks and refinements as thinking in other areas, otherwise the impression will be created that religion is 'above' the processes of rational thought. While one recognises the validity of the claim that the area of religion cannot be *confined* to the rational, one must nevertheless reject any suggestion that religion is essentially irrational and has no relationship with the ordinary demands of reason. Therefore the place where pupils are being taught to think about the experiences of life in general must inevitably be the place where they are taught to think about religion. If it is not, then religion will be regarded as something which is so special that it has nothing whatsoever to do with the rest of human experience or human thought.

The reverse of this coin is also true. If a school's curriculum does not include the study of religion then, as we have seen, the school might appear to be saying that religion is too special for it to handle; but it might equally appear to be saying that religion is so irrelevant to normal living that the pupils need not bother to take any account of it.

Perhaps the most contentious issue here is where a school can 'take account' of religion without actually having a subject called Religious Education on its time-table. Further consideration will be given to this question in Chapter 12, but it is worth reminding ourselves here and now of the exact wording of one of the most widely quoted official statements about religious education, namely the passage from the introductory chapter to the Crowther Report:

The teenagers with whom we are concerned need, perhaps above all else, to find a faith to live by . . . Education can and should play some part in the search (Crowther Report

1959, vol.I p.44).

It should be noted that the subject called Religious Education is not actually referred to in this passage at all. And indeed many teachers of other subjects, and many general, non-subject teachers, would claim that they were most definitely playing some part in their pupils' search for a faith to live by. Teachers of English Literature (or of the literature of other cultures), of all forms of Social Studies, of the arts, even of the sciences, are all developing perspectives on life which will help shape the pupils' beliefs about life, their attitude to life, their 'faith to live by'. Is it therefore necessary, if achieving just this is indeed our aim, to introduce a subject which deals specifically with 'religion' as such?

The answer to this question must depend on one's view of education as a whole. If one believes that basically education is 'enculturisation', then one can point out that it would be perfectly possible to develop the traditional perspectives of society through studying the society's literature, arts and so on, or through participation in ceremonies such as the more traditional types of school assembly. However, if one believes that education must involve some *critique* of the culture(s) which one has inherited, then it would seem a very strange approach to the study of men's beliefs if one were to look at beliefs solely as they are expressed through literature and the arts, and to ignore the conscious structuring and practical outworking of belief which is to be found in the religious systems of the world. Of course whether one actually sets aside a fixed period each week, carefully labelled, in which to carry out this task is another question. But, quite clearly, on the view of education which is being put forward here, *some* articulated programme of study of the phenomenon of religion must find its place on the curriculum of every school. (Or, where the pupils are too young to embark on actual study, the school must provide a conscious programme of preparation for subsequent study.) It is surely a betrayal of educational principles to suggest, even by mere implication, that the 'faith to live by', towards which each one of a school's pupils is struggling, should be anything other than an informed and intelligent faith.

The responsibilities of schools in this area are therefore clear and inescapable, whatever the legal requirements of any current Education Act may or may not be.

## References

Crowther Report (1959) *15 to 18: a report of the Central Advisory Council for Education (England)* HMSO.

R.J. Goldman (1964) *Religious Thinking from Childhood to Adolescence* Routledge.

P. Hirst (1972) 'Christian Education: a contradiction in terms' Learning for Living vol.II No.4 SCM Press.

Spens Report (1938) *Report of the Consultative Committee of the Board of Education on Secondary Education with special reference to Grammar Schools and Technical High Schools* HMSO.

# 3 The home, the community and the peer group

## KENNETH E. HYDE

*Dr Hyde is Staff Inspector for Religious Education for the Inner London Education Authority. The views expressed are those of the author and do not necessarily represent those of the authority.*

There is a growing realisation of the extent and importance of the social pressures which affect the developing attitudes and beliefs of children and young people. Teachers are aware that school is only one influence upon their pupils' development, and they face the considerable responsibility of enabling the young to understand the nature of these pressures and of helping them to adopt a rational rather than a prejudiced response to them. Just exactly what are these pressures? This chapter will examine briefly some of the issues in what is a very complex situation. How do social institutions affect religious beliefs?

### Religion in contemporary society

'Religious belief' is a phrase that is used in a number of different ways; some use it to imply commitment to credal statements of orthodox Christian institutions; others extend it to include those of other faiths. It is also used in surveys of popular belief to include assent to quite vague statements about belief in God, or in Jesus, or in the Devil, or in life after death. Comparisons between different surveys of beliefs need therefore to be made with caution. For such reasons, some more precise measure is often sought, and regularity of church attendance is frequently employed. Even here caution is needed. It has long been argued that the falling rolls of the churches point to a long period of declining belief; although different denominations arrive at their statistics in different ways, the trends are very similar.

There can be no doubt about this statistical decline within

the main stream of churches in the United Kingdom. Church statistics over a long period show a continuing loss; in the Church of England, with its statistics expressed as a proportion of the relevant population, the trend is very clear. Between 1930 and 1960 infant baptisms fell from 699 per 1,000 live births to 554, and by 1970 this had fallen further to 466. The decline in measurable activities has been very marked in the past decade; in 1960 of the age-group 12–20, 34.2 were confirmed, but in 1970 this had fallen to 19.7. Easter communicants in 1960 were 70 per 1,000 of the population aged 15 or over; in 1970 this had fallen to 51 (*Church of England Year Book* 1974). Similar figures can be cited for the Free Churches; the Roman Catholic Church is least affected, and some pentecostal 'sect' type churches flourish.

Martin (1967) has made a careful analysis of findings from many surveys, and shows that in fact something like 45 per cent of the population attend church at least once a year; 35 per cent never attend, and 20 per cent come for special occasions. It appears that with the many social changes of recent years, church attendance and support has changed its pattern; Martin suggests that the same total number of people come to church, but simply appear less frequently. Even so, a quarter of the population is in church at least once a month.

This is important, because it has been shown that young people who attend church at least once a month tend to retain positive religious attitudes, whereas non-attenders deteriorate not only in their attitudes, but fail to gain insight into simple religious ideas (Hyde 1965).

Patterns of church attendance and belief are also affected in other ways. Nelson and Clews undertook a study in Dawley, the original centre of Telford New Town in Shropshire. They developed a measure of urban mobility related to the period of residence, distance moved, density of population, and time since leaving the parental home, and found that high mobility was correlated with non-orthodox beliefs and with non-attendance at church. Social mobility in which people move to another position within the social hierarchy was associated with a higher proportion claiming church membership and higher rates of church attendance; it was not closely related to denominational change, as it is in

the United States. It must be remembered that the consequences of increasing urban and social mobility affect
families, and not just individuals; children and young people
will be more subject to these changes in their families.

Yet in spite of much social change, a great deal of stability
remains. Alves, using an attitude scale developed for his
particular research, found marked regional differences in
secondary school pupils' attitudes to religion, ranging from
the least favourable in London and the South East, through
those of the Northern industrial conurbations, the Midlands,
the South West and the North, to Wales, where the most
favourable attitudes were found. This finding is strikingly
similar to the data for overall church attendance gathered by
the count on a national scale in 1851 (see Gay 1971 and
McLeod 1973).

But when the counts have been completed of what is
specific and measureable, considerable vestiges of religious
belief remain. Because 35 per cent of the population never go
to church at all, it cannot be assumed that all of these are
committed atheists or agnostics. Working-class communities
are well-known to be considerably estranged from the
churches. This is true even for the Roman Catholic church,
which has in some places the reputation of being the church
of the poor. A recent study by L. Moulin has shown that in
England, just as in the United States or on the Continent
there is a marked social distance between this church and the
poorest social classes. For all denominations, this may be
affected by the social mobility of those poised between
clearly manual and clearly middle-class positions, especially
when a move towards higher status is reflected in the social
status of the housing area in which individuals live (Panton
1973).

However, local knowledge can be a corrective. By its level
of church attendance the East End of London must be one of
the least religious areas of the country. The twenty-five
parishes of the Church of England have between them an
electoral roll of no more than 1,400 out of a population of
168,000 for the borough of Tower Hamlets. Contact with
local people shows that many of them have a simple
traditional set of religious beliefs: clergy refer to the large
number of 'God-fearers' in their parishes, and inscriptions on

even the most recent head-stones in Tower Hamlets cemetery
bear tribute to this innate belief. Little study has been made
of this area of subterranean theology, although some start has
been made by Towler and Chamberlain (1973) who have
described some of the religious beliefs of what they call
common religion, the large grey area which exists as an
important part of the religious orientation of ordinary
people. These beliefs are thematic in form, not systematically
elaborated, and bear little reference to the beliefs and
practices of the recognised religious denominations. Christianity is seen primarily as a system of ethics — doing good,
helping lame dogs, and living decently. Prayer or religious
belief is seen to have an efficacy that presupposes some kind
of supernatural power; such belief is thought to be natural,
most people were brought up to believe in this way. Belief is
related to problems of the meaningfulness or the meaninglessness of suffering and evil.

One other reservation must be expressed regarding surveys
of beliefs and conclusions based on them. Many such surveys
have shown that those professing religious belief tend as a
group to be prone to conservatism, racially prejudiced and
authoritarian. Since this is evidently not true of a sizeable
minority of believers, attention has been given to different
styles of religious belief, notably by G.W. Allport. It is
beyond dispute that some people out of strong religious
conviction have been intolerant, cruel, censorious or self-
righteous, while others have shown kindness, humility and
patience and have been open to new vistas of goodness and
truth. Allport thus distinguishes between intrinsic and
extrinsic belief. Extrinsic belief is the characteristic of those
who use religion, who turn to God but do not turn away
from self; prejudice enhances their esteem; religion provides
them with a tailored security. It offers relief from guilt,
promise of reward in heaven against fear of failure in the
present. The broad spectrum of those thus described is so
considerable that some further classification has been suggested, to cover the 'indiscriminately pro-religious'.

The intrinsically religious person, on the other hand, is
seen as subordinating personal motives and practices to the
precepts of religion. For such people religion is open and
growing, individual and exploratory; even though strongly

committed to active membership of religious organisations, they do not depend on them for support for their beliefs, and may quite likely be found to disagree with many orthodox positions. (A brief summary of this position is to be found in Wright [1972]; longer discussions are offered in Strommen [1971].) It could be that in periods of reduced religious practice, the decline more affects extrinsic belief; there is however no evidence to support such a conjecture, even though it helps to explain current trends.

## Home influence

The work of our schools has to be seen against this background of social interaction. Pupils will be the products of their society, affected by the conventions and traditions which are accepted by their particular social group, focused in the attitudes of their homes. They are likely to have some knowledge of people with different styles of religion; they probably react against established ideas and institutions, but are sympathetic to what seems radical and sensitive to human need.

There can be little doubt that the strongest single influence upon any child is that of his home. The roots of maladjustment in most cases lie in the home; equally the child who develops normally, enjoying happy and satisfying relationships alike with friends and adults, has learned this adjustment from his home. The results of the deprivation of affection in early life are now well-known; similarly, children who grow in an atmosphere in which there is frequent expression of warmth and affection, identify themselves with these same parental attitudes. In terms of moral development, there is evidence that the use of physical discipline, in which in any way the parents' power over a child is asserted, leads to the development of a moral attitude based on fear of detection and punishment, whereas a much healthier moral development results from the psychological appeal to the child's need for affection, or to his self-esteem and his concern for others (Allinsmith 1960).

Much less attention has been paid to the influence of parents in the development of religious attitudes, but it may be surmised that similar processes are at work, so that a strongly religious authoritarian parent is likely to see — to his satisfaction – a similar religious attitude developing in his children. Whether this continues into adult life, or whether it is rejected in adolescence, is difficult to predict; the latter alternative is not uncommon. That parental influence is a strong factor in establishing religious attitudes is well attested. Thus, Wright (1958) in a study of 300 sixth-form boys found that parental influence appeared to be the strongest of all external influences in the formation of religious attitudes.

There are many exceptions; some children who have been without any religious influence in their home lives have later accepted a religious commitment with eagerness, while others have rejected the religion of their childhood. In a study of Jewish university students in England, West found that the students' commitment to their community was closely related to the participation of their parents, yet although many parents succeeded in influencing their children not to leave the Jewish community, they had less success in teaching them the Jewish faith. Even among those who had also attended Jewish schools some were rejecting their Jewish religion. It was also established that those who moved away from the position of their parents were not much influenced by their university experience; they had decided what life they wanted to lead before coming to university, that is, while they were still at school.

*The influence of school*
How much influence has school in the formation of religious attitudes? Taylor was at pains to compare attitudes of sixth-form pupils from county secondary, Church of England and Roman Catholic schools. In his sample he found little difference between the attitudes of students in the county and Church of England schools, whereas those of the Roman Catholic students suggested a much greater school influence, though only when the school was supporting parental attitudes. Without this support, church schools had no more influence than county secondary schools. Similar results can be cited from some interesting studies carried out in the United States (Greeley and Gockel 1971); the importance of this study is that in a very different educational system, the same effects are observed. There is however nothing

startling in these conclusions; school life suggests very many areas where only with parental support can the school's values be accepted by their pupils; the school reinforces home influence, it does not supplant it. In their Dawley survey Nelson and Clews asked adults about the schools they had attended in childhood, but were unable to find any evidence that attending a church school affected church attendance later in life.

A not dissimilar problem has been faced by the Farmington Trust in ascertaining the effect of particular schools in helping pupils to become morally educated persons. Sugarman (1973a) observes that if some variation in a school can make its influence more effective, it follows that the inverse can make it less effective, and that in some circumstances, 'less effective' crosses the zero point and becomes 'detrimental'. He says this in the light of his hope that next to the home, school is a more formative influence than the mass media, the neighbourhood, and other social influences. He argues that given the home background that children have, the school may make a difference in their moral development. He cites a study by Power of delinquency in twenty secondary boys' schools, which found that there was within any school little difference in the delinquency rates of boys from different districts, but substantial differences between boys from similar districts in different schools. Statistically the effect of the school was greater than that of the district. Similarly, in a study of his own, restricted to five schools concerned with the attitude of altruism, when allowances were made for home background, in two schools altruism scores tended to rise with the age of the pupils, in two more they tended to stay at about the same level, and in one school they declined with age, so that two schools seemed to have increased altruistic attitudes while one actually decreased them (Sugarman 1973b).

When Alves looked for factors within schools which had associated with them pupils with more favourable religious attitudes, he noted that the teachers had more than five years teaching experience, and that much longer teaching service was associated with the most favourable pupil attitudes. He commented that a third of the teaching force in religious education had at the time less than five years experience. The status given to the subject proved to be important, and apart from other considerations, the younger and the older teachers were related to higher attitude scores than those in the middle of their careers. The teacher's involvement with the social activities of the school and the methods he employed in the classroom were also to some extent contributing factors.

### The influence of the peer group

The influence of the peer group in adolescent development is considerable; while there has been no significant study of its effect on religious development, more general studies give an indication of its importance in this area.

Dunphy (1963) provided some insight into the function of the adolescent group. It begins at an earlier stage of development as a small clique of about six friends of the same sex; the friends are chosen because they subscribe to a similar system of values (and in consequence will tend to reinforce parental norms). There is strong conformity within a clique to its leader, who exercises a great deal of authority. As adolescence is reached, there comes the beginning of group interaction between cliques of opposite sexes which develops into a full 'crowd' structure, with up to four cliques involved. The leaders begin to form a mixed group, and the fully developed 'crowd' results, with new cliques of mixed sexes. By late adolescence the crowd has begun to disintegrate, breaking into smaller cliques of couples, each of whom has only a loose association with a group of a few other couples. Seen from this perspective, the peer group offers a very effective means of social growth during a period of rapid development and personal uncertainty. Security is found in the various styles of group membership and participation, and the apparently aimless chatter of such groups gives in fact an opportunity to develop powers of conversation with others of similar ability and background. The adolescent finds in the peer group support and approval from his peers; he cannot risk the ridicule of his friends, and so his behaviour is very conformist. 'While it endures, it is the most formative influence in the life of the average boy or girl . . . [it] does more to bring about normal social growth than do teachers and parents combined' (Cole and Hall 1969 p.347).

There is nothing in the many studies of peer groups' influence to suggest that in respect of moral or religious matters they normally exert any influence other than that of society as a whole. But Sugarman (1967) has suggested that a high commitment to the teenage role involves a rejection of subordination to adults, and thus leads to poor conduct in schools and low conformity to school norms. This he found to be particularly true when pupils came from home backgrounds of a lower intellectual quality, in itself also associated with under-achievement at school. Ambitious pupils find cliques of comparable peers; those who are strongly committed to the youth culture rebel against the norms of the school, academically they perform below expectations, and have poor chances of a successful career. This youth culture is that of the non-mobile working-class, and for its heroes there are the 'pop singers, song writers, clothes designers and others [who] have mostly achieved their position without long years of study, work or sacrifice'. This Sugarman compares with the lower-class youth culture described by Hollingshead in the United States, in contrast to the middle-class youth culture that is strongly focused in the High School, with its wide range of extra-curricular activities. By comparison with the latter, English secondary schools have nothing like the range of social activities, and are far less willing to accept adolescent norms, for example in matters of dress, than the American.

It would seem that the only strong religious influence is to be found in the specifically church-based youth groups, voluntarily selected by young people, usually with parental support or sympathy. In such groups the same pressures are exerted, but now in a positive religious manner; adolescents in such groups tend to find, with growing maturity, partners from the same group, and in time become the young marrieds by which the life of the churches is perpetuated. But for the most part, the general pressure of peer groups would seem to be opposed to church affiliation, and to discourage religious attitudes.

*Changing attitudes among pupils*
An interesting comment on the extent to which the attitudes of young people have changed in recent years was provided

by replicating in 1970 a survey that was first carried out in 1963 (Wright and Cox 1971a). As part of his study of Sixth Form Religion, Cox (1967) had included in his survey a number of questions relevant to a protestant ethic. The respondents had been asked to indicate whether ten issues, such as gambling, drunkenness, sexual intercourse before marriage, war or use of nuclear weapons was always wrong, usually wrong, sometimes wrong but usually excusable, never wrong, or if they had not made up their mind. Seven years later the survey was repeated in the same schools. It was found that apart from an increased polarization about smoking, there had been a shift of judgment in every other area towards a more qualified, lenient or undecided position, although there was a strong condemnation still against stealing and colour bar. A very significant shift towards a more permissive sexual ethic was found.

The results also showed that these changes were as marked among the frequent church attenders as among the non-attenders. This is more surprising when it is recalled that girls tend to be more religious; yet the survey showed a trend for girls to change more than boys. Although the association between religion and moral judgment is still strong, it has nevertheless become weaker than it was, and offers some challenge to the widely-held point of view that religious commitment conserves religious belief, or that religious and moral beliefs are functionally related. It is a striking indication of the sensitivity of young people to contemporary attitudes and values, and shows how quickly they respond to them.

In parallel analysis of these findings (Wright and Cox 1971b) a considerable decline in support for the legal provision for religious education was found, and much less general acceptance of the divine authority of the Bible. While the sixth-form girls remained significantly more favourable in their attitudes than the boys, they had nevertheless changed more than the boys in virtually every instance explored. The authors commented that they had no evidence with regard to changes in the content and method of religious education in the schools sampled, but were inclined to think the situation was much as it was seven years earlier.

*Some effects of immigration*

So far this discussion has been almost entirely concerned with the Christian faith and with indigenous white children. Yet in most of the urban areas large numbers of school children have parents who were born abroad, especially in the West Indies or in Asia. Their presence in the community has brought a growing awareness of other great world religions, or of different styles of Christianity. But little attention has been given to the religious and moral problems of the children of these minorities, although schools inevitably become aware of them, and in some ways, actually create them. It is in school that cultural adjustment begins to take place, and for some groups this is critical, as for example, the insistence by some – but not all – Muslim groups that their daughters must be educated in single-sex schools. In a conference of Sikh teachers working in English schools it was reported that 'since Christianity was predominant in schools, Sikh children often considered their own religion inferior and did not want to adhere to it' (*The Times Educational Supplement*, 29 June 1973).

There are obvious strains for new immigrants which are bound to be known to their community, and can affect the attitudes of their adolescents. Thus Hashmi (1966) while explaining the Muslim attitude to sex and marriage, which is almost puritanical, remarks that many men, particularly those that have left home for the first time, tend to behave in a rather immature fashion during the settling-down period in this country, and take liberties with their cultural code of behaviour. It is not surprising that in our contemporary society Hashmi wonders if the next generation will continue to be loyal to the ways of their community, or will become 'dark Englishmen'. He thinks that religious and family ties are likely to diminish, though he hopes that despite the problems, a new generation of British Muslims will arise with a blending of the healthier aspects of both societies and perhaps the best of both worlds. Seen by an external observer, it becomes more clear that the problem will be whether the second generation will find a restriction of opportunities; if so, they are likely to become inward-looking with less chance of a multi-racial adaptation developing. But perhaps the Muslim world is ripe for the kind of upheaval

that took place in Christendom at the Reformation (Butterworth 1969). Meanwhile, Muslim religious instruction is
organised at local mosques, and peripatetic Muslim teachers
visit some schools for withdrawal classes where there are
sufficient pupils to warrant such an arrangement.

Rather more than half the New Commonwealth immigrants come from the West Indies and by religion are
Christian. Despite their faith, they have many cultural
differences from the indigenous community in the urban
areas where they have settled. Hill (1970) has described how
in these depressed working-class areas, most of the churches
are at their weakest, lacking lay leadership and resources.
Unable to make any appreciable impact on the neighbourhood, these tiny communities have been bewildered by the
rapid changes immigrants have brought, and have not been
able to provide an effective ministry for them. For a number
of reasons relatively few West Indians have settled in English
churches, and instead have turned to the new Pentecostal
Assemblies, wholly organised and led by immigrants, a
movement which Hill sees as a religious response to the
experience of social deprivation, and which he expects to
become a major religious movement within the next decade
or so. Schools with West Indian pupils are well aware of the
exclusive nature of the beliefs and practices of sect members;
it is an interesting comment that in many schools traditional
biblically-based religious education is much more acceptable
to the pupils than the religious studies which elsewhere are
slowly taking its place.

*New religious movements*

In the meantime, significant religious movements are taking
place in which some young people are closely involved. At a
time when there has been a widespread movement away from
the churches and traditional expressions of religious belief,
there has been a noticeable degree of attention given to
astrology and various forms of occultism, so that the first
issue of the magazine *Man, Myth and Magic* sold 800,000
copies. Students and older pupils may have periods of
fascination with the ouijah board; the practices of witchcraft
which have had some occasional press notoriety seem to
attract mostly a somewhat older age-group. But there can be

no doubt that there is a great deal of popular attention to various forms of Asian meditation in which the young are much involved. Transcendental meditation groups are multiplying, and several Indian gurus such as the Maharishi Mahesh Yogi have their English following. Yoga, which in recent years has exploded as a gentle form of physical education for the not-so-young, is now beginning to attract a thoughtful audience interested in its philosophy. In the United States the 'Jesus People' have become part of the religious scene, and in some parts of England indigenous communes have been established. Leech (1973) thinks that the Mod/Rocker period and the hippy period, with its overtones of interest in drugs, have proved to be dead ends, and have been replaced by a new search for spirituality by adolescents, and claims a basis for this in the ideas of the musical hits of the day.

The more extreme instances of these movements are mainly to be found in the larger cities, especially London, but their presence is an indicator such as Leech suggests. A great majority of religious education teachers would probably agree that while many adolescents are quite unattracted by the churches, most of them are very much interested in fundamental religious questions, and are in the process of finding their own individual position and philosophy.

*Religion in an open society*
It is important to look at the general social trends that are affecting the growth of religious and moral attitudes in the light of the discussion in the previous chapter of the nature and place of religious education in an open society. A truly pluralistic society does not merely tolerate diversity, but values and nurtures it. There is an evident danger that minorities may at best only be tolerated, and a probability that some will continue to be effectively ostracised and rejected. In contemporary society there is an increasing emphasis on achievement, and at times there can also be seen the emergence of new minority groups of the weak, the mentally and the physically handicapped, and the old.

To what extent is society open, or becoming more open? If religion is thought of as belonging to the realm of the optional, thus making it a private affair, ways must be found to prevent conflicting and contradictory values dividing society to the point where there are no shared values. It is the task of religious education to work towards a climate of opinion that respects the choice by an individual of a religious commitment that really makes a difference to his personal and group style of life, rather than towards a society in which people of different faiths live side by side only to the extent that they do not find anything seriously at stake in their differences. But with this must go an openness that is constructive, appreciative, ready to learn and willing to share.

## Conclusion

In such a complex area as the formation of religious beliefs, no single factor can be seen as dominant. The acceptance or rejection of religion, and the particular style of religion which is accepted or rejected, seems to depend most of all upon the idiosyncrasies of particular personalities. Different research studies accept different criteria for what comprises religious belief and behaviour, which adds further confusion (Spilka 1971). For the present purpose it is sufficient to see the greatest single influence as that of the family, in which children's attitudes are first shaped. Family life can have bad effects — it is the principal source of maladjustment in childhood — but fortunately most families are supportive and genial. The attitudes they pass to their children are those of their own social group, modified by particular parental points of view. It is within the family that children are first exposed to the values of the mass media — television, radio and newspapers are for home consumption — and these values are accepted or modified by parental attitudes.

Next to the family the school may be the greatest single influence upon children; schools can reinforce the positive attitudes of parents, but have little power to substitute alternative systems of values. Much work needs to be done to help children and adolescents look objectively at the whole inherited spectrum of values, attitudes and beliefs. Home and school together (both products of particular social backgrounds) considerably influence the choice of a peer group in adolescence; the attitudes of this group become determinative through adolescence, and are not likely to be modified until full adulthood has been achieved.

In this situation, young people are very sensitive to

changes in public attitudes, and in this sense are indeed the children of their time. Part of today's situation is the increasing pluralism of society, and here the task is to assist pupils towards a sympathetic knowledge of the different systems of belief they are bound to encounter, rather than to encourage a superficial tolerance which can be easily shattered in situations of stress.

# References

W. Allinsmith (1960) 'Moral standards: II The learning of moral standards' in D.R. Miller and G.E. Swanson, eds. *Inner Conflict and Defense* Holt, New York.

C. Alves (1968) *Religion and the Secondary School* SCM Press.

E. Butterworth (1969) 'Muslims in Britain' in D. Martin, ed., *A Sociological Yearbook of Religion in Britain* 2 SCM Press.

L. Cole and I.M. Hall (1969) *Psychology of Adolescence* Holt.

E. Cox (1967) *Sixth Form Religion* SCM Press.

D.C. Dunphy (1963) '. ᵉ social structure of urban adolescent peer groups' *Sociometry* vol.26 pp.230–46.

J.D. Gay (1971) *The Geography of Religion in England* Duckworth.

A.M. Greeley and G.L. Gockel (1971) 'The religious effects of parochial education' in M.P. Strommen, ed. *Research on religious development* Hawthorn, New York, pp.264–301.

F. Hashmi (1966) *The Pakistani Family in Britain* Community Relations Commission.

C. Hill (1970) 'Some aspects of race and religion in England' in D. Martin and M. Hill, eds. *A Sociological Yearbook of Religion in Britain 3* SCM Press.

K.E. Hyde (1965) *Religious Learning in Adolescence* Oliver & Boyd.

K. Leech (1973) *Youthquake* Sheldon Press.

H. McLeod (1973) 'Class Community and Region: The Religious Geography of Nineteenth-Century England' in M. Hill, ed. *A Sociological Yearbook of Religion in Britain 6* SCM Press.

D. Martin (1967) *A Sociology of English Religion* Heinemann Educational.

G.K. Nelson and R.A. Clews (1971) *Mobility and Religious Commitment* University of Birmingham Institute for the study of worship and religious architecture.

K.J. Panton (1973) 'The Church in the Community' in M. Hill, ed. *A Sociological Yearbook of Religion in Britain 6* SCM Press.

C.H. Povall (1971) 'Some factors affecting pupils' attitudes to religious education' M. Ed. thesis, University of Manchester.

M.J. Power et al (1967) 'Delinquent Schools?' *New Society* 19 October.

B. Spilka (1971) 'Research of Religious beliefs: a critical review', in M.P. Strommen, ed. *Research on Religious Development* Hawthorn, New York, pp.485–520.

M.P. Strommen, ed. (1971) *Research on Religious Development* Hawthorn, New York.

B. Sugarman (1967) 'Involvement in Youth Culture, Academic achievement and conformity in school' *British Journal of Sociology* vol.18 pp.151–64.

(1973a) *The School and Moral Development* Croom Helm, London.

(1973b) 'Altruistic Attitudes in School' *Journal of Moral Education* 11 February.

H.P. Taylor (1970) 'A Comparative study of the religious attitudes, beliefs, and practices of sixth formers in Anglican, State and Roman Catholic schools' M. Phil. thesis, University of London.

R. Towler and A. Chamberlain (1973) 'Common Religion' in M. Hill, ed. *A Sociological Yearbook of Religion in Britain 6* SCM Press

V. West (1968) 'The Influence on parental background on Jewish university students' *Jewish Journal of Sociology* vol.10.2.

D. Wright (1958) *Problems of Religious Education in Grammar Schools*, M.A. thesis, University of Birmingham.

(1972) *A review of the empirical studies in the psychology of religion* Association for Religious Education, Sutton Coldfield.

D. Wright and E. Cox (1971a) 'Changes in moral belief among sixth-form boys and girls over a seven-year period in relation to religious belief, age and sex difference' *British Journal of Social and Clinical Psychology* vol.10, pp.332-341.

(1971b) 'Changes in attitudes towards religious education and the Bible among sixth-form boys and girls' *British Journal of Educational Psychology* vol.41, pp.328–341.

# 4 Morals and religion

PETER GEDGE

*Millions of words have been written and spoken in attempts to clarify and define these two concepts. In this chapter 'Morals' will refer to theoretical and practical answers offered to the serious question 'How ought we to live?' As space is limited, 'Religion' is here limited to the Christian religion, although the problem of the relation between morals and other religions is increasing in importance in British education.*

### Morals without religion?

'Please Miss, I don't believe in God. Why shouldn't I steal?' This question from a teenage girl typifies a still common view about the relationship between morals and religion. British Protestantism has traditionally had a strong moralistic strain and ordinary people have tended to summarise Christianity by Christ's second great commandment 'Love your neighbour' (at least to some extent) while rather neglecting the first, 'Love God', except at times of crisis like birth, marriage, death or Dunkirk. When the 1944 Education Act was drafted amid the physical and ideological conflicts of the Second World War and decreed that Religious Instruction should be given in every County and Voluntary school, leading Christians might well have thought that this gave the churches a chance to save the country for Christianity, but public opinion was more vague. 'Parents think it's good for their children in the same way as school milk,' one headmaster is reported as saying. In practice the work in schools tended to continue the tradition enforced in 1870 by the London School Board, which decided that in its schools the Bible should be read and such moral instruction should be given based thereon as was suited to the children's capabilities. Post-war Agreed Syllabuses may have included sections for older pupils on ethics, but the material suggested was almost always confined to biblical references, bearing witness to the almost universal assumption, at least among leaders in education if not the teachers, that morals depended on the Christian religion for their basis.

However in 1955 Margaret Knight, a Humanist psychologist, prevailed upon the BBC to allow her to broadcast on 'Morals without Religion', thus bringing to more public notice a philosophical commonplace — the view that morals and religion had perhaps no necessary connection. Moreover deteriorating figures for juvenile delinquency and crime in general were said to cast doubts on the effectiveness of a moral education based on religious instruction. That the popular press then saw fit to make this a headline story and that vigorous protests were made by hundreds, from archbishops to housewives, serves to show how far public opinion on this subject has changed in the last twenty years.

The 1960s saw searching criticism directed against RE both by teachers themselves and by people outside the schools. This reflected the secularisation of society increasingly noted and discussed throughout the decade and the theological and ethical uncertainties illustrated by John Robinson's famous book *Honest to God*. Surveys demonstrated the futility of the traditional Bible-based syllabuses. Loukes summed it up well. 'Let them know the Bible, it was said. We tried with a wealth of ingenuity and concern to let them know it. And at the end they hardly knew the first thing about it.' (Loukes 1965, p.57.) Nor did adolescents show much grasp of the meaning of the biblical narratives. What they were interested in, according to Loukes, were ultimate questions of meaning and purpose, provided that these were discussed openly and seriously at a level relevant to their own experience and progressing through analysis to the pupil's personal choice.

He made the claim: 'Religious Education and Moral Education both begin in the same area and are searching for the same discovery. The experience and first analysis of it are the same. So while, in principle, it would be perfectly possible to conduct ME and RE in separate courses, it would be difficult to avoid such an interaction between them as this would make the exercises a little absurd.' (Loukes 1965, p.109.) If ME were 'properly conducted, . . . it would soon begin to raise religious questions.' This approach to the problem of RE was a valuable suggestion. However, the label subsequently attached to it, the 'Implicit Religion' approach, indicates that if it is adopted as the sole approach to RE and ME, it may not do justice to a proper concept of RE, because it is too easy for the distinctively transcendent elements in religion to escape attention, and it might hinder a proper treatment of ME by assuming a theistic basis to morals.

## The independence of morals and religion

A common educational aim now is personal autonomy based on reason. Supporters of this view tend to insist on the independence of morals from religion and their arguments can be roughly divided into three groups.

First it is maintained that there is no logical connection between the two. Although leading philosophers have for centuries put forward with impressive detail the view that man's sense of obligation — the sense that there are certain things that he 'ought' to do — implies a transcendent personal will as its source and ground, equally important philosophers have insisted that this is not a logically valid argument but rather a valuable insight for many which expresses the importance to be attached to moral claims. Against the view that the existence of God and theological facts about his nature show that man is subject to a moral law, is put the almost universally-held philosophical tenet that no moral judgment can be made on the basis of a factual premise, usually summed up as 'You cannot deduce an "ought" from an "is".' Similarly those theologians who claim that man's relationship with a Creator-God leads to moral obligation base this claim on a prior assumption, that man ought to obey his Creator, quite apart from the problem of whether he is God's creature or not.

The second group of arguments turn on the ancient question: 'Is good good because God commands it, or does God command the good because it is good?' The attempt to define 'good' as 'what God commands' faces two types of objection. The first is empirical. There is the question which perennially puzzles even religious people: 'How can we be sure that we know what God's commands in a given situation are?' Then can we be sure that religion in general, or

Christianity in particular, really shows us what true goodness is? The other type of objection centres on another common tenet of moral philosophy, 'the autonomy of the human will', that is, the fact that ultimately our actions depend on our own free choice in the light of good reasons. Such objectors ask 'Why ought I to obey God's authority?' since it is not logically inconsistent to say that God is omnipotent and omniscient and yet also wicked; also no amount of theological statements of fact can relieve man of the need to decide morally for himself. The attempt to base morals on Christ's example meets similar objections. Even more fundamentally some insist that an action done in obedience to an external command is not really 'moral' at all but simply 'infantile'.

The alternative probably more acceptable to most Christians, that God commands the good because it is good, is held to demonstrate the 'autonomy of ethics', that ethics is independent of religion altogether. For it makes sense for a believer to ask if God's commands are really good, in which case he is on the same footing as a non-believer in that both accept in practice that the sole morally good reason for doing good is that it is good; no link with God is logically necessary.

The third group of arguments are more empirical and centre on the effects on the agent of his particular views about the basis of his morals. If someone is good for the prudential reason that good actions will be rewarded by the God who lays down the rules, some thinkers regard this as a despicable motive quite contrary to the disinterested morality advocated at the end of the previous paragraph. The utilitarian argument that morals should be linked with religion because moral action is thereby made likely is criticised on the ground that the empirical evidence to support such an argument is hard to obtain, since it would require very large-scale research to test for any association between religion and morals, even assuming that one could measure such an association and be sure that no third factor was involved. Actually it does seem safe to say that there are and have been people who have firmly declared their agnosticism or atheism and whose behaviour has been at least as 'moral' as that of contemporaries who claimed religious faith; and many Christians are very sceptical of arguments purporting to show that the 'good atheist' is a crypto-Christian.

## Moral education in the curriculum

This philosophical climate is affecting the schools, and ME is beginning to emerge as a curriculum area separate from RE. Further justification for this is found in the philosophy of the curriculum based on Phenix's 'Realms of Meaning' and Hirst's 'Forms of Knowledge' (see Phenix 1964 and Hirst 1965. These argue that the total curriculum should cover various areas and involve the use of various modes of experience and forms of knowledge which are fundamentally different in character and employ distinctive concepts. Among these areas are aesthetics, the sciences, religion – and ethics. Teachers are beginning to support this move towards an independent ME on two practical grounds, even if the evidence is inconclusive. Some doubt if RE contributes much, if anything, to the shaping of pupils' moral attitudes. Also the traditional link between morals and religion is being queried more on the ground that any negative attitude to religion and RE might have adverse effects on a pupil's own morals. So in the past few years there have been two notable attempts in England to apply current findings in philosophy, psychology and sociology to the specific problems of ME. The two research teams involved were led by John Wilson and Peter McPhail.

Wilson has been developing his theories for some years, with a greater emphasis on the philosophical analysis of what constitutes a moral person. His team was financed by the Farmington Trust and its first major publication was *An Introduction to Moral Education* (Wilson et al 1967) which became a standard text. It is a sign of the times that Wilson tried to avoid such traditional issues as specific authorities or sets of moral values and concentrated instead not on the content of morals but on the criteria by which we judge between moral principles. He set out to show people 'how to do morality', on the analogy of doing science as opposed to doing, for example, literary criticism. The result was the discovery of a creature known widely as 'Farmington Man', a valuable analysis of what Wilson claimed to be the skills necessary to make good or reasonable moral decisions and to act on them. He gave these skills four basic titles derived from Greek for convenience (the basic meaning of the Greek term is added in parenthesis): PHIL (like) i.e. the attitude that other people matter; EMP (experience) i.e. insight into others' and one's own feelings; GIG (know) i.e. knowledge of relevant facts and mastery of relevant social and moral techniques; KRAT (control) i.e. bringing the above components to bear on situations, and the translation of decision into action. 'Farmington Man' has appeared in various versions since and the most up-to-date and complex model appears in Wilson's useful 'compendium' on ME (Wilson 1973, pp.36ff), perhaps to be known as 'Warborough Man' after the new Trust sponsoring his research. Wilson's pioneering work has been valuable in clarifying issues in ME, but his *Teachers' Guide* is rather authoritarian in argument and, in spite of his attempt to concentrate on skills, he has based his system on the central 'component' (p.28) or 'principle' (p.31) of 'treating others as equals' which is not so self-evident as he seems to think.

McPhail came into ME via Social Psychology, and after leading a Schools Council Project on ME in Secondary Schools went on to similar work with younger pupils. The emphasis of his first project was not on philosophical analysis but on meeting the expressed needs of adolescents for help in increasing their understanding of what makes an action good or bad, and in finding solutions to inter-personal difficulties by educating them to choose. The Project's first handbook, *Moral Education in the Secondary School* (McPhail et al 1972) contains some theoretical discussion, including a survey of various forms of motivation for moral behaviour, which was a crucial issue for the Project. But the main emphasis of the book is on discussing the application of research to practice, referring to the well-received 'Lifeline' series of materials published for the Project by Longman's. These take situations within adolescents' experience and use them to help young people to 'a considerate style of life' based on rational choice, sometimes in conflict with social norms. The team's view on the relation between ME and RE is that, although not identical, they inter-relate, if well taught, and are not or ought not to be, in any sense in competition. It is argued that ME is best given not as a separate subject but as part of the work of various Departments, and their illustrative time-table assumes that in fact RE and the Humanities will take the major responsibility.

### Moral education as part of religious education

This view that ME should be more consciously provided for — though on a clearly 'open' basis making no necessarily religious assumptions — had been drawn quite prominently to teachers' attention in 1969 by a pamphlet entitled *Humanism and Christianity: the common ground of Moral Education* (Hemming and Marratt (1969), pp.38–165). In this James Hemming, a Humanist educational psychologist, and Howard Marratt, a Christian RE lecturer in a college of education, summarised the results of over three years' discussions among a group of Christians and Humanists involved in education. This concluded that between the extremes of those who would base ME on a Biblical, or Christian, content or would exclude almost all reference to religion as a source of ME, there was a growing body of opinion which held that children's moral insight might best be developed by bringing them into contact with a variety of material revealing common and differing viewpoints, both religious and non-religious. Dearden's influential *Philosophy of Primary Education* (Dearden 1968, p.88) strongly supported such an approach and maintained that in the Primary school the teacher's task in education about values is not that of firm insistence so much as of disclosure, which could take place through the history of religion and religious literature among other subjects.

That ME should be part of the RE curriculum can also be argued from the logic of the concept of religion itself. Religions normally involve a creed, a cult and a code of behaviour, or, as Ninian Smart suggests in Chapter 1, religion is a phenomenon with six major dimensions, one of which is ethical. Therefore, if one accepts the major aim of RE as being to create the capacity to understand and think about religion as a phenomenon and not just one religion in particular, and if an adequate presentation of religion is to be given to a pupil, then during his school career the total RE curriculum should include study of ethical aspects of more than one religion and/or philosophy. A corollary of this, of course, is that to teach a religion simply as a code of ethics is not doing justice to the religion. This caveat is worth making since there is a widespread tendency at all levels of education to reduce RE to ME.

Wilson arrived at a similar conclusion from another direction in his book on *Education in Religion and the Emotions* (Wilson 1971, pp.62ff). If one accepts that ME is concerned with the education of behaviour (what to do) and the emotions (what to feel) and defines ME as education which aims to develop the moral components of 'Farmington Man' (described above), then RE will be one of the curriculum subjects contributing to ME, especially in the development of EMP and KRAT.

*Implications for teachers of religious education*

What are the implications of this discussion for teachers of RE? First we must take note of the recent change at all levels in the climate of opinion about ME. The former assumption that morals were linked in some way or other with religion in general, or Christianity in particular, is no longer so widespread. The dominant philosophy of education aims at developing knowledge and understanding in pupils leading to a personal autonomy based on reason. This attitude is increasingly to be found among teachers entering the profession and among the pupils they try to teach. So those RE syllabuses which simply try to give teaching on morals supported by Christian texts may well be inadequate for the present situation, as even many Church schools recognise.

ME, instead of being a minor offshoot of RE, is emerging as a curriculum area in its own right which deserves conscious effort by all schools. The public sees teachers not simply as purveyors of skill and knowledge but as moral agents, and they will continue to be called on to exercise a very real moral function. However this function is exercised indirectly as well as directly, and there is a reluctance to attempt to confine ME to specific periods on the time-table. RE is considered to be only one of several subjects which can contribute to ME, and this should encourage RE teachers further to greater cooperation with colleagues. On the other hand, some are beginning to say that RE and ME should be kept entirely separate lest any negative feelings aroused by RE should have an adverse effect on the other.

No RE is adequate which fails to include in its total syllabus over the eleven to thirteen years of a pupil's schooling suitable study of the ethical dimension not just of one religion but of alternative systems of belief and non-belief. Young people expect this, and Christians can accept that a mature faith entails personal choice which is not best served by education in only one tradition. This does not, however, mean that a teacher's position need be permanently on the fence. Pupils do not necessarily respect more the teacher who is always open and uncommitted. What is vital is that whatever a teacher's own commitments are, he must respect the individual pupil's integrity and leave him really free to come to his own decisions. This is not only good educational philosophy; it is good theology too.

RE cannot be reduced to ME without ceasing to be RE and depriving a pupil of what is claimed to be a justifiable part of his education. Equally, ME which confines itself to rationalist assumptions or fails to ask basic questions of meaning, purpose and value is inadequate. Such questions are common to ME and RE, so a proper ME will include not merely the skills of moral decision-making but also content, and a fair survey of the range of answers to its questions will include answers given by at least two or three alternative traditions, religious and non-religious. For, as the analyses of Wilson and McPhail show, the really crucial question in ME is how one is motivated to exercise fully one's personal autonomy based on reason. Paul's dilemma is still with us. 'The good which I want to do, I fail to do; but what I do is the wrong which is against my will.' Various ways of meeting this dilemma are still offered for our consideration. It is not quite as easy as some educators seem to think to answer the question which a lawyer once put to Jesus: 'Who is my neighbour?'

## References

N.J. Bull (1969) *Moral Education* Routledge.

R.F. Dearden (1968) *The Philosophy of Primary Education* Routledge.

Bishop of Durham (1970) *The Fourth R: The Durham Report on Religious Education* National Society and SPCK.

J. Hemming and H. Marratt (1969) *Humanism and Christianity: the common ground of Moral Education* Borough Road College, Isleworth.

P.H. Hirst (1965) 'Liberal Education and the nature of knowledge' in R.D. Archambault, ed. *Philosophical Analysis and Education* Routledge, pp.113–38.

E. Lord and C. Bailey eds. (1973) *A Reader in Religious and Moral Education* (Part II) SCM Press.

H. Loukes (1965) *New Ground in Christian Education* SCM Press.

P. McPhail et al. (1972) *Moral Education in the Secondary School* Longman.

C. Macy, ed. (1969) *Let's teach them right* Pemberton.

P. May (1971) *Moral Education in School* Methuen.

P.H. Phenix (1964) *Realms of Meaning* McGraw-Hill.

J. Wilson (1971) *Education in Religion and the Emotions* Heinemann. (1973) *A Teacher's Guide to Moral Education* Chapman (N.B. Bibliographies)

J. Wilson et al. (1967) *An Introduction to Moral Education* Pelican.

# 5 'Readiness' for religion

BRIAN GATES

'Don't call me a teacher; call me a fellow-learner.' In our contemporary concern with a child-centred curriculum or with personal autonomy as the goal of education, there is horror at the thought of imposing any ideas or beliefs on another. 'He must make up his own mind, work it out for himself.' To such thinking formal provision of RE in the home or in the school might qualify as the major offender. 'Give me a child until the age of seven, and you can do what you like with him later.' Once this kind of association is made, who could be surprised if a young Primary teacher, charged with the responsibility for RE, were to recoil at the prospect. But imagine the relief if he subsequently heard that on psychological grounds children cannot understand religious concepts before adolescence. Here would be final proof that RE is none of his business.

Psychological considerations are relevant to both the theory and the practice of RE. What understanding of religion are children and young people capable of? Is understanding religion the same as religious understanding? If not, how are they related? How does understanding develop? This chapter will seek to assess the conclusions drawn from recent research and comment on their potential application for the classroom.

*Religious development: the spectrum of research*
Two major emphases stand out in recent research on children's religious development. While they are sometimes presented in opposition to each other, it is helpful to see them as at different ends of the same spectrum, which runs between the purely cognitive and the purely affective approaches. We shall consider six writers in the order in which they would appear on this spectrum starting at the cognitive and finishing at the affective end. The writers are

Goldman, Elkind, Godin, Madge, Robinson and Paffard.

## COGNITIVE STAGE THEORY
Reference to a developmental sequence in the formation of concepts of number, space, time and of powers of logical reasoning has become a commonplace in educational psychology (see Beard 1969 and Furth 1970). Piaget's studies spread over half a century are better known today than ever. Latterly, attempts have been made to apply his approach to children's understanding of religion. The result is 'God-concept readiness' (Williams 1971). To demonstrate what is meant by this sort of talk we will take examples from three of its most influential exponents.

### Goldman: God and Jesus
If any one person is responsible for making teachers in England conscious of 'stages in religious thinking', it must be R.J. Goldman. His research at the beginning of the 1960s was widely reported and the evidence he presented of children's difficulties in understanding biblical concepts was a major factor in the shift from the Bible to a 'life theme' emphasis in the newer Agreed Syllabuses.

Goldman (1964) examined the understanding which boys and girls between six and eighteen years had of three biblical stories (Exodus, Burning Bush, Temptations) and the ideas of God and Jesus contained in them. By presenting three pictures with which those interviewed might identify, he obtained further comments on their notions of biblical authorship, Church and prayer. As a result he described three main steps in religious thinking corresponding to Piaget's own schema:

INTUITIVE (pre-operational, unsystematic, egocentric, till 7/8 years)
*Why was Moses afraid to look at God?*
'He hadn't spoken politely to God.'
'Moses didn't like to see God burning in the fire.'
*Why didn't Jesus turn the stone into bread?*
'God said that if you ate bread alone you wouldn't live . . . You should eat something else with it — butter.'

CONCRETE (Content-dominated, 8—13 years)
*Why was Moses afraid to look at God?*
'Moses thought God would chase him out of the holy ground because he hadn't taken off his shoes.'
*Why didn't Jesus turn the stone into bread?*
'Jesus didn't believe in the devil, he didn't want to do it just for him. He's bad.'

ABSTRACT (formal operations, hypothetical and deductive reasoning, 12/13+)
*Why was Moses afraid to look at God?*
'The sight of God was too much for human eyes. It's too tremendous a vision. Moses knew this and was afraid.'
*Why didn't Jesus turn the stone into bread?*
'It was a case of good against evil. It would be a victory for evil against God, if he did it.'

The order of these stages is invariant. Transition between them is apparently more related to mental age than chronological age. But at any age the limiting influence of this developmental sequence is such that all religious thinking is affected:

| | |
|---|---|
| Ideas of God: | omnipotence and omnipresence |
| Miracles: | their explanation and significance |
| Christology: | the distinctiveness of Jesus as a man, his perfection |
| Good and evil: | temptation, the devil, divine judgment |
| Bible: | its origin and authorship, its isolation in time or contemporary relevance |
| Church: | what it is and why people go |
| Prayer: | reasons for praying and the effectiveness of doing so |

Goldman points out that below the mental age of thirteen, thinking on any of these topics will be 'operationally' limited. This verdict applies to both the logical quality and the religious quality of thinking, since for Goldman 'theo-logic' depends on a prior capacity for logic. Not until late adolescence does genuine religious thinking become possible; previously it is better described as 'pre-religious' (stage I) or 'sub-religious' (stage II) (Goldman 1965).

Since the topics covered by Goldman's interviews were typical of the agreed-syllabus RE that had predominated in English schools until the 1960s, the implications for teaching were seen to be dramatic. To avoid misunderstanding that might persist into adulthood, the teacher was advised to beware of direct biblical (or doctrinal) teaching and instead to concentrate on enriching and enlarging children's general experience of life. Their lives could then be illuminated by the direct use of religious language at a later stage.

*Elkind: religious identity, denomination and prayer*
At the same time that Goldman was interviewing children in the West Midlands and South of England, David Elkind was extending his application of Piagetian methods to deal with children's understanding of religious identity in Massachusetts, USA (Elkind and Flavell 1969). But where Goldman had restricted his investigation to Anglicans, Nonconformists and 'Non-attenders', Elkind dealt successively with Jewish, Catholic and Protestant children (Elkind 1961, 1962, 1963). He concentrated on several components of religious identity (Elkind 1964a, 1964b):
  — what characteristics are shared by all members of the group?
  — how is membership attained?
  — what is the distinction between membership of a religious group and any other groupings — ethnic/national?
Again Elkind found that understanding of these various components of religious identity developed according to the familiar sequence of stages:

INTUITIVE (pre-operational, undifferentiated, egocentric, until 7/8 years)

*What is a Jew?*
'A person.'
*How is a Jewish person different from a Catholic person?*
'Because some people have black hair and some people have blond.'
*What's a Protestant?*

'I don't know.'
*Really?*
'Well maybe it's something that makes you feel happy.'

CONCRETE (8–11 years)

*How can you tell a person is a Catholic?*
'If you see them go into a Catholic church.
*What is a Jew?*
'A person who goes to Temple and to Hebrew school.'

ABSTRACT (formal operations, differentiated, 11+)

*How can you tell a person is a Protestant?*
'Because they are free to repent and pray to God in their own way.'
*What is a Catholic?*
'A person who believes in the truth of the RC Church.'

This was confirmed by his subsequent study of children's understanding of prayer (Elkind et al, 1967). Children spontaneously give meaning to religious terms that are beyond their level of comprehension, but few under the age of twelve years attain a 'proper' understanding of any religious concepts.

Especially interesting is Elkind's emphasis on denominational belonging and identity. The respective starting points of Goldman and Elkind may well reflect the different constitutional arrangements for religion in their two countries. In England, until recently, the plurality of religious communities has been 'contained' within the framework of a national Christian tradition: Protestant biblical teaching has been a common denominator for RE in schools. But in the United States provision for RE has been entirely separate from the schools and therefore carried on within the separate religious communities. Since English religious life is now increasingly recognised as plural, it is helpful to be shown what developmental considerations are operative within religious communities.

In the face of the likelihood of erroneous religious ideas being conceived during primary years, Elkind is more

sanguine than Goldman about the prospect of children
growing out of them. Just as Piaget showed that 'animistic'
and 'artificialist' notions are gradually replaced even without
systematic teaching (Piaget 1926–29–52) so Elkind anti-
cipates that greater socialisation and objectivity in thinking
will extend to religious matters too.

Nevertheless, he is sceptical about RE as a deliberately
intellectual enterprise during childhood. He prefers instead to
concentrate on 'training the emotions', especially through
exposure to the activities of the parent religious community.

### Godin: magic and sacrament

André Godin is a Belgian professor of psychology who, as
editor of *Studies in Religious Psychology* (Godin 1957–68)
and the Catholic RE Journal *Lumen Vitae*, has been engaged
in research on children's religious development for over
twenty years. He too accepts a psycho-genetic stage sequence
for religious understanding on the strength of various
research projects carried out under his direction. Following
Piaget he attributes magical notions to the primitive years of
childhood and of the human race: a child prays or performs
ritual acts with expectation that some aspect of the world
will automatically be changed. Thus magical mentality infects
a child's appreciation of the eucharist. This is illustrated by
responses to the following story put to ninety Catholic pupils
aged eight, eleven and fourteen years:

> *What do you think of this story: it is probably not true,
> but if it were true, what would you think of it?*

> A woman is busy cleaning in the sacristy. She finds a
> ciborium on the table with some consecrated hosts: the
> priest has forgotten to put it back in the tabernacle in the
> church. But the woman does not know that the hosts are
> consecrated; she thinks they are prepared for the morning,
> to be consecrated at the next day's Mass. So she eats two
> or three, just like that, to see what they taste like.

> *Have you understood? What do you think of it? If the
> story were true would the consecrated hosts have pro-
> duced some effect in the soul of this person?*

The responses reveal a sharp decline in magical thinking from 8–14. In contrast to older boys and girls, most of the younger children either convict the woman of sacrilege, or affirm that grace would be communicated anyway; or if they deny this, it is for 'magical reasons': 'She touched the host' (ten years) 'She ate three' (nine years).

On the basis of these and other findings Godin suggests there is a gradual evolution from 'magical' to 'sacramental mentality'. Not every teacher shares Godin's Catholic antipathy to magic, but RE does properly encourage pupils to understand what differences there may be between magic and other religious beliefs. It is however very noticeable that Godin is more emphatic than either Goldman or Elkind that Christian formation must have its own theological norms transforming any *naturally given* psychological structures (Godin 1960).

Godin is also critical about the extent to which Goldman fails to appreciate the expressive power of symbols in the experiences of young children. Piaget pointed to the dawn of symbolic sense in infant thumb-sucking and doll play; similarly Godin suggests that stories and ritual acts may be passively assimilated from first contact with religious teaching. Their significance to individual children would not 'meekly follow the curve of bio-physical maturation in childhood and adolescence'. But, in some hidden interior way, a child may find meaning there, deeply felt, in spite of conceptual limitations.

## THE PRIMACY OF FEELING

Alongside those who stress the importance of rationality in religion and the gradual construction of a conceptual framework of understanding between infancy and adolescence, there are others who focus primarily on feeling. This matches the currency of talk about fantasy and feeling in education, non-verbal methods of communication and the importance of the emotions in children's learning. Intellectual understanding is not necessarily excluded in this alternative focus; more often it is claimed that intellect without feeling is hollow. Again we will look at three examples of such an emphasis from recent research.

No one model is common to this second emphasis as

Piaget's was to the first. But there is a common ethos derived from the mystical tradition of mankind. This ethos may be in religious form (Otto's sense of the numinous) or poetic (Wordsworthian 'nature mysticism').

## Madge: childhood wonder

As if illustrating the contrast of ethos between the 'cognitive' and the 'affective' approaches, V. Madge relied much more on spontaneous talk and recollection than on Goldman's clinical interview technique. From extensive teaching experience in primary school, reports of student teachers and autobiographical references, she drew a picture of childhood and religion's part in it: 'children in search of meaning' (Madge 1965). Most obviously their search is represented by the varied range of questions they ask about any aspect of life:

> Who made the telephone?
> How does a cut in your skin heal?
> How do hedgehogs grow baby hedgehogs inside?
> Who is God's mummy?

In such questioning she sees the beginnings of both religious and scientific enquiry. But she also speaks of them as 'inner stirrings' of an 'elemental sense of the mysterious'. It might be prompted by iron filings wriggling under a magnet, by falling rain, or a bird:

> *Lark and Dove*
>
> One morning in
> lark song I heard a lovely
> tone; the dark was
> going, the sun was coming.
>
>> One night very early, still light,
>> Two loving doves came flying
>> To give spirit to everyone.
>> As they flew we saw them
>> From our window.          *Linda* (7 years)

A sudden consciousness of beauty can compel wonder in a child — awaken a sense of 'the numinous'. But so it can for an adult. One of Madge's 'humanist-agnostic' students writes as follows after an evening stroll by the sea:

> The sea pounding the beach under a starry sky is a
> beautiful sight any evening, but this night was different in
> some way. I stood there entranced, watching the endless
> cycle of the waves rolling forward, breaking on the beach,
> sucking back to re-form and advance once more. Some-
> thing of the wonder of those minutes caused me to
> understand the term 'eternal' rather better than ever I had
> before. . . . Although a 'humanist-agnostic' I definitely felt
> something I can only think was 'spiritual-wonder', an
> awareness of an inexplicable 'something'. It caused me to
> sit down and question myself more deeply than ever
> before; question myself on the nature of life, whether
> everything can be explained scientifically in logical terms,
> or whether I am mistaken in this belief. I am not yet
> satisfied (Quoted in Madge 1971).

RE, on this reckoning, from nursery onwards is rightly
dedicated to arouse the sense of trust and security, of love
and joy, of wonder and awe. Madge does not reject
Goldman's 'stages' of development but emphasises that
sensitivity to the way young children actually think and feel
is the key to religious development at this stage.

### Robinson: the taproot of experience
As Deputy Director of Sir Alister Hardy's Religious Experience Research Unit at Oxford, Edward Robinson followed
up all the references to important childhood experiences
mentioned in the first one thousand adult responses to the
Unit's national appeal:

> Those who feel that they have been conscious of, and
> perhaps influenced by some Power, whether they call it
> the Power of God or not, which may either appear to be
> beyond their individual selves or in part outside and in part
> within their being, are asked to write as simple and brief an
> account as possible of these feelings and their effects.

From Robinson's follow-up of these first returns he obtained
vivid accounts of childhood recollections. These speak of

powerful feelings erupting in immediate experience, but many go on to stress the long-term effect of growing on with the realisation that such experiences had been had.

Many, but by no means all, of the experiences which Robinson has quoted in articles have been triggered by nature:

> The first approach to a spiritual experience which I can remember must have taken place when I was five or six years old at the house where I was born and brought up. It was a calm, limpid summer morning and the early mist still lay in wispy wreaths among the valleys. The dew on the grass seemed to sparkle like irridescent jewels in the sunlight, and the shadows of the houses and trees seemed friendly and protective. In the heart of the child that I was, there suddenly seemed to well up a deep and overwhelming sense of gratitude, a sense of unending peace and security which seemed to be part of the beauty of the morning, the love and protection of my home and the sheer joy of being alive. I did not associate this with God, but I knew that in all this beauty was a friendliness, a protective and living presence which included all that I had ever loved and yet was something much more (quoted in Robinson 1972a).

The potency of such experiences for the people concerned convinces him that children are capable of far greater religious understanding than R. Goldman has seemed to allow: the fact that children may not be able to articulate their deepest feelings is no proof of their not having them or of their unimportance to children.

> I do not think it will ever be possible to do full justice to the religious experience of children unless it is unreservedly recognised that the higher (and rarer) flights of vision to which the word 'mystical' is generally applied are not generically distinct from the simpler intuitive insights which are probably a great deal more common in childhood than we are now willing to admit (Robinson 1972a).

Any attempt to deny this is insensitive to the 'living nerve' that makes child and adult the same person. The major priority in RE is for the teacher to be able to recognise the inarticulate sense of inner spiritual awareness which may be found at any age, and to help it find expression.

## Paffard: Inglorious Wordsworths

Robinson takes Goldman to task for rejecting the whole idea of religious experience as a mode of awareness different from any other. Evidence can be presented, however, which suggests that the religious distinctiveness of a sense of mystery or wonder is itself doubtful. This is the thesis of M.K. Paffard's 1964 Bristol M.A. thesis now published (Paffard 1973).

Moved by recollection of the significance of solitude in his own childhood, of spiritual longings both diffuse and intense during his years at boarding school, Paffard has searched for similar experiences recorded in autobiography and fiction, or as revealed by a questionnaire he gave to four hundred sixth formers and university undergraduates. He finds transcendental experiences in abundance: feelings that ordinary consciousness is transcended, maybe involving visions or a sense of physical presence, maybe feelings of oneness, ecstasy, joy, melancholy, or fearsom awe. A C.S. Lewis may describe this sense in religious terms, but an A.L. Rowse will insist that it is thoroughly aesthetic. The difference to Paffard is one of *overbelief*. Thus he quotes. 'No Buddhist ever had a vision of the Blessed Virgin Mary, and St Benedict never saw a vision of the Blessed Goddess, Kwan-Yin' (Paffard 1964). It is the experiences themselves which matter.

Few of the experiences reported in the questionnaire do actually come from the primary years; most are from adolescence. More English specialists and young people who have written poetry acknowledge having such experiences than any others. Outside, in evening solitude, is the most frequently mentioned occasion for them. All are transcendental, claims Paffard, whether the language is of communion with God, conversion experience, or sheer aesthetic delight.

Paffard's empirical work is with younger people than that of the Religious Experience Research Unit, but his sample is from beyond the compulsory years of schooling and 'academically selective'. In principle, however, there is no reason to suppose that the capacity for such experiences is not as widespread in junior school children as he (and Marghanita Laski) (Laski 1961) claim it is in the general population. But as was also the case in the example quoted by Madge, on Paffard's reckoning, many, if not all, RE concerns will be shared by those teaching English or encouraging 'creative writing'.

## INTERPRETING THE SPECTRUM

It is not my present intention to declare that any one of these research wavelengths is more finely tuned than the others. On the contrary, only by trying to see these and other wavelengths in relation to each other will the total spectrum be complete – the spectrum, that is, of research and of religion itself. What then emerges?

### (i)  *The spectrum of religion*

To a degree this spectrum of research views reflects the fact that there are many different ways of being religious and different emphases within any one religious tradition. Yet we have examined only two expressions of these differences. To one, sophisticated theological reasoning may be the all-important characteristic of mature religious belief and under-standing. To another, what matters most will be a personal encounter with God to which no words could ever do justice. It is easy enough for the philosopher to caricature all talk of mystery and mystic vision as muddle. 'The return to the catastrophic humbug masquerading as wisdom and insight that characterised medieval thought' was how one letter to *The Times Educational Supplement* dismissed an article by E. Robinson. But similarly a mystic or an evangelical of any tradition may ask to feel the pulse that beats within reason and reject the insulting implication that until the age of thirteen or fourteen a child is sub-religious or devoid of religious insight. There is a feeling side to reason, without which he could never understand another person or 'hunch' a hypothesis. And can he not begin to do both of these in infancy?

These and other ways of being religious need appreciation

by the teacher if religious development is to be understood.

## (ii) *The spectrum of research*

Words and how they can be used in different ways undoubtedly make problems for the researcher. Goldman entitles his book *Religious Thinking from Childhood to Adolescence*, yet says he does not think religious thinking is any different from any other kind of thinking. Godin is no less concerned with cognitive structures but insists that Christian cognition might be transformed by personal revelation at almost any age. Robinson reproves Goldman for the narrowness of his conception of what it means to be human or religious: but is he in turn perhaps too broad? Though he states that religious experience may be discrete and distinct, he comes close to embracing aesthetic responses with religious. In this he is near Paffard's description of any difference between religious and aesthetic experience as 'overbelief'.

For all these apparent differences of emphasis, each in his own way is seeking to fathom the childhood of man, religious or secular. In coming to terms with their different views it has therefore to be asked just how substantial their points of difference are; are they largely semantic? Infelicitous usage may account for much misunderstanding of the respective positions. For instance, despite what their critics say of them, advocates of the cognitive stage theory are flexible about the actual age when an individual child may learn to perform certain mental operations and admit the likely difference that home culture or teacher variable can make. Goldman himself, if his debt to a Froebel training is to be properly acknowledged (Goldman 1959), is well aware of unconscious, non-rational, emotional aspects of life and even of the centrality of mystery to religion — he simply 'bracketed' these for his research purposes. Robinson, for all his distaste for compartmentalising childhood, in turn accepts that certain qualities of mystical experience are adult phenomena. Differences remain, but not necessarily exclusive ones.

Each end of the spectrum of research on children's religious development is therefore helpful to the teacher. Between them they represent the child's gradual comprehension of the relationship between separate strands of knowledge, and the partial inaccessibility of that personal synthesis at every age to anyone but the private 'I' behind it.

### (iii) *Understanding religion and religious understanding*

Secular school and religious community are likely to have different ambitions for the children who come within their boundaries. The church, synagogue or gurdwara might well aspire to transmit the faith inherited from of old to a new generation in such a way that it becomes their own. The County maintained school can have no such commitment, however, to one particular religious tradition; it will seek instead to introduce its pupils to the religious facts of life as to any other aspect of human experience. In briefer terms, the hope of one will be for the child to become openly religious, of the other that he become 'religiate' (if we may use this term in the same sense as educators use the terms 'numerate' and 'literate' to describe a pupil equipped to deal with number and literature. An analysis of the aims of this kind of Religious Education will be found in Chapter 7).

The term 'religiate' is used as a way of highlighting the practical, educational value of trying to understand what men have meant, or mean today, when, as individuals or as entire civilisations, they have ordered their lives around specific beliefs in God or gods. Even in infant school, and without any word from the teacher, children can be well aware of the existence of different religious beliefs and practices: from parents and friends, from the near neighbourhood, or far-flung on the TV screen. They will try to make sense of this as of everything else, but the progress towards fully-fledged conceptual understanding may be slow, as we have seen. Yet no appreciation of the convictions and dreams that have motivated men will be complete without such learning.

The teacher in this situation is not called to proclaim his private faith or doubts. Faith and doubt are publicly represented in beliefs and actions which appear in stories, that are enshrined in history, in a contemporary documentary or in credal formulations; they may be the subject of songs or pictures, or even be conveyed by stylised ritual or simple gesture. In any of these forms the child and the teacher may approach them together and make of them what they are able at that particular time in their lives. Together they can talk about what they have just seen, heard, or performed; they can explore experiences just shared, checking for sense and meaning. The teacher forms a triangle, as it were, of himself, the children and the various expressions of religion (see Rosen 1967). He relates to the class and they to him, but they also each relate to a particular item in a whole range of experience — a specific story, ritual or example of religious truths (see Gates 1974). Concepts and feelings are both involved in the interplay. The end is understanding religion, but incidentally, it will also be an aid to a religious understanding of life.

In beginning, therefore, to open up with a class of children the manifold claims of religious belief and experience, the general Primary teacher or the Secondary specialist has firm ground on which to stand. In seeking an effective RE he need not apologise for being both learner and teacher. Religious *thinking* may begin to flourish in our 'teens, but religious education begins much earlier (Smith 1936) and for most people, as Gabriel Moran reminds us (Moran 1971), religious education takes about seventy years.

# References

R.M. Beard (1969) *An Outline of Piaget's Developmental Psychology* Routledge.

D. Elkind (1961) 'The child's conception of his religious denomination: 1 The Jewish child' *Journal of Genetic Psychology* Provincetown, Mass., USA.

(1962) 'The child's conception of his religious denomination: 2 The Catholic child' *Journal of Genetic Psychology* Provincetown, Mass., USA.

(1963) 'The child's conception of his religious denomination: 3 The Protestant child' *Journal of Genetic Psychology*, Provincetown, Mass., USA.

(1964a) 'Age changes in the meaning of religious identity' *Review of Religious Research* vol.6:1, Religious Research Association, New York.

(1964b) 'The child's conception of his religious identity' *Lumen*

*Vitae* vol.19, Lumen Vitae Press, Brussels.

D. Elkind and J.H. Flavell (1969) *Studies in Cognitive Development* OUP.

D. Elkind, D. Long and Spilka (1967) 'The child's conception of prayer' *Journal for the scientific study of Religion* vol.6, University of Connecticut, USA.

H.G. Furth (1970) *Piaget for Teachers* Prentice-Hall.

B. Gates (1974) 'Groundwork for the future — religious education and curriculum innovation' *Ideas* vol.29, Goldsmith's College, London.

A. Godin ed. (1957–68) *Lumen Vitae* quarterly, Lumen Vitae Press

A. Godin (1957) *Research in religious psychology* Lumen Vitae Press, Brussels.

A. Godin (1960) 'Magical mentality and the sacramental life in children' *Lumen and Vitae* vol.15, Lumen Vitae Press.

(1962) *Child and adult before God* Lumen Vitae Press.

(1968a) *From Cry to word: contributions to the psychology of prayer* Lumen Vitae Press.

(1968b) 'Genetic development of the symbolic function: meaning and limits of the work of R. Goldman' *Religious Education* vol.LXVIII, Religious Education Association, New York.

R.J. Goldman (1959) 'What is religious knowledge?' *National Froebel Education Bulletin* vol.117, Froebel Education Institute, London.

(1963) 'Children's Spiritual Development' *Studies in Education: First Years in School* Evans.

(1964) *Religious Thinking from Childhood to Adolescence* Routledge.

(1965) 'The Application of Piaget's schema of operational thinking to religious story data' *British Journal of Educational Psychology* vol. 35: 2, Methuen.

P.H. Hirst and R.S. Peters (1970) *The Logic of Education* Routledge.

ILEA (1968) *Learning for Life* Inner London Education Authority.

M. Laski (1961) *Ecstasy: a study of some secular and religious experiences* Barrie & Rockliff.

J. Macmurray (1935) *Reason and Emotion* Faber.

V. Madge (1965) *Children in search of meaning* SCM Press.

(1971) *Introducing young children to Jesus* SCM Press.

G. Moran (1971) *Design for Religion* Search Press, New York.

M. Paffard (1973) *Inglorious Wordsworths: a study of some transcendental experiences in childhood and adolescence* Hodder.

J. Piaget (1926) *The language and thought of the child* Routledge.

(1929) *The child's conception of the world* Routledge.

(1952) *The child's conception of number* Routledge.

E. Robinson (1972a) 'I called it "It" ' *Faith and Freedom* Manchester College, Oxford.

(1972b) 'How does a child experience religion' *The Times Educational Supplement* 15 December.

C. Rosen (1967) 'All in the day's work' in J. Britton, ed., *Talking and writing* Methuen.

J.W.D. Smith (1936) *Psychology and religion in early childhood* SCM

Press, revised edition 1953.

M. Strommen ed. (1971) 'Some developmental tasks in religious education' *Research on religious development: a comprehensive handbook* Hawthorn Books, New York.

R. Williams (1971) 'A Theory of God-concept Readiness' *Religious Education* vol.LXVI: 1, Religious Education Association, New York.

# 6 The language of myth

RAYMOND JOHNSTON

Many new demands are made upon today's RE teachers, and they can be forgiven for feeling aggrieved and dejected from time to time. Inadequate staffing, inadequate time, inadequate materials and resources can all hamper the proper execution of the teacher's task. Yet in some ways the most unsettling demand of all is to change the content of what is being taught. On grounds of social policy and of educational enrichment, a good case can be made out for a contribution from world religions in the school curriculum. Where more obvious to put this than in the RE syllabus? As this is introduced and the RE teacher tries to find his or her feet in the welter of materials on offer, a considerable amount of mythological data will be inspected, much of it unfamiliar to both teacher and pupil alike. Does it *really* belong to RE — or should it be in the English syllabus as world literature, or as poetry of other nations? This chapter attempts to show that myth is most closely connected with moral education, yet is also inescapably religious. If the argument has any worth, then there is a case for saying that any classroom time devoted to moral education should also include the myths of other societies. Yet ultimately social, moral and religious education are inextricably interwoven.

My main purpose is to show that myth is necessary for the normal healthy development of a child, that moral development in particular needs this kind of material, that myth is essential even for adult moral awareness, moral consistency and moral activity, and that this has, therefore, significant implications for religious education in school.

### The inner world of the child
In the world of the baby, fact and fantasy are blurred, the world appears monstrous, threatening, inexplicable. The needs of a child are very clear in these early months: warmth,

security and immediate bodily satisfaction, these being normally provided by a loving and affectionate mother. But soon the child begins to pick up other signals and to form some sort of picture of the world beyond mother. This is happening quite crucially, so the child psychologists tell us, between the ages of two and four. There is a fascinating chapter in D.W. Winnicott's book *The Child, The Family and The Outside World* (1964) entitled 'The World in Small Doses'. Winnicott's point here is that there are two worlds for the small child; the world of the physically experienced, that which is touched, seen or heard, but also the imaginatively grasped personal world, the world of feeling, imagination, pleasure, pain, jealousy, ideals and vision.

Now the emotional and psychic life of the child is fed by the stories which children are told. John and Elizabeth Newson in their study of the way four-year-olds were being treated in an urban community found story-telling a remarkably prevalent occurrence at bedtime (Newson 1968). It was a thing that parents of all types seemed quite naturally to indulge in. By this means parents are responding to very deeply felt needs in their children, creating a framework, weaving a tapestry. What they seem to be doing, and what the stories appear to do. is to give an appropriate ranking, ordering and evaluation to the otherwise chaotic world of the emotions and instincts and, thus, to some degree, to tame that world, making it comprehensible. In stories, the world of the imagination is peopled and painted and coloured. Using another metaphor, the child is being given a map on which to identify the strange and still incomprehensible features on the inner landscape of the soul. If this is true, then the child without stories is impoverished, deprived (to use the modern word) and very much at risk. He lacks a fundamental orientation, not simply an enrichment. If genuine moral thought and moral action demand some kind of consistency and control, as is generally agreed, then the part played by the story element in moral development becomes essential.

Stories, then, give us images which help in emotional development. But whence comes the power of these images, why are some stories, parables, pictures, so useful, so powerful? One or two things do stand out very clearly. One important psychological tradition maintains that there are present in every individual, besides his personal memories, the 'great primordial images', This hypothesis, it is claimed, explains the fact that certain myths and legends are found all over the world in almost identical forms. It might also explain why mental patients can reproduce exactly the same images and associations as are found in ancient texts. C.G. Jung called these images or motifs 'archetypes'. In addition to each man or woman's personal unconscious, he suggested, there is a trans-personal or collective unconscious, made up of primordial images. These images Jung saw as 'the most ancient and the most universal thought forms of humanity. They are as much feelings as thoughts – indeed they lead their own independent life' (Jung 1919). So the great myths, the most pervasive patterns in the human stories that have been told down the generations, correspond to something essentially human. They speak of elements or patterns of our basic humanity which can only be discovered or expressed in images and parables, in stories and symbols. The wounded king, the dying god, the slaying of the dragon, the cheating of the oracle, the ring of power – all these draw a strange and deep response from us. And perhaps they also correspond to something more real than the 'real world' of popular empiricist twentieth-century speech.

A fascinating interview with a ten-year-old boy, whom he names Alfred, is recorded by Winnicott in his book of case studies *Therapeutic Consultations in Child Psychiatry* (1971). He encouraged his young patient to draw imaginatively as they talked, and the boy eventually illustrated some of his own dreams. On one picture, drawn as they talked, Winnicott comments thus:

> This is a dream that is full of symbols that belong to myth and fairy story – the three legged stool, the fire, the tail, the witch with tall hat, the pots and pans, indicating something cooking or being concocted, and the darkness indicating the unconscious. The whole thing goes right down to deep unconscious material but not, of course, to the deepest. The deepest unconscious material is indescribable. As soon as one has found ways of describing it, one has left the deepest layers. Society offers names, verbalisation, fairy story and myth to the child to help him or

her to deal with the unnamed fears that belong to the unnameable.

Here, of course, as in all areas of psychiatry, there are complex problems of validation and interpretation. Winnicott's phrase 'dealing with unnameable fears' sounds dramatic, and it is difficult to know how one could conclusively verify that this has taken place. But whatever one might think of the model of the psyche used by psychotherapists, few would deny that this kind of mastery or control contributes to stable behaviour. It favours the development of a balanced emotional life, in the light of which our consideration of the interests of others may develop.

## Reason and morality

So far, we have thought of the young child, and we have thought of myth simply as a story element which helps in his development and his coming to terms with his inner world.

Turning now to recent discussions of moral education, we find that the most widely influential school of thought has been based upon the work of a number of leading philosophers who have interested themselves in reason and morals. The background to their important contributions is the post-war analytical and linguistic emphases sometimes known as 'Oxford philosophy'. The most significant books are R.S. Peters' *Ethics and Education* (1966) and Wilson, Williams and Sugarman's *Introduction to Moral Education* (1967). Other distinguished philosophers have contributed at the level of academic interchange and in learned journals, but it is Peters and Wilson who are most commonly prescribed reading in University Departments and Colleges of Education where the study of education is taken seriously. Yet it is not unfair to say that the eminence and intelligence of the moral philosophers concerned has not resulted in large-scale clarification of issues among the whole body of the teaching profession, or in significant practical advances in the actual moral education which schools provide, implicitly or explicitly. We must briefly delineate the emphases of this approach however (and doubtless administer some rough justice through lack of space) before returning to our topic of myth.

As Peter Gedge pointed out in Chapter 4, the modern view begins by noting quite simply that moral discourse differs fundamentally from other spheres of discourse. Valuing, choosing and commanding are different from stating, describing, noting facts. Deciding what is right and good is different from deciding what is red or round. We must adopt a very general, cautious approach. How do we decide what is good morality? How do we assess the merits of a moral view? What are the rules and procedures of morality? All this leads to a reluctance to look at particular moral codes or the hard currency of specific moral commitments on which our confused age seeks certainty. The aim is not to establish a full set of immediate 'first order' moral values, but to look for something much broader — the general rules which characterise moral discourse. We find them set out for us by Wilson, for example, along the following lines (Wilson et al 1967).

To be thinking and speaking morally, we must be *rational* — stick to logic, use language correctly and attend to the facts. Genuinely moral beliefs and opinions come from someone who is *autonomous*, that is, he holds his views freely, not under compulsion; he holds these views *intentionally* and for a reason, being rational in that sense too. He is *impartial* — he has some kind of principle that all people on similar occasions ought to do similar things — this is the principle of universality, genuine moral principles being susceptible of maximum generalisation. Moral discourse is by nature *prescriptive*, it *commits* the speaker to actually acting on what he says, and its principles are *overriding*, in that they take precedence over all other types of principles of action. Similar considerations appear in Peters' book *Ethics and Education* where, in Chapter 11, he speaks of the emergence of rational morality with its fundamental procedural principles which he lists as 'fairness, freedom, considering other peoples' interests, and respect for persons'. These, says Peters, are the presuppositions of asking questions such as 'What ought I to do?' and these principles do not change. They derive from the philosophy of Kant, but some of them are to be found as early as Socrates. Thus, the content of morality may change, and particular applications within these broad structural principles may be different from time to time, but the form of the thing — what could be called the scaffolding — remains the same.

Certain critical comments need to be made on this new definition of morality. To begin with, it seems to be a considerable innovation as a definition of what 'moral' means. It appears at first sight to avoid any kind of commitment, to be neutral. This, of course, is always a useful thing to be in today's rather confused scene. But if it is applied vigorously, it denies the right to be called 'moral' to more than ninety per cent of the decisions of the vast majority of the human race. Most men most of the time do not rise to the heights of all these necessary criteria as they make up their minds what they ought to do. It is in fact a definition for highly intelligent philosophers rather than for most of us who live in the ordinary humdrum world, certainly for most of the children that we teach.

To judge between rival moral codes one needs a moral attitude for a basis, some sort of firm ground. The one adopted or assumed by these writers is basically the liberal democratic one, something that in Britain is born and bred into all of us. Its foundation is a type of anti-authoritarian conviction that nobody has the right to tell anyone else what to do, at any rate without very good and very convincing reasons. But this sort of stance is already a moral position in itself! Wilson, for example (in Wilson et al 1967) goes a long way towards adopting a particular moral code. Lying beneath Wilson's apparent neutrality is the position of nineteenth-century English utilitarianism. For religious people it is certainly not particularly obnoxious or un-Christian, but it is a specific position. And it is open to all the objections levelled at utilitarianism since it was first propounded.

The second aspect of this position which is obvious and important is that it is highly intellectual. This is scarcely surprising since it goes back to a great intellectual, to Kant himself. It demands a very high level of verbal sophistication and conceptual mastery. Only a very few can grasp and apply it. It is in fact an elitist view of morality. How ironical to be faced with this in our democratic age! It avoids emotional and metaphysical elements, but it certainly concentrates upon a highly sophisticated intellectual approach. Anyone who has tried to read the first section of *Introduction to Moral Education* will know that it is extremely demanding.

Thirdly, this approach is individualistic. Of course, the good moral philosopher must address individuals and he must disturb them and sting them into intellectual activity. And yet the social and the communal do not figure largely in this new approach. We remember the accusation against Socrates that he corrupted the youth of Athens, an anti-social activity. Few today would wish to condemn Socrates, or condemn him solely for asking deep and disturbing questions which would otherwise never have occurred to his hearers. Yet we should also remember that Socrates stood in the tradition of the Sophists, and the Sophists produced a certain type of intense intellectual activity whose weakness lay in its individualistic and rather cynical point of view. If you paid them, the Sophists could defend or destroy almost any case you would like to name. Spectators of this brilliantly individualistic sort of performance often find that it breeds scepticism and even despair. Where is *truth* in all this?

I have briefly indicated some of the weaknesses which seem to me to characterise the background to the moral education debate as it exists at the moment. Now if we consider the moral education of the older child and the adolescent and ask how something more positive can be supplied, an interesting fact emerges. The introduction of myth can broaden, deepen and enrich this rather bleak view which is at the moment predominant. Myth — whether in RE or in literature lessons — can be of real service in 'moral' education. Nor is this a new idea. Admittedly, by including religious myths we have broadened the definition of moral education' and what we include in it. We spill right over into religious education. But when we do broaden it, we find we are including elements which have been part of the tradition of the human race for centuries. We need not exclude the great majority of humanity as morally uneducated if we are willing to broaden our concept of morality in a way that Wilson does not seem very happy to do.

## The function of myth in society

In every society with any kind of social cohesion there have always been myths — myths which recur from mother's knee on to the teaching which adolescents need to master before they can become fully-fledged members of the community.

These shared ideas on which society and its institutions depend emotionally and imaginatively form a kind of mental structure which is typically enshrined in the form of story or stories. Without deciding at this point on the truth or the historicity of these narratives, this is a matter of simple fact about the educational form that has been taken, from time immemorial, by the shared patterns of ideas and values which any society takes for granted. The transmission of moral values has been achieved by these old stories. Symbolic ideas in story form give fuller meaning and fuller integration to the life of the society. Western civilisation has found the Christian stories its centre in this respect. Radical departure from this tradition has thus inevitably meant the creation of new stories, as the brief flowering of a national socialist culture in Germany and the more permanent Marxist ideology have demonstrated. From this viewpoint moral education in a very real sense depends on myths. Dr Margaret Clarke has made this point with very great force in her book *The Archaic Principle in Education* (1962). The aim of the old epics and legends supposedly enshrining the early history of the race and told by parents, recited by priests or sung by jongleurs, was not primarily to amuse (though of course they also served that purpose). 'The aim was to impart to youth the ethico-intellectual tradition of the race. For the moralising of youth was considered to be tremendously difficult. It was the whole task of education' (p.9).

The role of myths in this rather specialised sense has been strangely neglected, though it was recognised and studied in some detail in relation to society ancient and modern, by Sturt and Hobling in their *Practical Ethics* (1949). Margaret Clarke wrote her book in the early 1960s to provide a sharp reminder of what seemed to her to be a most disquieting event. As she wrote in her introduction, 'Something has disappeared today from education – something which has been associated with it during all the thousands of years of its existence, for primitive peoples in the West as in the East, in static as in progressive civilisations. A millennial pattern has vanished in a matter of fifty years; it has vanished and it has not even been missed' (p.9). Dr Clarke believes that Homer, Virgil and the biblical stories were our 'myths' in this sense. These have been mistaken by modern Europeans as 'mere story-telling'. Education has now no centre and has been absorbed by techniques. Literature is no longer read as the means of understanding and acquiring a tradition. It is studied from the aesthetic point of view, and if only a few people show the aptitude for such detailed and sensitive study, then so much the worse for the rest. We therefore end up by confining the study of literature to the supersensitive, the experts.

It is hard to refute these accusations. Something like this *has* happened. The shift took place between the two world wars. Certainly the social purpose which appears to have been served by the central literary tradition of Western Europe was forgotten. When texts had to be set for study, as in English and Modern Languages syllabuses, the demand for contemporary or near contemporary texts increased; the old was simply irrelevant. Perhaps the philosophy of John Dewey, stressing the fundamental importance of interesting the child and involving him in present-day society, has reinforced this demand. 'On the face of it,' writes Dr Clarke, 'Dewey's demand was unreasonable, as there was an obvious danger that the child would study what afterwards proved to be worthless. Notions of worth or worthlessness, however, were no longer apposite, as the one aim was to interest. Literature was now a source of feelings and sensations and was supposed to be good in itself' (p.51).

Dr Clarke's case may be somewhat overstated, but it is an important one. George Steiner has recently rephrased and re-echoed this theme. 'The end of classic literacy,' he calls it in his T.S. Eliot memorial lectures at the University of Canterbury in Kent, subsequently printed in book form under the title *In Bluebeard's Castle* (1971).

The question now arises: Can we rehabilitate morality and moral education in terms of vision and parable, that vital ingredient which the myths provide? Or is the very idea of such a project impractical and intellectually disreputable? We turn here to an important essay by Iris Murdoch which is printed in *Christian Ethics and Modern Philosophy* (Ramsey 1966). Iris Murdoch in this essay first characterises contemporary moral philosophy roughly in the way that has been described above in considering John Wilson's approach to moral education. The ideal is the altruistic, autonomous individual; moral activity concerns clarifying principles, arguing, choosing. This is the tradition of Hume, Kant and Mill with a dash of Rylean behaviourism. It implies, she believes, a denial of the inner life as illusory. It alleges that the whole business of moral duty is rational, to provide logically valid legislation for repeatable situations by the specification of morally relevant facts. She then goes on to give a critique; she points out all that is omitted from this view — imagination, creativity, mystery. These elements in our own real world and our own experience are missing. In a noteworthy phrase, she reminds us: 'A man's morality is not only his choices but his vision.' The current view, she says, neglects self-reflection and inner monologue, passing over a man's meditation or conception of his own life, the stories he tells himself about himself. There is a Walter Mitty in us all. Today's rational ethic takes no account of parables or speculations on human destiny, which all of us entertain at least occasionally, and it certainly has no visions of life and of the universe which guide our actual choices on many occasions. This view centres upon rational abstraction, generality, impersonal principles. But this rather bleak approach fails to grasp fundamental dimensions of human experience. Moral choices in this current orthodoxy take place in a kind of grey and lonely world where the individual is central, solitary and responsible. But for the vast majority of adults, fables and patterns rather than rules are the background of their choices. A man's morality is not only his choices but his vision, and this vision is so often given and sustained by parables or stories. These owe their point to the fact that they are concrete and particular, vivid and personal; they are suggestive, they conjure up a whole situation and their very ambiguity and even paradoxicality adds in some strange way to their enduring quality and their helpfulness. Can we, therefore, rehabilitate one or more myths to help us in moral activity in this present-day complex and somewhat chaotic moral scene?

More than one educational thinker has glimpsed a positive way forward. An essay written in 1960 on the professionalisation of teaching is an unlikely place to find anything about myth, but it is there we read the following (Bruner 1960):

With respect to the life of the society, there are similarly alternative models upon which one can pattern oneself. These are frequently called the myths of a society, and myth in this sense does not mean untruth. The enduring body of a culture's literature is a storehouse of myths, that symbolise and condense the myriad forms of the rather limited range of plights that characterise the life of a people . . . In contrast to the classic times of Greece, we are indeed without a unified corpus of myth. In its place have arisen ones of modern literature, notably the novel, and in the literature of the last century and a half, one finds traced, not so much externalised myth, as what might better be called a record of voyages into the interior. It is by knowledge of those voyages that one comes to a sense of the alternative forms of coping or fleeing; one gains a knowledge of life beyond what one might immediately encompass in direct experience, however one lives. And how does this relate to the function of teaching? I should like to propose that the teacher of literature has a function akin to the teacher of empirical subjects, such as Science and History, where the latter attempts somewhere to provide a model, indeed alternative models of the external world one encounters. It seems to me that it is a function of the teacher of literature to use the corpus of morals and drama, to elucidate the inner world and its alternative expressions.

There is a fascinating connection here with the words from Winnicott, with which this chapter began. Professor G.H. Bantock has further explored this whole area of educational theory in *Education, Culture and the Emotions* (1967).

But this idea of numerous alternative worlds is not completely satisfactory. Myths are *more* than simply alternative interior worlds, for myth is connected with religion; myth and ritual belong together. Myth explains, ritual depicts or embodies myth, so the anthropologists tell us. A myth is more than a story, or at least it certainly possesses a strange power beyond mere entertainment, when it is rooted properly in the culture to which it belongs. For the community sharing that culture, a myth is a way of apprehending reality, and reality includes what theists call deity. (Indeed reality may perhaps be reduced ultimately to nothing but deity.) But today we do not have free choice of myths for contemporary moral education. It seems to me naive to imagine that the myths of past cultures or of distant contemporary cultures could ever become formative and deeply felt influences in the lives of most modern European children. Not only are such myths not learned and studied reverently and exclusively (as in their home cultures) but they also lack the power and colouring given by that specifically worshipping element which is the essence of the religious attitude. John Wilson has more recently written another book *Education in Religion and the Emotions* (1971) which redresses the balance of his exclusively intellectual earlier work somewhat by an examination of the religious attitude grounded in awe and worship.

For a religious myth to be its full self, it needs to be seen and apprehended in a religious context, a worshipping context with more than a tinge of awe. We are back in the realm of religious education. But let us be clear on the magnitude of the task confronting us. However eagerly we have promoted the study of world religions in education, however energetically we may offer the legends and myths of Greece and Rome, of Iceland, or India, or Ancient China, to present-day Western children, these stories cannot give us a sufficient basis for the myth component of moral education. Their spell is diminished by time and distance, since we can no longer believe in them in a fully religious sense. They are hard indeed to respond to as literature. As moral example, they may perhaps serve a useful purpose. As entertainment for the young, or as raw material for religious studies for some of the older age-group they are splendid, but they are not acting as they did in their home communities as myths in the deepest sense. So where must the teacher turn?

## Today's competing myths

Our problem is not in the absence of candidates — there *are* myths available today. Myths can be created, as Plato thought they should be. In our own century Hitler managed it. Feeding on the German romantic tradition which came through Herder, Hegel, Fichte and Nietzsche, he had plenty of raw material. A deadly myth emerged. Marx had managed it, feeding again on Hegel and Feuerbach amongst others. And with our intrusive modern media of communication, the enforced national adoption of a mythology becomes a real possibility; compulsory mythical indoctrination could be achieved. Typically, quasi-religious rituals can embody and support the myth in the societies on whom it is imposed. This has happened in Nazi Germany and it happens in Marxist countries. On this sort of basis, moral education becomes more clear-cut and manageable for the youth of the society; though to us in Western democratic lands, it seems far too constricted. The price of this stability is, of course, individual freedom. No one may reject the myth and yet prosper, as Solzhenitsyn reminds us.

Yet in the West we face the scramble of evanescent, competing myths. What Professor Bantock has called 'the babel of rhetorics' is really the product of a coarse and unprincipled commercial approach to the young who are offered one myth after another. No wonder they are confused. Ever-changing myths stimulate consumption. Myth has fallen sick, a prey to the perversions of the market-place. One of the most popular myths of recent years, now on the decline, has offered us as a model for the masculine ego-ideal, the figure of the fictitious spy James Bond. Books and films about 007 produce astronomical profits. Yet the effects of identification with the Bond myth are serious in the extreme, as the literary critic David Holbrook has shown in his book *The Masks of Hate* (1972) in which he attempts a full scale psychiatric analysis of James Bond. In his concluding chapter on the Bond myth, which is the centre of his book, he summarises his analysis in this way:

> Through the writer Ian Fleming's paranoia we are encouraged to feel that any relinquishing of assertiveness and hate behaviour may bring about annihilation, and yet our anxiety is focused on our fear that hate will lay the world waste. Here we have the clue to the widespread appeal of Fleming's books for those living in a world deficient in opportunities for true solutions, one which is full of fear prompted by false solutions, including the confrontations of the Great Fear, and violence itself. Their symbolism of a

hate which threatens to reduce the world to ashes reflects our fear that this will actually happen in human affairs. But Fleming's contribution is to make matters worse by recommending implicitly that we take to the ways of hate and contribute to those cycles of aggression, egocentricity and destructiveness which threaten survival . . . such culture can provide no lasting satisfactions, but only a temporary sense of being alive by bad thinking or some other manic ploy (Holbrook 1972, pp.136–7).

This bad thinking Holbrook attributes to 'the false mythology of our civilisation'.

One other myth deserves mention and it is perhaps rather more respectable. It is the evolutionary myth and it has a strange fascination. It was born and flourished in the nineteenth century. Chesterton demonstrated its illogicality and inconsistency as a basis for religion or morals but World War I was eventually thought to have given it a death blow. Its progressive optimism seemed shattered by the slaughter. Yet in the late twenties it revived, only to receive another crushing blow from World War II with its ghastly revelation of man's inhumanity to man. Just what was the evidence for such a positive and noble view of man and human destiny? Yet it revived again post-war, principally in the often eloquent writings of Julian Huxley. It was again demonstrated to be rationally inadequate by C.S. Lewis, particularly in his essay 'The funeral of a Great Myth' now printed in *Christian Reflections* (1967). But despite this James Hemming, the atheistic psychologist, can write enthusiastically in his book *Individual Morality* (1969) 'our prime duty is to serve evolution.'

The inadequacy of this myth lies firstly in its irrationality, which Lewis has shown. It cannot stand up to serious examination outside the biological field. Of its capacity to function as a powerful imaginative focus for some individuals in society there can be no doubt. Lewis admitted this, and Huxley has written some splendid pages on this assumption. But in a critical age, if a myth is to live it must not offend the canons of rationality where these are relevant (though of course there is much more to life and to myth than rationality). However, the inadequacy of the evolutionary myth for moral education is even more serious. At the beginning of the century G.K. Chesterton recorded his own intellectual pilgrimage in a book which is still in print, *Orthodoxy*. He declared his view of Darwinism as a guide for morality in a characteristic passage:

> The kinship and competition of all living creatures can be used as a reason for being insanely cruel or insanely sentimental, but not for a healthy love of animals. On the evolutionary basis you may be inhumane or you may be absurdly humane but you cannot be human. The fact that you and a tiger are one may be a reason for being tender to a tiger or it may be a reason for being as cruel as the tiger. It is one way to train the tiger to imitate you; it is a shorter way to imitate the tiger. But in neither case does evolution tell you how to treat the tiger reasonably — that is, to admire his stripes while avoiding his claws.

Yet, as we know, this evolutionary myth lingers on in the 'naked apery' of much modern popular science and journalism. It is in fact still a kind of coarse-grained myth by which it becomes possible to justify animal behaviour in man, and sometimes behaviour worse than that of animals. There is little here for moral education to get a grip on, or for religious education to teach or to foster.

In conclusion perhaps a more hopeful approach might be indicated. Why should we not try to make explicit the criteria which a myth for today would have if it is to be any use, especially in moral education? The following are a few proposed criteria and then some suggestions of what might satisfy them.

A myth for moral education today must firstly offer some satisfaction to the deepest longings and aspirations of man for meaning in life, coherence in experience — 'food for the soul', to use old fashioned language. Much well-intentioned moral education material comes nowhere near to making this provision. Secondly, such a myth must be able to satisfy both the emotional needs of the individual and offer guidance on the social needs of the community, as has been indicated earlier. Thirdly, it must offer a vision of the ideal which all may grasp, at least in outline. A dazzling platonic vision for the philosopher only will not do for the average man. We cannot turn to formulations of great intellectual sophistication, nor to the dreary utilitarianism which is often the only ingredient of a lot of moral education material on offer today.

Fourthly, if the stories of an appropriate mythical tradition for today make any affirmations which involve historical events, or historical individuals, these affirmations must be open to investigation and in principle to falsification. Only then can it be granted that these aspects of myth are in any sense true.

And fifthly, and rather obviously, it must offer something which children can apprehend yet be flexible enough and many-sided enough to apply to adult situations without any feeling of constraint or infantile regression. Having laid down these criteria I can only say that for me the 'mere Christianity' to which both Chesterton and Lewis found their way eventually, seems to offer a myth, a vision and a story, a uniquely suggestive principle of coherence which satisfies these criteria. Let Lewis express this in his own words:

As myth transcends thought, Incarnation transcends myth. The heart of Christianity is a myth which is also a fact. The old myth of the Dying God, *without ceasing to be a myth*, comes down from the heaven of legend and imagination to the earth of history . . . By becoming a fact it does not cease to be a myth; that is the miracle . . . But Christians also need to be reminded . . . that what became Fact was a myth, that it carried with it into the world of fact all the properties of a myth. God is more than a God, not less; Christ is more than Balder, not less. We must not be ashamed of the mythical radiance resting on our theology. We must not be nervous about 'parallels' and 'pagan Christs' — they *ought* to be there — it would be a stumbling block if they weren't.

So our brief examination of myth and its relation to moral education has led us back to religious education, where myth is most truly at home — in so far as it is at home anywhere in today's uneasy school time-table. RE teachers can take heart. In bringing children into contact with the mythical inheritance of the human race they are attempting to compensate for what may well be the ultimate deprivation. They are not simply feeding the starved English imagination – together with the teacher of literature. They are also attempting a task of supreme social significance. They are bringing water to the dried roots of the soul. They have a chance to bring some life into the 'heap of broken images'. For cultural and historical reasons, the Christian story is, and ought to be, at the heart of the British RE teacher's thinking and planning. In addition, as we have seen, it can be maintained quite pragmatically that society needs something of this nature, and that there is no other contender for the task. By all means let us read and enjoy all the myths. As long as we and our youngsters are prepared to discover that one of them stands up and looks us straight in the eye – searchingly, uncomfortably. For one of them can turn out to be myth, fact and truth itself.

Let Lewis have the last word as he concludes the essay quoted above:

> We must not, in false spirituality, withhold our imaginative welcome; if God chooses to be mythopoeic – and is not the sky itself a myth? – shall we refuse to be *mytho-pathic*? For this is the marriage of heaven and earth, Perfect Myth and Perfect Fact, claiming not only our love and our obedience but also our wonder and delight, addressed to the savage, the child and the poet in each one of us no less than to the moralist, the scholar and the philosopher (Lewis 1967).

### References

G.H. Bantock (1967) *Education, Culture and the Emotions* Faber.
J. Bruner (1960) 'The Function of Teaching', reprinted in W.E. Drake, ed. (1969) *Sources for the Intellectual Foundations of Modern Education* Merrill.
G.K. Chesterton (1909) *Orthodoxy* Bodley Head.

M. Clarke (1962) *The Archaic Principle in Education* W. Maclellan, Glasgow.

J. Hemming (1969) *Individual Morality* Nelson.

D. Holbrook (1972) *The Masks of Hate* Pergamon.

C.G. Jung (1919) *The Psychology of the Unconscious* Kegan Paul.

C.S. Lewis (1967) *Christian Reflections* Bles.

J. and E. Newson (1968) *Four Years Old in an Urban Community* Allen & Unwin.

R.S. Peters (1966) *Ethics and Education* Allen & Unwin.

I.T. Ramsey ed. (1966) *Christian Ethics and Modern Philosophy* SCM Press.

G. Steiner (1971) *In Bluebeard's Castle* Faber.

M. Sturt and M. Hobling (1949) *Practical Ethics* Routledge.

J. Wilson, N. Williams and B. Sugarman (1967) *Introduction to Moral Education* Penguin.

J. Wilson (1971) *Education in Religion and the Emotions* Heinemann.

D.W. Winnicott (1964) *The Child, the Family and the Outside World* Penguin.

D.W. Winnicott (1971) *Therapeutic Consultations in Child Psychiatry* Hogarth Press.

# IN THE CLASSROOM

# 7 Agreed syllabuses, past, present and future

JOHN M. HULL

*The present legal position*

The 1944 Education Act requires that religious education in England and Wales 'shall be given in accordance with an agreed syllabus adopted for the school . . . ' The Fifth Schedule of the Act prescribes the procedure for the adoption of an agreed syllabus. The local education authority shall convene a 'conference' consisting of representatives of

(a) such religious denominations, as in the opinion of the authority, ought, having regard to the circumstances of the area, to be represented;

(b) except in the case of an area in Wales or Monmouthshire, the Church of England;

(c) such associations representing teachers as, in the opinion of the authority, ought, having regard to the circumstances of the area, to be represented; and

(d) the authority.

Each of the four 'committees' so constituted has one vote and all four must vote in favour of the proposed syllabus. They may decide to adopt an existing syllabus prepared by another authority, or parts of several such syllabuses, or they may prepare their own syllabus.

The resulting syllabus is also to be used in the controlled schools although denominational teaching may also be given in certain circumstances. In aided and special agreement schools, denominational teaching may be given in accordance with the trust deeds or the customs of the school, but in certain circumstances teaching according to the agreed syllabus of the area may also be made available.

These provisions are unique to religious education. Religion is the only subject which by law the schools are required to teach, and the agreed syllabus is part of a wider agreement by means of which the church schools and the county schools have become more closely integrated.

*Earlier history of the agreed syllabus*

From 1870 to 1944 religious education was not required by law in England and Wales. Whether religion should be taught or not was a matter for local decision. But if such teaching was provided, then it should include 'no religious catechism or religious formulary which is distinctive of any particular denomination'. This, the famous Cowper-Temple clause of the 1870 Act, was repeated in the 1944 Act. If the schools were not to teach anything distinctive of the various denominations, what were they to teach?

In fact, almost all the school boards or the local education authorities did require the schools in their areas to offer religious instruction, and from the earliest days of the public educational system, local authorities would issue guidance to the schools on the content of the instruction they were to give their pupils. Many of these syllabuses were modelled on syllabuses already in use in the church schools but with denominational peculiarities removed. The Anglican catechism would thus disappear but the Apostles' Creed and the Ten Commandments would remain. Some ecclesiastical authorities issued revised editions of their own syllabuses for use in the 'council schools'. Sometimes a local authority would ask local clergy to help in the drawing up of a special School Board Syllabus and clergy were often entrusted with the task of inspecting the instruction given in the council schools.

These early syllabuses were very brief, being perhaps no more than a paragraph or two in the local school regulations or perhaps a page of biblical passages and other materials to be studied and memorized. But as the denominational rivalry of the nineteenth and early twentieth centuries declined, more substantial cooperation between the local authorities and the churches appeared, and by 1920 many quite detailed, thorough and relatively enlightened syllabuses were circulating between the various areas.

It is not possible to point to any one document as being the first of the modern agreed syllabuses, but developments in Cambridgeshire were certainly amongst the most important. In the years after the First World War the Cambridgeshire Education Committee had been trying to reorganize its schools into senior schools (eleven plus) and 'tributary junior schools'. This was possible in areas where all the schools were of one type, that is, all were council schools or all were church schools. But where (as was the case in most parts of the country, particularly the towns and cities) there was a mixture of types of school, the religious problems created some difficulty. Not only was there the problem of how the schools were to be administered, but what was to be done about religious education?

In March 1923 two Advisory Committees were set up, one to consider the practical problems of a single administration and the other to see if it might be possible to draw up 'an *agreed* [their italics] Syllabus of Religious Instruction and observance which would be acceptable to all religious bodies' (Cambridge 1924). The result was *The Cambridgeshire Syllabus of Religious Teaching for Schools*. The committee, although not divided into representative groups as became the later practice, did include head teachers, churchmen and academics, both Anglican and free church.

The appearance of this syllabus gave considerable prestige and inspiration to what was rapidly becoming a national movement. Within five or six years numerous authorities had appointed committees of teachers and clergy and had adopted the results as an 'agreed syllabus'. By 1934, 224 of the 316 local education areas had adopted syllabuses of this sort and about forty different syllabuses were in circulation. The Cambridgeshire syllabus was easily the most popular, being used in 87 areas, but there were still some 90 areas in which the older kind of syllabus was still in use (Yeaxlee 1934). In 1939 Cambridgeshire added still further to its influence by issuing a new edition of its now famous syllabus.

So it was that, when the agreed syllabuses became mandatory and the machinery for their production and revision was codified in 1944, a tradition had already been well established and the syllabuses themselves had already reached a certain maturity and stability. Not until the later 1960s was there to be any substantial change in the directions laid down in the 1920s and 1930s (Hull 1975).

## A typical syllabus of the older type

The agreed syllabus, as it evolved between about 1924 and 1964, was almost entirely a syllabus dealing with the past.

Interest in the present was directed towards the nurturing of
the religious lives of the pupils. But the present was not
*studied*; the present was nurtured through study of the past.
The Bible was studied, including the history of Israel, the life
and teachings of Jesus, the growth of the Church in New
Testament times and the history of Christianity in particular
areas. The latter was often the only distinctive feature which
a particular syllabus could offer. There might be religious
biography, usually missionary and social reforming heroes,
and, usually in the sixth form only, some discussion of social
and ethical problems studied from the Christian point of
view. There might be some comparative religion (as it was
called) in the sixth form. But usually the sixth form syllabus
consisted of more advanced biblical study with some systematic or philosophical theology.

Let us take, as an example, the widely used 1945 Surrey
Agreed Syllabus:

> The aim of the Syllabus is to secure that children attending
> the schools of the County . . . may gain knowledge of the
> common Christian faith held by their fathers for nearly
> 2,000 years; may seek for themselves in Christianity
> principles which give a purpose to life and a guide to all its
> problems; and may find inspiration, power and courage to
> work for their own welfare, for that of their fellow-
> creatures, and for the growth of God's kingdom (Surrey
> 1945).

The suggestions for infants (ages three to seven) include a
good deal of material which twenty years later might have
been called 'experiential'. Talks on light, food, shelter,
flowers and trees are suggested under the heading 'God's gifts
to His children', and 'God's wonderful world' and 'God's
provision for Animals' are found under the general heading
'God our Heavenly Father – His Love and Care'. But
although 'the child's interest is in his immediate surround-
ings' many of the lessons 'may appropriately consist of
simple, fully-illustrated talks about the objects, animate and
inanimate, which form the background of the Bible stories,
(Surrey 1945). A good deal of the work may thus be thought
of as emotional and conceptual enrichment with a view to

the appreciation of the Bible. There are, of course, many stories from the Bible, both Old and New Testaments, suggested right from age three. The reference to 'God's provision for the Animals' in fact occurs under the main heading 'The Bible and its Teaching'.

Throughout the whole syllabus, from infants to seniors, the work for each year falls under two main sections. Section one is 'The Bible and its Teaching'; section two is 'The Christian Life'. Section two of the final course for seniors deals with 'Christendom' and consists of an outline of Church history concluding with the appearance of the British denominations followed by 'Christian work in the Modern World'. 'Some of the Problems of Religion and Life' appears only as an Appendix. This then is a typical syllabus of what might be called the classical period of agreed syllabus creation.

## The agreed syllabuses of the later nineteen sixties

From the late 1950s there was, in religious education, a much more thorough emphasis upon the centrality of the experience of the child, and in response to an upsurge of activity and renewal in the early 1960s, a new generation of agreed syllabuses began to appear. The first, and still one of the most influential, was the West Riding Agreed Syllabus: *Suggestions for Religious Education* (1966). The custom of arranging the work in yearly units was abandoned, and greater stress was laid on the development of the child by arranging the work into broad categories such as 'late childhood' and 'early adolescence'. The material for each stage was headed 'Themes and Activities' and it was emphasized that the pupil needed to discover Christianity for himself. Much more material was concerned with the present. For middle adolescents, two of the three themes suggested are 'Personal relationships — Discovering oneself' and 'Christianity in the modern world'; and for 'late adolescence' there is but one theme, 'Religion and Life in Contemporary Society'.

The other influential syllabus of this period was that of the Inner London Education Authority *Learning for Life* (1968). Here the techniques of theme teaching are developed more thoroughly, with material on 'neighbours', 'holidays' and 'the

family' for juniors, and a thematic presentation of the
Gospels dealing with work, death and money is offered to
adolescents as an alternative to a more traditional type of
study of the life of Jesus. (See also Wiltshire 1967,
Lancashire 1968 and Northamptonshire 1968).

*Cambridge, Hampshire, Essex and Cornwall*
By 1970 it was becoming clear that the machinery of the
agreed syllabus was not sufficiently flexible and rapid for the
needs of religious education. Designed as a system of checks
and balances between the denominations, the authority and
the profession itself, it supposed tensions which in fact
seldom existed. Cambridge had asked its Standing Advisory
Council on Religious Education in 1966 to consider the
possibility of a revision of the Cambridgeshire Syllabus and
while discussions were in progress, the Advisory Council,
thinking that teachers might be too scrupulous in teaching
from the existing Syllabus, issued a statement to schools
'assuring them that trial and experiment in religious education were not only permissible but warmly supported by the
council' (Cambridge 1970). Following discussion with
teachers, a Religious Education Development Centre was set
up at Homerton College, Cambridge. In September 1968,
three working groups of teachers began to meet at the Centre
under the auspices of the Advisory Council to prepare
material for trial in schools. This material was published in
1970 and by then it had been decided that there would be no
more Cambridgeshire agreed syllabuses. The existing syllabus,
although not formally suspended, was by-passed in the
decision to encourage wide ranging experimentation, and
when the Chief Education Officer wrote the Foreword to the
1970 collection of papers he said 'Some other Authorities
have recently produced revisions of their Agreed Syllabuses
but our Standing Advisory Council have decided to encourage in religious education the same sort of development
which is taking place in other areas of the curriculum.' The
Education Committee, in their own Introduction, remark
'These suggestions are not in any way a new syllabus; they
are to be considered as part of continuing curriculum
development . . . ' (Cambridge 1970).

In 1967 Hampshire had convened a statutory Conference

to consider the question of its agreed syllabus. The Hampshire Syllabus then in force was the 1954 Syllabus and the 1967 Conference gave approval to the additional use of the 1966 West Riding Syllabus. But no revision of the existing Hampshire Syllabus was to be attempted. Instead, the two working parties of the statutory Conference produced a 'Handbook of Suggestions' which 'is not a new agreed syllabus; nor, indeed . . . is it a syllabus at all. It is quite deliberately compiled in a form different from that of any previous agreed syllabus of Religious Education produced by the Authority' (Hampshire). The Handbook is intended to offer teachers practical help and consists of many articles, collections of ideas, work units for classroom teaching, resources and so on.

The Essex Education Committee authorised the use of the West Riding Syllabus (1966) in September 1969, and, rather like Hampshire, decided to supplement it with a series of papers for teachers. As in Hampshire, the Primary and Secondary Working parties, originally set up to consider revision of the syllabus, undertook the production of this material. It was felt that 'in a climate of much educational change there should be continued consultation and discussion, looking forward to a possible new syllabus' (Essex). The material was published under the title 'Interchange' two or three years later.

In Cornwall, the Agreed Syllabus of 1964 was in need of revision and a Standing Advisory Council met in 1968 and established working parties, and the new Syllabus was published in 1971. As the Chairman of the Education Committee pointed out, 'This is probably a unique Syllabus as it was, with the approval of the various Church authorities, written by teachers for use of teachers in all types of schools' (Cornwall 1971).

In these four developments we can see the machinery of the agreed syllabus being used in a fairly flexible way. The distinction between a Conference for the recommending of an agreed syllabus (which an authority *must* set up) and a Standing Advisory Council for Religious Education (which it *may* set up for general purposes) is becoming blurred, teachers are taking a more prominent role, the problems of reaching agreement between the churches on what they hold in common are not in evidence, and the materials in use are open to continuous addition. Agreed syllabuses are becoming instruments not of syllabus creation but of curriculum development. Bath took a slightly more radical view towards both the machinery and the content than any of the four authorities we have just considered; Birmingham used the machinery with scrupulous exactness and came to grief because the letter of the law was invoked against it – an ironic fate for a syllabus which had made a greater effort than most in the early seventies to observe the customary legal procedures. (For a summary of agreed syllabus revision to date see Birnie 1971.)

### The Bath Agreed Syllabus

Although it has received little national attention, the Bath Syllabus (1970) presents us with an interesting example of the changes which agreed syllabuses are undergoing at present.

The City of Bath Conference to revise the 1953 Bath Agreed Syllabus had its first meeting in May of 1969. The Fifth Schedule of the 1944 Act was strictly observed. Ten of the thirty-two members of the Conference were representing the churches and sixteen members represented the teachers. The Conference began by considering the aims of religious education. A statement was drawn up which was presented for approval to the Education Committee in October 1970 and went forward to the full City Council the following month.

In this three-page statement, the Conference recommended that the 1953 Agreed Syllabus should be withdrawn. No revision was to be attempted. The Conference also recommended that no 'independent syllabus' for Bath be prepared but 'teachers will be encouraged to make use of suggestions in some of the new syllabuses (e.g. West Riding, ILEA, Wiltshire, etc.) and also to devise schemes of work particularly suited to their own situation, which shall be incorporated into the handbook' (Bath 1970). A loose leaf handbook would be issued. This would contain the opening statement itself, a number of other papers prepared by the Conference on aspects of religious education, and 'occasional working papers' would be circulated from time to time for addition to the folder.

The Conference next recommended that a working party 'mainly representing the teachers' should be set up 'to act as a clearing house for ideas' and to stimulate new work in religious education. This would be channelled through the existing Teachers' Centre. The statutory Conference would then consider its obligations under the 1944 Act to be complete and would continue as a Standing Advisory Council 'to cooperate with teachers'.

The statement then discusses the aims of religious education.

> The primary aim of religious education is to help young people to understand the nature of religion. This does not simply mean teaching about religion if by that is implied an historical survey of the doctrines, practices and institutions of the major religions or even of only the Christian religion. It means helping young people to understand and appreciate religious phenomena, to discuss religious claims with sensitivity, to be aware of the nature of religious language and to recognise the criteria and standards by which truth and falsehood in religious beliefs are distinguished . . . (Bath 1970).

Several implications of this basic aim are then stated. The first is that 'religious education must remain open . . . both in its selection of material and methods of enquiry and in its respect for the individual so that pupils can eventually make free and responsible decisions about the claims of religion.' The second implication is that while in this country 'it is appropriate to examine the Christian faith more closely than other faiths' nevertheless 'in a pluralistic society there must also be an attempt to understand views other than Christianity (eg Humanism, Communism, Buddhism etc)' (Bath 1970).

When the document was discussed in the Bath City Council, several councillors expressed concern about the single reference to Humanism and Communism. The debate was reported in the *Bath and West Evening Chronicle* on 4 November 1970 under the heading 'Religious education report starts row'. The report, the newspaper account said, 'could lead to the revolutionising of religious education in schools' but 'a move to get this reference [to Humanism and Communism] removed from the report before its adoption by the council was defeated.' One councillor, urging that the report be rejected, said 'It is the duty of a Christian council to oppose this insidious breach and erosion of the [agreement about religious education] which has been arrived at over several life times.' Another commented 'If they want to teach atheism in schools, why don't they just call it atheism?'

A lively correspondence on the subject was published in the newspaper in the next few days. 'Lessons that make me see red', 'Christianity is best', 'The truth about that "teach Communism" report' and 'Hysteria sets in' were some of the headlines.

The Chairman of the Education Committee of the City Council made a statement in which it was made clear that there was no intention to 'support the teaching of Communism . . . [but] that an attempt be made to "understand" what Communists believe'. The Conference on the Agreed Syllabus met again in December 1970. The section in question was reaffirmed and not altered. When this recommendation came back again to the Education Committee and in due course to the full City Council no objections were offered. The matter received but the barest mention in the local press and there was no further public controversy. In effect, this document became the adopted Agreed Syllabus of Bath and so replaced the 1953 Agreed Syllabus.

From this time the Standing Advisory Council for Religious Education (the heir to the Conference although a smaller body) fostered the idea of a 'developing syllabus' which would in principle be unfinished. The folder was issued and the document which the City Council had approved, now called 'Introduction: Suggestions for Religious Education' became the first paper in the folder. Between May 1971 and February 1974 five more papers were circulated for addition and just before the new administrative area of Avon was created on 1 April 1974 a paper from the Bristol Agreed Syllabus was added to the Bath collection in order to unite these two parts of the new unit.

The Bath events throw some interesting light on the problems of producing an Agreed Syllabus in the conditions of today. What the City Council adopted (Paper one, 'Suggestions for Religious Education') is not a syllabus at all and does not claim to be one. It is a statement about the aims, principles and difficulties of constructing a religious education syllabus but it is not actually a syllabus. Paper three, 'Using the New Syllabuses' (May 1971), fulfils the intention declared in the opening paper that teachers would be asked to consider materials from several of the new agreed syllabuses and it sets out a number of headings of work, themes and topics from these other syllabuses; but this paper never came to the attention of the Education Committee let alone the full City Council. What the City Council had done, in effect, was to offer religious education complete freedom of content, subject only to the guidance of the opening paper and the continued cooperation of the Standing Advisory Committee for Religious Education. Religious education was thus set free to pursue the normal paths of curriculum development followed more or less by other subjects through teachers' centres, work parties, conferences, publication of experimental work and so on. Although the main procedures of the 1944 Act were followed and although there was certainly a *bona fide* intention to meet the legal requirements to the full, the Bath Agreed Syllabus is a departure from the tradition and a radical reinterpretation of the workings of the Act. There was no legal challenge.

Many other matters which became burning issues only two or three years later in Birmingham were raised in Bath. The question of Humanist participation was discussed at the very first meeting of the Bath Conference. It was decided to invite Humanist comment at a later stage. The procedures adopted gave very much more responsibility to classroom teachers than had normally occurred before. The question of the inclusion of secular philosophies and movements was the most controversial one and the area which gave rise to maximum misunderstanding between religious educators and the public. On the other hand, because of the absence of significant immigrant communities in Bath, the question of participation by the non-Christian religions did not become prominent nor was the question of school worship resolved.

*The Birmingham Agreed Syllabus*

The first Agreed Syllabus of the City of Birmingham was adopted in 1950 and reissued in 1962 with an expanded section of suggestions for teachers. The syllabus and the accompanying articles have no particular merit but simply restate or reprint material which was standard in such works.

> We speak of religious education, but we mean Christian education. To believe that Jesus Christ is the key to reality, that the full revelation of God's nature in a human life has been made in Him, that through Him alone we have peace with God, is not to deny that the Holy Spirit has been and is at work in other religions and philosophies. But the aim of Christian education in its full and proper sense is quite simply to confront our children with Jesus Christ . . . (Birmingham 1962).

By the late 1960s it had become obvious that a new agreed syllabus was needed. Considerable numbers of Sikh, Muslim, and Hindu children were attending Birmingham schools and religious education was seen as a key point in community relations. The Conference was convened in 1970. The committee representing the 'other denominations' included not only Catholics, Orthodox and free churches but also representatives of the Jewish, Sikh, Hindu and Islamic faiths. At a later stage, a Humanist was co-opted on to several of the working parties and on to the Coordinating Committee with speaking but not voting rights.

The Religious and Cultural Panel of the Birmingham Community Relations Committee had been meeting since March 1969 and spent some time in discussing what kind of religious education would be suitable for the city in the 1970s. The panel, which included Sikhs, Jews, Muslims, Hindus, all the major Christian churches and representatives of the teachers' organizations, presented a paper to the Agreed Syllabus Conference called 'Religious Education in a Multi-Religious Society' (Hull 1971). The panel recommended that:

> it should be part of an education for life in this country that children come to know something of the traditional

religion of the land, namely Christianity . . . children should not be ignorant . . . of the main features of the major world religions; and that in Birmingham . . . Christian children should know something about Hindu, Islamic, Judaic and Sikh faiths . . . just as children of these various faiths should know something both of Christianity, as the majority faith of the country, and of the other minority faiths . . .

The panel concluded that there should be

a deeper and more particular study of one religion, normally the tradition to which the pupil adheres. In multi-religious schools this would be made possible by allowing in the new Agreed Syllabus for options in part of the curriculum, the particular options that would be appropriate in a particular school depending upon the composition of its pupil body (Hull 1971).

Work on the Syllabus and the Handbook which was to accompany it was virtually complete late in 1973. It was decided that the Syllabus itself should be very brief, merely setting out the broadest principles of the syllabus and giving some slight indication of its content. This one-page document was recommended by the Conference as the statutory syllabus and it was that which required the statutory agreement of the four committees of the Conference. The 1970–3 Conference was at this point following the example of its 1962 predecessor. In the 1962 Birmingham syllabus, the actual syllabus is printed in red on the two-and-a-bit central pages of the book and described as 'Basic Syllabus'. The rest of the 1962 book of 107 pages is accompanying articles and suggestions for teachers. The syllabus for the age range twelve to sixteen in the 1973 document said

Three areas of investigation should be studied. A (i) Religion as it manifests itself in our own and other societies, and the claims upon which it rests. (ii) Non-religious stances for living, their basic assumptions and their outworking in personal and social life. B Aspects of

personal life and behaviour which call for moral judge-
ments. C The problems currently facing mankind nationally and internationally which involve ethical and religious
considerations. (At the time of writing, the Birmingham
Syllabus and Handbook have not been published. I quote
from my own documents as a member of the Conference.)

The Handbook which accompanies this brief syllabus, part
of which has just been quoted, is a bulky volume of some six
hundred pages, with extensive articles on aspects of religious
education, and detailed courses for every level of the school
with lists of resources and bibliographies.

In the present Syllabus and Handbook religious education
is seen as an intrinsically valid educational activity,
justified by its particular contribution to preparation for
life in contemporary society. It is not propaganda for a
given religious standpoint . . .

The Introduction continues by pointing out that previous
agreed syllabuses when dealing with world religions tended
'towards a comparison of other faiths with one considered as
self-evidently superior to the rest; whereas the approach now
is to study them objectively and for their own sake.' In the
secondary school there should be

a detailed study of at least one religious tradition in all its
dimensions. Each pupil should have the right to choose for
himself or herself the subject of this study from the
following options: Christianity, Hinduism, Islam, Judaism
and Sikhism. In addition to this detailed study some
further study of one or more of these options should be
undertaken, including Christianity if this is not the religion
chosen for detailed study. All secondary school pupils
should also study one, at least, of the non-religious stances
for living.

At the secondary stage, the handbook then sets out for both
detailed and less detailed study courses in all five of the
prescribed religions and courses for less detailed study in two
non-religious stances for living, viz. Humanism and Commun-

ism. It is anticipated that a detailed study would occupy about a year and a less detailed study about a term.

At a final meeting of the full Conference in the autumn of 1973 all four committees voted in favour of the Syllabus and recommended the Handbook. These documents went on to the Finance and General Purposes Committee of the Education Committee of the City Council in February 1974 where they were accepted subject to the deletion of the references to Communism. This decision was front page news in the local press and was also reported in several national newspapers. The Education Committee and the City Council itself refused to delete the offending portions, and a controversy developed along party political lines, with the minority Conservative party opposing the Communist course and the majority Labour party seeking to retain the Syllabus and Handbook intact. The fact that this affair coincided with a national election did nothing to calm things down. A lengthy correspondence was published in both the *Birmingham Post* and the *Evening Mail* with headlines such as 'Subversion', 'Communist Textbook', 'The Teaching of Communism' and 'Happy Marx'. Publication of the Syllabus and Handbook was delayed.

The legality of the Syllabus was questioned and counsel's opinion was sought. In June 1974 the barrister retained by the City's Solicitor expressed the view that the Syllabus did not fulfil the requirements of the 1944 Education Act. The Bishop of Birmingham had also expressed some reservations about the Syllabus and Handbook and his Director of Education sought the advice of the National Society (Church of England) on the legality of the documents. Legal opinion was again quoted against the syllabus. 'Communism in syllabus is outside law, says Church' was the headline in *The Birmingham Post* on 10 June.

Section 10 of the Fifth Schedule of the 1944 Act provides for appeal from the local authority to the Minister should the conference be unable to agree or should the authority fail to adopt a syllabus unanimously agreed upon by the conference. The legal opinion engaged by the City thought that the City, although believing it had adopted a syllabus, had not in fact done so because what the conference had submitted to it was not in fact a syllabus of religious instruction. It was not a syllabus, because the brief document in question did not provide sufficient indication of the main heads of the proposed content, and it was not entirely a syllabus of religious instruction because it included non-religions, to be studied in their own right. These could only be included, counsel thought, if their study contributed to the advancement of religious knowledge. The matter was therefore referred to the Secretary of State for Education in Mr Harold Wilson's government, Mr Reginald Prentice. In the late summer the City was advised that the Conference to draw up the Agreed Syllabus had not yet completed its work. Until it had done so, no opinions on the legality of its recommendations could be given.

Many of the problems glimpsed in Bath came to a head in Birmingham. Since affairs in Birmingham present us with the clearest case to date of the difficulties and the profound changes taking place in the agreed syllabuses, we must examine some of them in greater detail.

## What does 'agreement' mean in an agreed syllabus?

The agreed syllabus had always been an ecumenical document in the sense that the churches, agreeing not to permit the teaching of anything denominationally distinctive, agreed to teach what they held in common to be the truth. The Bath syllabus revealed how irrelevant this kind of ecumenical cooperation has become today. In any maintained school in the future, when religious education deals with Christianity, it will do so 'without implying the need to commend or to be exclusive'. Not only is religious education not 'teaching Communism' in that it is not fostering belief in Communism; it is not teaching Christianity either, in that it is not concerned to foster faith in Christianity. When the aim of religious education is 'to secure an understanding and appreciation of religion' then the subject will be controlled by whatever methods might be suitable to the study of religion. Statements from Christians about what they believe in common will of course be valuable in helping the teacher to present Christian beliefs accurately; but the assumption that the churches needed to agree about a syllabus because their common faith would be taught as being true can no longer be viable.

The Bath syllabus revealed the irrelevancy of the older assumption but the Birmingham documents replaced it with a new assumption. All the Conference today is required to agree about is that the various subjects it recommends are all worth including. That is all. Christians after all do not believe that Humanism is true and Muslims do not believe that Hinduism is true. Although from time to time during the meetings of the various working parties the view was expressed that belief in God was the common affirmation which linked the Syllabus together (Buddhism is not presented in detail until the sixth form) this can hardly include the non-religious stances for living, and since these are treated in exactly the same spirit (descriptively and sympathetically) as the religions, the theistic basis collapses. Agreement is thus not about the truth of the content at all. The various groups represented all agreed that their respective beliefs were worthwhile, noble, and that a child's education would be the poorer if he were denied some opportunity to encounter them. This new assumption about agreement cuts the ground from under the whole philosophy and rationale of the older agreed syllabuses including those which appeared in the 1960s.

## A descriptive approach to the world religions

Non-Christian religions were included, if at all, in the older syllabuses only in the sixth form and only in an apologetic or missionary context. The London 1968 Agreed Syllabus created an important precedent when it included representatives of the Jewish and Muslim communities. But although the contribution of the Asian pupil to religious studies is emphasized, London does not recommend any specific study of a religion other than Christianity earlier than the sixth form. The problems of teaching other religions are discussed in a helpful way, and it is rightly pointed out that religions not actually represented in the school will be more difficult and less valuable to teach, but in a city like London there must have been many schools even in 1968 where something more than this would have been appropriate well before the sixth form. The biographies suggested for study in the primary school may, it is suggested, include people of all beliefs and none, but leaders of the non-Christian faiths are not mentioned by name as are the Christian heroes. Similarly, the joint work of Christians and Humanists is commended but no Humanist seems to have been co-opted on to the conference at any stage, and although the contribution of the uncommitted teacher in religious education is recognised, the usual description of the religious education teacher is 'the Christian teacher'. Nevertheless, London had blazed the trail which Yorkshire and Birmingham were to follow.

Early in 1974 the West Riding of Yorkshire Education Committee published a Supplement to their well known 1966 *Suggestions for Religious Education* (Agreed Syllabus). Called *Religious Education in the Multi-faith Community*, it appears to be the first recognition through an agreed syllabus that in a religiously mixed society religious education in the county schools cannot commend one faith and simply refer in passing to others. Such a policy would force the non-Christian communities to withdraw from religious education and would encourage the development of whole new systems of aided schools.

We have seen how from its inception, the Birmingham Conference was committed to a religious education syllabus which would make a positive contribution to community relations in the city. It was gradually realised that this meant the creation of a syllabus which could be taught by any well informed teacher of good-will, regardless of his faith, to any interested pupils, regardless of their faith. So, in the Birmingham documents, a new relation between the teacher's teaching and his personal faith is envisaged. Previously a teacher taught what he believed (Christianity) although the Cowper-Temple clause might prevent him from teaching *all* he believed. Now he is asked to teach (that is, encourage pupils to study) many things which he does not believe and to refrain from commending in any special way the things he does believe. The abandonment of the Christian hegemony in the agreed syllabuses in these various ways represents a small but significant shift in the relations between church and state in Britain.

*The non-religious stances for living*
Previous agreed syllabuses made tentative steps in this direction. The Lancashire Agreed Syllabus of 1968 mentions

'Humanism' and 'Dialectical Materialism' as possible discussion topics in the sixth form, and in a somewhat similar
context the London 1968 Syllabus refers to 'rationalism,
materialism, Marxism, existentialism'. But these secular life
styles were approached from a Christian point of view; they
were thought of as 'challenges to faith'. The 1966 West
Riding Syllabus describes Communism and Humanism as
'alternatives to the Christian faith' and the short book list
contains only works by Christians.

The tendency to include the non-religions in religious
education received significant support in *The Fourth R*
(Durham Report) in 1970.

> By religion we mean some pattern of belief and behaviour
> related to the questions of man's ultimate concern. For
> some, it is an Eastern religion; for some it is Christianity;
> for others it is one of the secular creeds of the West, for
> example Marxism; for others it is agnostic humanism . . .
> (p.100).

*Religious Education in Secondary Schools* (Schools Council
1971) remarks

> It may be argued that some of the alternatives to religious
> faith, such as secular Humanism, Marxism and Maoism
> deserve the same sympathetic study and attention. We
> would agree (p.66).

There is a well established group of new textbooks for
religious education which deal with the non-religions alongside the religions. (See, for example, Herod 1969 and
Sherratt and Hawkin 1972.)

The Birmingham Handbook goes much further than
previous agreed syllabuses in that, instead of a few words
directed at the sixth form, it provides thorough courses for
the fourth or fifth forms in both Humanism and Communism, and accepts the advice of Working Paper 36 that such
beliefs should receive 'the same sympathetic study' as the
religions themselves.

The fact that the Birmingham documents are not concerned with the teaching of politics is apparent from the fact

that Humanism has been chosen, along with Communism, as an example of a non-religious stance for living. Humanism has less organised political expression than either Christianity or Communism. But what then are the criteria for the inclusion in a religious education syllabus of non-religious stances for living? A candidate for admission must satisfy all three of the following criteria. First, the ideology or way of life must explicitly reject religion. Second, it must claim to be a substitute for religion. Third, it must nevertheless exhibit certain characteristics of the religions, such as a theory of history, a total view of man and his destiny and a system of ethics. Although a necessary ground for inclusion, these criteria are not a sufficient ground. Fascism for example, although it meets the three criteria, may not be thought sufficiently significant in Britain today to justify inclusion in a hard-pressed curriculum, or it may be deemed morally unworthy of inclusion. The main British political parties are clearly excluded by the criteria. The Liberal party does not offer itself as a substitute for religion, the Conservatives do not claim to present a comprehensive interpretation of every aspect of life, the Labour party does not reject any doctrine of Christianity. Such influences from Christianity as there may be in any of these political philosophies would be dealt with in Christian Studies. Capitalism is an ambiguous case. Perhaps it would be helpful to make the same sort of distinction between the implicit and the explicit in the study of the non-religions as it is customary to make in the study of the religions. Capitalism would then be seen as an *implicit* non-religious stance for living. No doubt it is full of all sorts of implications for ethics and religion. Capitalism implies a view of man but it does not preach a doctrine of man. It adopts an attitude towards the world but it has no teaching about the world. In these respects it differs from Communism and should probably be excluded.

Doubts about this widening of the content of the agreed syllabuses have been expressed in two quarters, and they are concerned mainly with Communism. There is a significant body of Christian opinion which is doubtful (and other religions are similarly sometimes doubtful). The debate turns upon problems to do with the Christian response to secularity and the nature of Christian mission. The relationship between Christianity and education is also an important problem. There is also a significant opposition from politicians, both at the local and the national level. This opposition springs from a misunderstanding of the task of the religious education teacher. The politicians assume that if a teacher teaches about Christianity, it is because he is a Christian and wants others to share his views. Similarly, they assume that if the teacher wants to teach about Communism, it is because he is a Communist and wants others to share his views. Just as the clergy used to interpret trends in religious education in terms of the pulpit so now politicians are interpreting them in terms of the hustings. It seems difficult for them to understand that the teacher is neither an evangelist nor a propagandist but an educator. The teachers' unions have taken a lively interest in the controversies about the Birmingham documents because they have seen that the professional integrity of the teacher is at stake.

*An assessment of the continued significance of the agreed syllabuses*

It seems unlikely that agreed syllabuses will ever regain the influence which they had from about 1924 to about 1970. This is partly because there have appeared other sources of authority and guidance. These include the Schools Council curriculum development projects, the materials published by the Shap Working Party on world religions, the Primary Mailing of the Christian Education Movement and the broadsheets prepared in many counties by the many Advisers in Religious Education employed by the local authorities. It is also clear that, because of the cumbersome machinery required to bring them into operation and the limitations presented by such elaborate committee work, agreed syllabuses will normally be rather conservative documents. Teachers are asking for a more active role in shaping their own syllabuses, and the patterns of teacher training and the work of the many in-service centres encourages this. It is symptomatic of this trend that many local authorities have published recommendations for religious education which have by-passed the agreed syllabus machinery entirely. Use has been made of the Standing Advisory Councils which the Act permits the authorities to establish, or the authority has published work submitted by teachers. These documents have no statutory authority but they have tended to present the more active growing edge of the subject. We may also notice the tendency in the agreed syllabuses to present articles rather than a detailed syllabus, and it is interesting to notice that, even immediately after 1944, the syllabuses, in spite of the fact that they really did have mandatory power, continued to insist in their forewords 'and introductions that they were only suggestions and that teachers were to be encouraged to be selective and creative.

In spite of all this, the agreed syllabuses retain a certain moral and professional weight which no other document has. They give official approval and recognition to trends already well established. They offer a platform for public discussion and for cooperation between many interested parties. Their most significant feature is usually not merely what they say but how they came to say it. Change in the classroom is not effected by presenting to a fully trained teacher a syllabus in the making of which he has had no direct part. But the agreed syllabuses do a great deal to register the climate of the subject and to set out its norms.

In the future some means must be found which will retain the interest and commitment of local authorities and churches in religious education and which will provide a forum for the sharing of concerns between the teachers and the public. There must however be no more statutory controls. Officially sponsored advisory bodies seem the most promising solution.

## References

Bath (1970) *Agreed Syllabus of Religious Education* City of Bath Education Authority.

Birmingham (1950) *Agreed Syllabus of Religious Instruction* revised edition 1962, City of Birmingham Education Committee.

I.H. Birnie (1971) 'Carry on Agreeing' *Learning for Living* vol.II no.1, SCM Press.

Cambridge (1924) *The Cambridgeshire Syllabus of Religious Teaching for Schools* Cambridgeshire and Isle of Ely Education Committee.
(1970) *Religious Education: Suggestions for Teachers* Cambridgeshire and Isle of Ely Education Committee.
Cornwall (1971) *Handbook for Religious Education* Cornwall Education Committee.
Durham Report (1970) *The Fourth R* National Society and SPCK.
Essex (n.d.) *'Interchange' Working Papers in Religious Education* Essex Education Committee.
Hampshire (n.d.) *Approaches to Religious Education: a Handbook of Suggestions* Hampshire Education Committee.
F.G. Herod (1969) *What men believe* Methuen.
J. Hull (1971) 'Religious Education in a Multi-Religious Society' *Learning for Living* vol.II No. 1 SCM Press.
J.M. Hull (1975) *School Worship — an obituary* SCM Press.
ILEA (1968) *Learning for Life* Inner London Education Authority.
Lancashire (1968) *Religion and Life* Lancashire Education Committee.
Northamptonshire (1968) *Fullness of Life* (Primary) and *Life and Worship* (Senior section) Northamptonshire Education Committee.
Schools Council (1971) Working Paper 36 *Religious Education in Secondary Schools* Evans/Methuen.
B.W. Sherratt and D.J. Hawkin (1972) *Gods and Men* Blackie.
Surrey (1945) *Syllabus of Religious Instruction* Surrey County Council Education Committee.
West Riding (1966) *Suggestions for Religious Education* County Council of the West Riding of Yorkshire Education Department.
(1974) *Religious Education in the Multi-Faith Community* County Council of the West Riding of Yorkshire Education Department.
Wiltshire (1967) *Religious Education in Wiltshire* Wiltshire County Council Education Committee.
B. Yeaxlee, ed. (1934) *Religious Education* vol.1.

# 8 Curriculum development

DAVID NAYLOR

Even a cursory look at current syllabuses in Religious Education reveals the urgent need for a strategy for making decisions about the curriculum. Kerr (1968) argues that too often presuppositions about content predominate and asserts that 'For the purpose of curriculum design and planning, it is imperative that the objectives should be identified first as we cannot, or should not, decide "what" or "how" to teach in any situation until we know "why" we are doing it.' Such a warning is nowhere more necessary than in Religious Education. Agreed Syllabuses even as recent as 1970 show an alarming tendency to advocate content based on traditional assumptions and presuppositions and unrelated even to the stated aims. The Lancashire syllabus (1968), for example, advocates for thirteen-year-olds the aim 'Becoming an adult in the community' and 'finding an authority by which to live.' The recommended content begins with Bible passages which create difficulty for the modern reader and goes on to list Abraham, Moses, Elijah, Amos, Hosea, Isaiah etcetera. A later section deals with the Kingdom of God and admits 'There is no more debatable or debated question in the whole field of New Testament scholarship.' Clearly the aims have been forgotten, there is no rational plan and the content from a Biblical Studies degree syllabus has filled the gap.

It will be the purpose of this chapter to convince the practising teacher that curriculum theory has direct relevance to the classroom, to outline models for the curriculum, and by way of wide references, to indicate further reading and critical commentaries on the subject.

What has been called the 'process' approach to curriculum planning has much to offer in this situation although, as will be argued later, it cannot be adopted uncritically. Sadly, this approach to curriculum planning has often been obscured by unnecessary jargon. It does, however, offer some very useful vocabulary and concepts. It would be a pity if its form proved a, stumbling block to religious educators, so that the dichotomy between educational theory and practice is increased rather than decreased.

It may be helpful to see the development of the 'process' approach in its historical perspective. Tyler (1949) identifies four fundamental questions which must be answered in developing any curriculum:

1 What educational purposes should the school seek to attain?
2 What educational experiences can be provided that are likely to attain these purposes?
3 How can these educational experiences be effectively organised?
4 How can we determine whether these purposes are being attained?

This brief 'lineal' view of the process introduces common sense and would have saved a few trips down blind alleys for RE if taken seriously during the past twenty years. Its most serious defect is its apparent lineal and static nature. Kerr (1968) produced a model (Figure 1) which is probably more helpful.

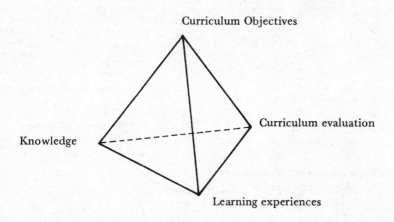

Figure 1

The important point made by this model is that no one of the four factors can be considered independently without reference to the other three. Thus, for example, objectives can only be stated with reference to a content area and this in turn suggests particular kinds of learning experiences. Teachers are frequently irritated when some enthusiast for the 'process' approach insists that aims and objectives must be discussed before content and methods. Hooper (1971) makes the point well when he says 'Effective curriculum design requires an iterative process where each question is constantly being processed in the light of answers to subsequent questions.' Much frustration could be avoided if curriculum models of the type mentioned above were used as a check list for analysis rather than as a blue print to be followed slavishly. The *logical* priority of objectives over content must nevertheless be reiterated if teachers of religious education are to be prevented from resurrecting content which makes little educational sense.

Wheeler (1967) constructs his curriculum model as a cyclical process (Figure 2) and this helps to focus attention on the continuous nature of curriculum planning.

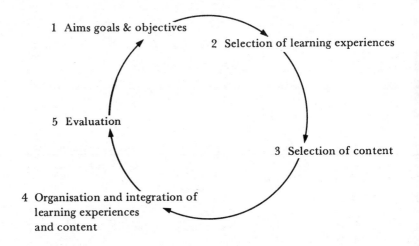

1 Aims goals & objectives

2 Selection of learning experiences

5 Evaluation

3 Selection of content

4 Organisation and integration of learning experiences and content

Figure 2

Each process is constantly reviewed and modified in the light of the feedback obtained by evaluation. The approach can be contrasted with the tendency in the past to launch an Agreed Syllabus as a finished product.

None of these models is completely adequate, and one needs to espouse the virtues of all three in such a complex undertaking as designing curricula. It will be convenient to outline the five phases (objectives, content, learning experiences, organisation and integration, and evaluation) with examples from RE before dealing with criticisms of the procedure made by several writers.

## Aims and objectives

These terms are frequently used in a fairly loose fashion and sometimes taken as synonymous because the distinction between them is not clear-cut. It is, however, worth making a distinction in the interests of clarity. Pring and Harris (Pring 1970) argue that aims contain value judgments in stating what is worth achieving. Statements of objectives, on the other hand, describe what the learner will be able to do when he has completed a given piece of learning. Decisions about aims are not easily made but once they are hammered out the next task is to reduce them to specific educational objectives. It is at this point that the celebrated *Taxonomies of Educational Objectives* (Vol.1 Cognitive Domain and Vol.2 Affective Domain) (Bloom 1956 and Krathwohl 1964) are of great assistance — though at the sound of this kind of language, the average practitioner begins to be wary of the theorists. The word 'taxonomy' simply means 'arranging in order'. The taxonomies were in fact formulated by practising teachers and researchers to aid them in team planning. The classification is content-free and the organising principle is increasing complexity. Let us take a scheme on Judaism as an example and use the 'cognitive domain' of the 'Taxonomy' to formulate clear objectives from the general aim: 'Pupils should develop a sympathetic understanding of Jews and Judaism.' Only the main categories will be used; the reader is referred to the handbooks for the finer sub-divisions.

## LEVEL 1: KNOWLEDGE
This is the lowest cognitive level involving simple memory

recall. Eg pupils should be able to plot on a timechart the key events in Jewish history from the Exodus to the New State of Israel.

## LEVEL 2: COMPREHENSION
This level involves the using of knowledge in a familiar way. Eg after watching a filmstrip on the Passover festival pupils should be able to identify the signs and symbols used.

## LEVEL 3: APPLICATION
At this level the pupil is required to *apply* what he has comprehended to concrete situations. Eg after visiting a synagogue pupils should be able to compare and contrast the service with a Christian Service.

## LEVEL 4: ANALYSIS
This slightly more difficult cognitive process involves the breakdown of information into elements for the purpose of clarification. Eg after learning about key festivals in Judaism, pupils should be able to identify the common elements, eg the making present of past events through symbolic action.

## LEVEL 5: SYNTHESIS
At this level the learner is required to put together elements to produce a pattern which is unique to him and which was not clearly there before. Eg pupils should be able to compose (in writing, speech or action) an account of a day in the life of a Jewish boy (a) in the first century AD or (b) in a modern Kibbutz.

## LEVEL 6: EVALUATION
This is the highest cognitive level and involves the passing of value judgments based on internal and external criteria. Eg pupils should be able to examine critically some anti-semitic literature and write a review of it.

The second volume of the Taxonomy on the 'Affective Domain' is generally considered to be of less direct practical value. It attempts to classify objectives in the important area of attitude formation. The organising principle in this case is internalisation. The lowest level (*receiving, attending*) is achieved when the pupil attends in the RE lesson most of the time but does not respond with any great enthusiasm. The second level (*responding*) is achieved when the pupil shows interest, likes answering questions and occasionally does not hear the bell for the end of the period. At level three (*valuing*) our hypothetical pupil shows signs of commitment, follows up references in his own time, and seeks out additional data. Level four (*organisation*) is reached when the learner successfully internalises values, eg he becomes as keen on Religious Studies as some boys are on football. The highest level can be said to have been reached when, over a period of time the pupil looks at human life in the world through the eyes of a student of religion.

When we teach, we develop attitudes at the same time. If the above attempt to summarise the second volume of the Taxonomy makes it seem all too obvious it at least draws attention to the need to take seriously the question of attitude development. Having set ourselves such objectives it will then be incumbent upon us to engineer learning experiences and select content likely to achieve them and, as far as possible, to systematise our attempts to measure and record progress towards them.

It should be noted that objectives are stated in terms of what the learner will be able to do and that unambiguous action words such as list, plot, identify, compare, contrast are used (see Mager 1962 and 1968). In my experience many teachers are only operating at levels 1 and 2 of the Taxonomies and one hopes that attempts to carry pupils to higher cognitive levels may transform the subject. On the other hand the 'behavioural' aspect of this approach has come in for some heavy criticism as we shall see later.

*Content*

The knowledge explosion through which we are living highlights the importance of developing criteria for the selection of content. Work of vital significance on this aspect of the curriculum has been progressing steadily over the past decade and has much to offer to the teacher of RE. The rapid evolution of the subject which may be summed up crudely by noting the shift from Theology to Religious Studies, has left some teachers bewildered, others clutching at passing straws and others reacting conservatively. As mentioned in Chapter 4, one key development had been the placing of religion on the epistemological map by identifying it as one of the forms of knowing and experiencing the world. Hirst (1970) identifies seven distinctive 'forms of knowledge' and includes religion. Phenix (1964) differentiates six 'realms of meaning' and includes religion under the .heading of 'synoptics'. His thesis is that these are the areas of understanding required for a person to function in civilised society. He goes on to claim that, if any one of the six is missing, the person lacks a basic ingredient of experience.' Against this background Hull (1974) is able to argue for an educational treatment of religious and secular faiths in schools as 'one of the most significant duties of the school in a pluralistic society' and to conclude that, without this,

> We would have a silent school, a school which hid from its pupils the great faiths by which men live, for which they struggle and die, a school which offers no information, no clarification, no preparation for responsible life in society where these things are debated. Then indeed we would have a vacuum, and the school would fall prey to those whose interest it is that young people should become unreflective consumers.

The identification of religion as a 'form of knowledge' or 'realm of meaning' only brings us to the starting gate in the curriculum stakes. The massive task of selecting, sequencing and pacing content still lies ahead. What is needed is a set of criteria for the task. The total subject matter (or schema) of religion is boundless, and selection from this field involves asking such questions as How much Christianity? Which secular faiths? Will it be a 'Cook's Tour' of World Religions or one religion in depth? If it is to be one religion, which one? These decisions can only be made when the aims are clear and this supplies the first criterion for selection, *validity* (see Wheeler 1967 and Nicholls 1972). To be valid the particular content must be likely to lead to the achievement of the objectives of the course. There will, of course, be more than one piece of 'valid' content capable of leading to the achievement of the pre-determined objectives. The second criterion, according to Wheeler, is *authenticity,* ie true to the canons of the subject and accurate. There is a warning in this to the RE specialist launching into another culture and religion without adequate preparation and the use of 'authentic' sources. It is in this aspect that the teacher needs the active help of the academic institutions. A current problem is that there is more 'authentic' classroom material coming from the pens of scholars in the field of non-Christian religions than from the Christian apologists who outnumber them.

The subject matter we select should also be *significant*, ie we should not simply pour out content but should select material which illustrates principles or what Phenix calls key ideas. At the practical level this means asking such questions as 'Can we afford to teach Micah or the Maccabees when Marx and Martin Luther King are possibilities?' Our work on the Maccabees may be authentic but what is being asked here is whether 'the content is logically central enough to apply to a wide range of problems' (Wheeler 1967). As Musgrove (1968) points out, 'Every curriculum has a "cost" and the cost of the curriculum is the other curriculum that might have been.'

Wheeler goes on to list minor criteria: (a) needs and interests of the learner (these have already been taken into account in determining aims and objectives) (b) utility (c) learnability (d) consistency with social realities.

A further checklist for use in selecting material is the widely used list of dimensions of religion outlined by Ninian Smart in Chapter 1. A balanced diet from these dimensions (doctrinal, mythological, ethical, ritual, experiential, social) within a programme involving both the personal quest for meaning — implicit religion (Schools Council 1971) — and the objective empathetic study of the phenomena of religion (explicit religion) is what is required. Phenix's description of the teacher as the 'humaniser of knowledge' sums up his role in this aspect of curriculum planning. His task is to sequence material to suit the pupils in accordance with the logic of the subject. In respect of the latter he will need to analyse in order to pass on findings and he will also be responsible for facilitating discovery in the field through the direct application of the appropriate methodologies. All this seems a tall order for the teacher with hundreds of pupils passing through his hands in the course of a week and it is therefore most appropriately carried out by teams both nationally based and school based. Proper organisation for developments of this kind is lacking from our present system.

*Learning experiences*

There are many ways of learning the same content. The next aspect of rational curriculum planning concerns decisions about learning experiences. It involves asking what the pupils will be doing during their course. As Tyler (1949) points out, it is 'not what the teacher does but what the learner does that matters'. Unfortunately there are so many constraints on RE teachers in terms of resources and time that some potentially potent learning experiences are not available to them. To take a trivial example, most of us have experienced the projector with a 13-amp plug for a room with a 15-amp socket for which Mr X has lost the adaptor. The first need is a base for the subject and some essential equipment, the second is a fair allocation of time.

The essential criteria for selecting learning experiences according to Nicholls and Nicholls (1972) can be summarised by saying that they should be (a) appropriate to the group (b) recognisable by the pupil to be useful (c) varied (d) possible and practical. Eaton (1973) suggests

> one good idea is to make a list of all the possible sorts of activities that go on in your classroom, eg teacher talks, teacher asks questions, pupils explain, small groups tackle a problem, pupils watch a film or filmstrip or slides or TV, read individually, listen to tape recording or record, make models, find out answers to questions on a work card etc.

Learning experiences designed for 'implicitly religious' topics will be more difficult to engineer than those designed for 'explicit religion'. The important thing is to find the most potent experiences. Clearly first-hand experience, where possible, will be more effective than vicarious experience. Thus if the objectives and content are in the area of understanding Greek Orthodox Christians and comparing and contrasting selected aspects of the ritual and doctrinal dimensions with Protestant Christianity, then the best learning experiences would involve meeting Greek Orthodox Christians in work, worship and home, with a visit to Greece to conclude the unit of work! Obviously this is impractical and expensive so we must move down the ladder of learning experiences until we find the best possible practical solution allowed by the limitations imposed by the classroom and its resources. Is there a film we can use, or tape recording with pictures? Is there an Orthodox priest who might visit the school?

The importance of variety in learning experiences needs to be stressed, but two notes of warning should be added. First, we should beware of gimmicks, only use hardware when it is the best approach. Second, it is important to remember that we are dealing with the sensitive area of private beliefs. When we organise learning experiences such as visits to places of worship and encounters with committed people it is a difficult task to ensure that a genuine encounter takes place. A great deal of skill, sensitivity and empathy is required on the part of the teacher. At the same time he needs to recognise his limitations, for example, he is most likely an Anglo-Saxon product of a Christian culture and not a meditation master or a guru.

*Organising and integrating the experiences and content of learning*
This stage in the planning process is important for several reasons. First it draws attention to the fact that organisation is an open question, that is, it is a matter for decision and not simply of tradition. Second, rational consideration of these matters enforces clarification of the widely misused term 'integration'.

The subject of integration and RE will be discussed in Chapter 9 (see also Birnie 1972 and Warwick 1973). It will be sufficient here to highlight the main issues. The word 'integration' tends to be used in a variety of contexts. It is possible to integrate either the time-table (integrated day or week) or pupil groups (not segregating pupils according to age and ability) or teachers (team teaching) or lastly to

integrate subjects. It is the latter with which teachers of
Religious Education are most concerned at the present
time — the place for RE in the curriculum either as a separate
subject or within an area called Humanities or Integrated
Studies. Much loaded language is used in favour of integration. Knowledge, it is argued, is a 'seamless robe' and
ought not to be 'pigeon holed' into 'watertight compart-
ments' so that pupils have to perform 'mental gymnastics'
every thirty-five minutes. Four possible approaches to the
integration of subject matter can be illustrated diagram-
matically (see Figure 3).

TYPE 1 The Subject Curriculum        TYPE 2 The Topic or Theme-
                                                       Based Curriculum

TYPE 3 The Core Curriculum          TYPE 4 The Problem-Centred
                                                       Curriculum (interdisciplinary
                                                       enquiry)

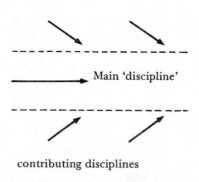

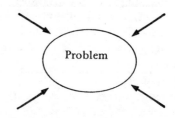

contributing disciplines

contributing disciplines
illuminating the problem

Figure 3

In my opinion, where RE is operating on a Type 1 curriculum it is starving to death for lack of time and support. Where Type 2 is in operation it is dying by being dismembered. For example a topic on 'fishing' degenerates into 'fishing in Palestine' and one on 'flight' has an RE component 'the flight into Egypt'. Clearly this kind of work contributes nothing to the pupils' understanding of religion in general and Christianity in particular. Types 3 and 4 hold more promise since they can overcome problems of isolation and time shortage and yet allow for religion as a *distinctive* 'form of knowledge' or 'realm of meaning' to be explored.

The problems of organisation and integration will not solve themselves. They need friendly cooperation, hard bargaining, planning and decision-making within a defensible theoretical framework provided by the procedures of curriculum development.

*Evaluation*
This phase of the curriculum process can be considered in two senses. First there is the evaluation of the course which results from feedback from both the pupils and the teachers involved. Second it is concerned with the evaluation of pupils' work and progress. In relation to course evaluation, the continuous nature of curriculum development and the importance of feedback has been stressed earlier. It will be more useful here to concentrate on the second aspect, by outlining definitions and criteria evolved by curriculum theorists. The following working definitions may clear up some terminological confusion. The term *measurement* is concerned with quantifying the nature and extent of changes in the pupils' performance and attitudes. *Assessment*, on the other hand, considers this measurement in the light of the expected outcomes, whilst *evaluation* involves the making of judgments about the nature and desirability of the recorded changes. Different types of assessment are possible as shown on the diagram. (Figure 4.)

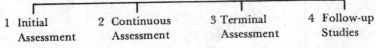

| 1 Initial | 2 Continuous | 3 Terminal | 4 Follow-up |
| Assessment | Assessment | Assessment | Studies |

Figure 4

There is a tendency to concentrate on 3 and 2, although 1 and 4 might also provide equally interesting data for the teacher.

Wiseman and Pidgeon (1972) rightly argue that 'evaluation starts with knowing what is to be evaluated.' Unless the expected outcomes are specified as clearly as possible, measurement, assessment and evaluation are likely to be inaccurate. If our assessment is to be *valid* it must test all the objectives and not simply those which are easily measured. Lower cognitive levels (Bloom levels 1 and 2) are easier to assess and traditional school procedures tend not to test the higher skills. Since the assessment tail tends to wag the objectives dog there is a danger that in such a situation the teaching will concentrate on memorisation and simple comprehension.

Wilhelms (Hooper 1971) puts forward a very important criterion when he argues that 'Evaluations must facilitate self-evaluation.' The learner's self-image is built up through the feedback that he receives, and the consequences of one-sided feedback are obvious. The aims should be to encourage the growth of a healthy and valid self-image and to develop the learner's capacity for self-assessment. At the same time the assessment procedures should have the minimum 'backwash' effect on the curriculum as a whole. Many teachers of RE avoid examinations for this reason, but this itself may have a 'backwash' effect in down-grading the subject in the pupils' estimation. There is probably room for more development along the lines of CSE Mode III.

The survey of the key aspects of curriculum development is now complete and we must now take account of the criticisms which have been made of the 'process' approach in general and behavioural objectives in particular. Over the past few years there has been a steady stream of articles, and many of the doubts and reservations expressed are very telling as far as religious education is concerned. The main critics and criticisms can be summarised briefly and additional references given for the interested reader who wishes to pursue the problem further.

James, in her provocative book *Young Lives at Stake* (1968), considers the approach I have outlined to be far too simplistic. Aims, she points out, are heavily value-laden and are not so easily formulated. The needs of the pupil, the demands of society and of the subject-matter are not as easy to reconcile as is suggested. Furthermore, teaching involves complex human encounters with unique individuals, and to suggest that this can be reduced to objectives concerning observable behaviour is to confuse education with training.

Stenhouse (1970) points to difficulties which are particularly acute for religious education. He points out that the content of a work of art or a piece of literature (and one might add, a religious phenomenon like a Cathedral or a Quaker meeting) cannot be reduced to a student's behaviour in terms of acquired skills. The student in such situations may demonstrate satisfactorily the mastery of certain skills and, outside the classroom, show that he missed any *genuine* experience of the subject matter.

Other writers (eg Gribble 1970, Eisner 1971, MacDonald-Ross 1973) make similar criticisms; it is alleged, for example, that the Bloom categories are not always satisfactory; a pupil may appear to be synthesising or evaluating when he is really involved in a piece of memory-recall. Also there is a danger in pre-specifying objectives; it may be appropriate in some cases to experiment not knowing the outcome. Moore (1973) in a critical article called, 'Measuring the Measurable', concludes 'it is a very short step from an overriding concern for the measurable to the notion that the measurable is all that should concern us.'

These objections must be taken with great seriousness and divert us from an over-zealous literal interpretation of the 'process' approach. Nevertheless it must be said that an assertion such as 'my subject cannot be tied down in this way' can be a smoke-screen for lack of clarity about what the outcomes of the teaching are to be.

There must be some happy medium between the rigidly structured behavioural objectives approach and the 'play it by ear' curriculum. In the latter connection I am reminded of the ex-colleague to whom the children said, on seeing his rather blank expression, 'Don't worry, sir, you'll think of something.' In spite of her criticisms of the objectives approach, Charity James lists the advantages of the rational approach of the curriculum theorists whose work has been outlined in this chapter.

Rational planning of the curriculum does not stand or fall

with behavioural objectives. A means-end approach, as Hirst points out, is central to a planned curriculum but 'ends can be specified in enormously varied ways, some specific, some general, some behavioural, some not' (Taylor and Walton 1973). This seems to me to be a helpful mediating position for the teacher of Religious Education to adopt. The subject will only move forward at both national and local levels if we adopt and adapt some of the strategies advocated by the curriculum theorists.

## References

I.H. Birnie ed. (1972) *Religious Education in Integrated Studies* SCM Press.

B.S. Bloom ed. (1956) *Taxonomy of Educational Objectives* Handbook 1: Cognitive Domain, Longman.

J. Eaton (1973) 'Planning the curriculum', booklet for use by students at St Martin's College, Lancaster, unpublished.

E. Eisner (1971) *Confronting Curriculum Reform* Little, Brown, Boston.

J. Gribble (1970) *Journal of Curriculum Studies* vol.2 no.1, Faber.

P. Hirst and R.H. Peters (1970) *The Logic of Education* Routledge.

R. Hooper, ed. (1971) *The Curriculum: context, design and development* Oliver & Boyd.

J. Hull, ed. (1974) Editorial, *Learning for Living* vol.13 no.5, SCM Press.

C. James (1968) *Young Lives at Stake* Collins.

J.F. Kerr, ed. (1968) *Changing the Curriculum* ULP.

R. Krathwohl (1964) *Taxonomy of Educational Objectives* Handbook 2: Affective Domain, Longmans.

Lancashire (1968) *Religion and Life* Lancashire Education Committee.

M. MacDonald-Ross (1973) 'Behavioural Objectives — a critical review' *Instruction Science* 2.

R.F. Mager (1962) *Preparing Instructional Objectives* Fearn.
(1968) *Developing Attitude towards Instruction* Fearn.

G. Moore (1973) 'Measuring the measurable' *The Times Educational Supplement* 9 November.

B. Musgrove (1968) 'Curriculum Objectives' *Journal of Curriculum Studies* vol.1, Faber.

A. and H. Nicholls (1972) *Developing a Curriculum: a practical guide*

Allen & Unwin.

P.H. Phenix (1964) *Realms of Meaning* McGraw-Hill.

R. Pring (1970) *Education Course 283* Unit 7, Aims and Objectives, Open University, pp.80 ff.

Schools Council (1971) Working Paper 36, *Religious Education in Secondary Schools* Evans/Methuen.

L. Stenhouse (1970) *Education Course 283* Unit 7, Open University, pp.96 ff.

P.H. Taylor and J. Walton (1973) *The Curriculum: Research Innovation and Change* Ward Lock.

R.W. Tyler (1949) *Basic Principles of Curriculum and Instruction* Chicago University Press.

D. Warwick ed. (1973) *Integrated Studies in the Secondary School* ULP.

D.K. Wheeler (1967) *The Curriculum Process* ULP.

S. Wiseman and D. Pidgeon (1972) *Curriculum Evaluation* NFER.

# 9 Religious education in integrated studies

MICHAEL C. BROWN

Considerable confusion surrounds the notion of educational integration. To one side of integration stand various forms of assimilation of one method or subject to another; to the other side stand various forms of complementary or parallel studies.

Many of our traditional school subjects themselves are in fact based upon assimilation of a number of logically irreducible methods. The results are not entirely unsatisfactory, provided always that people understand what is happening. For example, certain approaches to History involve the use not only of factual information about the past but also the application of judgments which are the 'norms' of other disciplines. Some of the best History teaching deliberately takes up moral and religious questions, not as if they were part of History itself, but as worthy of consideration in their own right. It is, moreover, a traditional role of historians (questioned by some contemporary scholars) to turn History itself into a kind of broadly philosophical study. In this setting conclusions are drawn about the 'meaning' of the facts about the past. Similarly, Social Studies, and to a lesser extent Environmental Studies, also adopt a deliberate assimilation of methods. In popular terms they are both concerned to blend fact and interpretation.

This kind of assimilation becomes confusing either when it is forgotten that a given subject may be making use of a number of logically distinct methodologies, or when the subject is taught as if such distinctions simply do not exist. This mistake lies behind those theories about General Studies which suggest that somewhere over and above specific 'realms of knowledge' there exists a general kind of knowledge in which a new kind of general understanding replaces the separate understandings of the traditional disciplines of knowledge. It has been cogently argued that, in fact, such general principles, concepts, methods and categories for the organisation of knowledge do not exist (see Pring 1972). On the contrary, it can be demonstrated that there are a number of different ways of looking at the world, each with its proper approach.

What purport to be integrated studies often turn out to be parallel, complementary or correlative studies, in which a given topic is examined from a number of different viewpoints without any attempt at either true integration or even a blending of methods. This is no bad thing. Why should we not hear the views of, for example, ecologists, lawyers, moralists and theologians respectively on some such subject as environmental pollution? This is the kind of thing that goes on at many levels in thematic teaching. But it is not an integrated exercise in the strict sense of the word. Its aim is not so much to examine the theme 'in itself', as to exemplify various ways of understanding the theme, that is, from the standpoint of a variety of realms of meaning.

Final integration in education is more than correlation between realms of meaning or assimilation of one method to another. It is a matter of the integration of curriculum content by way of such integrative methods as will contribute to the integrating personality. Integration is in the mind of the learner and such ultimate integration of experience is the business of religion and philosophy. These are the realms of meaning which serve to provide total or 'synoptic' views of reality in experience, and by analogy it is, in the last resort, only religious and philosophical types of study which by virtue of their own structure are in the position to provide a total or 'synoptic' view of the meaning of the curriculum.

One of the most interesting aspects of modern philosophy has been the attempt to analyse the structure of knowledge itself. In 1933 Oakshott published a work under the title *Experience and Its Modes*. Earlier, between 1923 and 1929 Cassirer had produced a monumental work in eight volumes on the structure of knowledge which he used as the basis for *An Essay On Man* (1944). He treats the structure of knowledge in terms of the history of culture and the different kinds of understandings of the cosmos which have been given symbolic form by mankind. The most specific attempt to relate the theory of the structure of knowledge to educational practice came with the publication of Phenix's *Realms of Meaning* (1964). Phenix's conclusions have recently been popularised in slightly modified form by Professors Hirst and Peters. Each of these authors, in one way or another, has stressed the peculiar nature of the religious mode of experience. Oakshott describes it as the consummation of 'practice', the conative principle at its most all-inclusive. Cassirer describes the centrality of myth and religion in man's symbolic self-understanding. Phenix is concerned with the 'synoptic' function of religion in drawing together the totality of experience.

For the purpose of the present chapter, Phenix's analysis of the formal characteristics of the realm of religious meaning is particularly important. Phenix first describes those areas of meaning concerned respectively with formal or analytical understanding, with empirical facts, with aesthetic experience, with intuitive 'direct' knowledge and with ethical norms. He then considers what he terms the 'synoptic' realm of meaning, that which includes both philosophy and religion. Of religion he writes:

> When all kinds of knowledge are comprehended within a synoptic perspective controlled by the normative quality, the resultant discipline is religion. Religious knowledge is regarded as an apprehension of the Ultimate Good — a Harmony of the Whole, a Complete Truth — that is not contained in any of the more limited ways of knowing. Religious Knowledge is usually thought to require an act of faith by which a total commitment is made to whatever is regarded as ultimately worthy of devotion. In this essentially normative act all the various classes of knowledge are synthesised (Phenix 1964, p.27).

Philosophy also, or at any rate that kind of philosophy which purports to make objective statements as to what the world is ultimately like, is also an all-embracing, 'synoptic' mode of understanding. These apprehensions, whether religious or philosophical, are those which gather together other modes of experience and provide a comprehensive understanding of them. That is why, for example, there is at least a grain of truth in the popular claim that morality 'depends' upon religion. This might be better expressed by pointing out that ethical systems and decisions do not exist in a vacuum, but find a context in some more inclusive religious or philosophical interpretation of life.

A traditional view of religion is that its synoptic role arises from its interpretation of the world *sub specie aeternitatis*, from an absolute perspective beyond space and time. Such integration of experience may arise either by way of the objectivity of philosophy or by way of commitment to a religious faith, or indeed by way of a combination of the two. By analogy, within the school curriculum, true integration is only present when pupils are faced with those ideas and feelings which arise within these synoptic realms of experience. Religious Education, therefore, is not merely something to be integrated with other content matter, let alone something to be assimilated to or correlated with other types of knowledge; rather, by virtue of the logic of its own subject matter, it provides an ultimately integrative principle for the interpretation of other realms of meaning.

A religiously educated person is one who is in a position to integrate different ways of looking at the world in a peculiarly comprehensive manner. Such a person, in the first place, knows what religion is; and, in the second place, has developed such reflective qualities as are required in order to apply what is known about religion to other general or particular ways of looking at the world. The profile of such a person is that of one who

1 Is able to *recognise* religious issues, their interrelationships and their interrelation with issues in other fields;
2 Discerns what is *said and done* in the realm of religion;
3 Discerns what is *felt and meant* in the realm of religion;
4 Is able to master the *categories* which are required in order to understand and evaluate what is said, done, felt and meant in the realm of religion;
5 Is sensitive to the *symbolic* in the realm of religion;
6 Is sensitive to his *own being*;
7 Is sensitive to all that *transcends* his own being;
8 Is open to the challenge of the *unexpected*;
9 Is disposed to assign a *positive* value to and to affirm an ultimate confidence in life;

10 Is disposed also to become an *interpersonally, ethically and aesthetically* educated person and thereby to be in a position to integrate his experience in itself and with that of others in a total value system.

The first five items in this profile cover the study of what may be termed the 'explicit' manifestations of religion. These comprise all those ideas, feelings, words and actions which are normally thought of as peculiarly religious. Such a study may at times be a highly specialised exercise and call for a degree of separate teaching in classes set aside for the purpose. The integrative function of such teaching is not, therefore, immediately apparent; nor in the modern world, is the integrative function of religious symbolism.

The second five items are readily seen as being somewhat different. These dispositions, listed as being required of the student of religion, are particularly important in relation to the study of religion in its 'implicit' dimension. This is concerned, as it were, with the religion behind religion; it consists of a stance in respect of the world which lacks any specifically religious expression and yet is characterised by its integrative function. Teaching directed towards an appreciation of this dimension of religion, based as it is on broad attitudes and dispositions, and not confined to a religious context, is unlikely to be restricted to a programme of Religious Education as such, but will be diffused throughout the curriculum.

### Types of knowledge

Phenix has made the point that knowledge may be classified in respect of quality under three headings. Some knowledge is about facts, other knowledge about formal relationships, and a third category is concerned with norms.

Factual knowledge may be either empirical or direct, that is intuitive. The physical and social sciences serve as a paradigm for the empirical kinds of factual knowledge. Factual knowledge about religious rites and ceremonies, sacred times and seasons, and knowledge about the contents of the scriptures is of this kind. Experiences are also facts; all those direct apprehensions of persons and things that are described in literature and by the human sciences belong equally to the realm of fact. Not only can a man be said to know certain facts about his home town; he also simply knows it. He has both empirical knowledge and a direct 'appreciation' of it. Both his empirical and his experiential knowledge belong to the world of fact.

'Formal' knowledge is that which gives shape to reality by defining relationships between ideas. Mathematics, logic and philosophy are all concerned with 'formal' relationships. Much ordinary conversation is also of this kind — the cat is on the mat inside the front door and cannot therefore be making that horrible noise in the front garden. Art in all its manifestations is also concerned with form — each and every work of art bears a singular formal relationship to reality as a whole.

Lastly, knowledge is concerned with norms. Morality and religion are the paradigms of such 'normative' knowledge and experience. Just as science and mathematics are confounded in the popular mind, because both are concerned with general laws (formal or factual respectively), so also morality and religion are mistakenly seen as one and the same thing. They are rightly seen as 'normative' approaches to life but they are not sufficiently differentiated in respect of what Phenix would call their quantitative characteristics. Morality is concerned with 'general' rules and 'singular' (specific) actions; religion is concerned with 'comprehensive' apprehensions of what is to be accorded supreme devotion.

In the second part of this chapter, I shall attempt to relate the realm of religion in turn to those parts of the curriculum which deal with factual and with formal knowledge respectively. This will be done largely in terms of the traditional secondary school curriculum. The question of the relation between the moral and the religious types of normative knowledge are dealt with elsewhere in this volume.

## Religion within the curriculum

Facts may be either empirical or experiential. Items 2 and 3 in the profile of the religiously educated person, as outlined above, are concerned with empirical facts about religion. They are facts like any other facts. 'Religious' facts do not exist in the sense that they demand a different method from that to be adopted in the study of other facts. This is important when one is faced with the claim that only believers can properly teach about religion. The basic facts about religion are not the exclusive preserve of the believer or even of the teacher of Religious Education. Indeed, a somewhat distanced approach to the facts may be a positive advantage. For example, if one adopts such an approach, the most obvious fact about the Resurrection of Jesus is not that it happened, but that certain people believed that it had happened, preached that it had happened, and that certain historically verifiable effects followed from this preaching. Many believers, however, may be inclined to put their efforts into giving the Resurrection itself the status of an empirical fact, and in so doing fail to recognise it as being more of a unique object of religious faith than an empirical fact in the normal sense of this term. The notion that the Resurrection cannot be presented as a fact like other empirical facts may simply not occur to the believer, and by the same token he may also overlook the significance of those undoubtedly empirical facts which are associated with the Resurrection faith of the early Church.

The scope of the more strictly empirical facts about religion is enormous. Such facts, in general, are the preserve of historians, archaeologists, human geographers, economists and the teachers of all manner of social sciences. There is a case for urging that as much as possible of this empirical content of Religious Education be dealt with by those who normally attended to such matters. Children themselves often think it odd when Religious Education forsakes such obviously germane topics as God and Allah, the meaning of the lives of Jesus and the Buddha, the study of the Bible or the Vedas, or even the 'implicit' dimensions of religious experience, and becomes an exercise in the history and geography of the Holy Land. It is no answer to the problem of Religious Education merely to replace the Bible story lesson with lessons in historical, geographical and social background. The background is important but it is not at the heart of Religious Education in any serious sense of the term. Let as much as possible of this empirical study be in the hands of historians and geographers. It may be that the teacher of religion is a geographer or historian as well, or even a generalist accustomed to performing more than one role. But the integrative function of Religious Education is not well served by the teacher of religion becoming amateur historian, geographer, economist, political scientist and psychologist rolled into one. It may well be that the distinctively integrative concerns of Religious Education are best served by a degree of separateness on the part of those concerned to raise these issues, and by the leaving of the more empirical studies to those best equipped to deal with them.

There is, however, another side to the question. In that they are so many and so varied, it is doubtful whether the more obviously 'religious' phenomena, in the sense of those which arise largely as a consequence of and as an expression of man's religious experience, can be fully dealt with by the historian or geographer as such. In this empirical area the teacher of Religion should have three distinct contributions to make. He should have a clear idea as to precisely what religious problems are best illustrated by the study of particular factual information. In this respect he will, secondly, be able to advise his colleagues in the construction of all manner of integrated programmes. Lastly, he will himself be able to teach the more obscure of the specifically religious phenomena and the less familiar items of background information.

In this way it may be possible to transfer much of the study of the more general background phenomena to the sphere of those who normally deal with such matters. It is also important to open the way for social scientists to study religious phenomena from the viewpoints of their own particular disciplines. There remains, however, a considerable area of empirical study to which only the teacher of religion has ready access and from which he alone will be able to make a significant selection.

Before leaving the realms of factual knowledge we must consider what Phenix calls the realm of 'synnoetics'. This has already been described as the realm of 'direct' or intuitive knowledge. 'Sensitivity training' is not a subject taught in schools and is very little considered in the construction of the curriculum. But simple direct awareness, the fact of oneself in relation to other persons and things, at a psychological level the question of giving one's attention to things, is basic to the entire educational venture. The act of attending to the fact of relationship is also at the heart of religion. A general disposition to attend directly to persons and to things, to 'know' them, is a prerequisite of that more particular attention to persons and things which appears in several items in the profile of the religiously educated person. Religious Education must proceed hand in hand with any attempts that are being made to open up to pupils the 'synnoetic' realm of experience.

I have selected two only of the various types of formal knowledge for discussion – the study of language as such, and the study of literature and the arts. A great deal will have to remain unsaid about the relationship between religion, mathematics, logic and philosophy.

Items 1 and 4 respectively of the profile of the religiously educated person call for understanding of what characterises the realm of religion and of the concepts used within that realm. Item 5 is also concerned with language. It is surely reasonable that matters relating to language should be in the hands of those chiefly concerned with the teaching of language. One cannot expect teachers of language to be experts in the conceptual, linguistic and operational bases for each and every known mode of discourse; but one may reasonably expect such teachers to point out that various ways of using language operate in different contexts. To teach *how* to operate within each realm is the business of the specialist in each realm. There is nothing particularly abstruse about this exercise. I have on many occasions asked a class of twelve-year-olds to write three short pieces about the stars – one as if from a science text book, one in the form of a poem and one in the form of a myth of origin. The point is immediately taken by even the least able children and a session at once creative and analytical becomes possible. However, in the context of my role as a teacher of religion, I have had the suspicion that I have been trespassing on the ground which belonged more properly to the teachers of language, and had it been they that had made the basic distinctions, I would have had all the more time to have investigated with the pupils the more specific characteristics of myth as a mode of religious discourse. Some form of team teaching was probably called for.

Such teaching is also called for as between the teacher of

religion and the teacher of history. In many recent programmes of Religious Education there has been some stress
laid on the distinctions to be made between the various
literary genres to be found in the Bible and other sacred
texts. There is much (often grossly over-simplified) talk of
history, myth and legend. The problems are complex and
require cooperation between language teachers, historians
and teachers of religion. *That* such distinctions exist is the
business of the teachers of language; *how* myth differs from
legend is the business of the teachers of history; the specific
characteristics of religious myth that of the teacher of
religion.

The case for linking the study of religion to that of
literature and the arts is perhaps stronger than the more
commonly advocated case for a liaison between the study of
religion and the social sciences. The reason that the latter
association comes so readily to people's minds is that religion
is so easily confounded with social morality. The case for the
former association is based on the very real shading off of the
realm of religion into that of aesthetics. Insofar as literature
and the arts can carry content, that content is frequently
religious; indeed, religions would not survive apart from their
symbolic forms. It is interesting to note that the contemporary crisis, amounting to near break-down, in man's symbolic
understanding affects both religion and the arts. It is also
interesting to note a further link in that such literary critics
as Northrop Frye are suggesting that the study of literature
should not be built upon the notion of 'appreciation' but
upon the more objective notion of structural 'understanding'.
This view is parallel to the notion that the purpose of the
study of religion is not the inculcation of faith, but the
'understanding' of religion through the adoption of an
objective, although sympathetic, approach.

It is my experience that teachers of literature and the arts
are divided as to whether it is allowable to 'use' these studies
as vehicles for teaching about ethics or religion. On the one
hand there are schools in which the teachers of English
appear almost to have absorbed the roles of teachers of ethics
and religion, often with highly 'confessional' and moralistic
presuppositions. On the other hand there are institutions
where the art-for-art's-sake school of thought reigns supreme.

The teachers of the performing arts are at times particularly suspicious of any attempt to 'use' music, drama or dance to any ends beyond the purely aesthetic. In this context moral and religious content is regarded as either irrelevant or as non-existent. Again, the resolution of this conflict calls for team teaching. The close logical links between the realms of aesthetics and religion demand that these be complementary studies. The teacher of religion must perforce make considerable illustrative, and perhaps more importantly participatory, use of literature and the arts. The teacher in these areas must give due weight to the religious content of his material. Both sides must respect the autonomy of the realm of meaning with which the other is concerned. There must be mutual interchange of expertise.

*True integration*

We have seen that both at a logical and at a practical level the realm of religion stands in a particular relationship to various modes of formal and factual knowledge. It is also related to the 'normative' realm of ethics. These logical and practical relationships do not suggest that one should stand out either for the sanctity of separate disciplines or for the shibboleth of 'breaking down the subject barriers'. The important thing is that each and every realm and type of knowledge should be seen for what it is and allowed to exercise its proper function. Integration of the curriculum is achieved by the raising of integrative issues and by the exploration of the integrative emotions. These issues, ideas and emotions belong to the 'synoptic' studies which are based upon the concerns of religion and philosophy. Integration does not arise merely by rearranging subject areas; it does not proceed by way of finding the correct formula for the association of departments in like or complementary clusters; it does not arise simply by the abolition of subjects nor by the introduction of an integrated day.

On the other hand integration does entail a considerable degree of team teaching and specialist expertise. In both secondary and primary schools it is desirable that each teacher be an expert, if not in a 'subject' in the old sense of the word, at any rate in a particular approach to knowledge. It is also desirable that each teacher be a generalist, not in the old sense of a Jack-of-all-trades, but in the sense of understanding in broad outline the methodologies proper to other approaches to knowledge.

Dare one imagine an ideal school in which the headteacher is a philosopher who is able to adopt a synoptic but reasonably objective stance, and can thus give shape and form to the whole operation? Dare one imagine that he or she will appoint to his or her staff a team of specialists: one expert in matters empirical; one concerned with the formal operations characteristic, in the first place, of the 'tool' subjects; one expert in the matter of aesthetics; one whose main concern is in the realm of 'synnoetics'; and one whose field is ethics? Dare one, further, imagine that the welding together of the curriculum at those points where ultimate questions touch the heart and mind will be in the hands of the teacher whose business is religion in the widest sense of the word?

In the early 1960s far-sighted educationalists such as Jeffreys and Niblett suggested that religion as a separate subject was a nonsense and called upon Christian teachers to strive to bring their faith to bear upon their teaching at every level. Today, in a more secular age, many would question the 'confessional' assumptions of their vision of a Christian education. But the insistence upon the need for a more open and objective approach to religion in schools should not lead us to overlook the radical implications of the logic of religion itself. Religious Education is in danger of being 'integrated' out of existence by assimilation to moral and social studies. To become itself it must, in fact, insist on a central, but not a 'confessional', role. In this way it will not provide dogmatic-ally-based answers but will bring to the surface the thoughts and feelings with which pupils must come to grips if the integrating personality is to be taken seriously as an ultimate goal of the educational venture.

## References

E. Cassirer (1944) *An Essay on Man* Yale University Press.
P.H. Hirst and R.S. Peters (1970) *The Logic of Education* Routledge.
M. Oakshott (1933) *Experience and its Modes* Cambridge University Press.
P.H. Phenix (1964) *Realms of Meaning* McGraw-Hill.
R. Pring (1972) 'Forms of Knowledge and General Education' *General Education* Autumn, Longman.

# 10 Catechesis and religious education

RICHARD M. RUMMERY

In August 1970 the Australian Catholic Episcopal Conference officially approved and commended as a set of norms for catechetical activity the guidelines of a document entitled *The Renewal of the Education of Faith* (Australian Episcopal Conference 1970). The issuing in the past year of this document with a separate introduction by the Roman Catholic hierarchy of England and Wales for the use of Roman Catholics of those countries, seems to me an event of considerable importance for Roman Catholic religious education.

As I have set out at greater length elsewhere (Rummery 1974), there have been many attempts in the Catholic Church in the past century or so to impose a uniform catechism of Christian Doctrine on the whole church. In some ways, this kind of activity may have confused the ideas of unity and uniformity, as for example in the decision of the 1950 Catechetical Congress in Rome to press for a uniform wording in national catechisms 'so that the same words will be used to convey the same truths' (Sloyan 1964), a resolution which remained unimplemented in most cases. The Second Vatican Council, despite the recommendations of a working party that the task of any catechetical commission of the Council should be to produce a uniform and definitive catechism for the whole Church, did not set up an explicitly catechetical commission and, indeed, moved only in a very limited fashion to the broader area of Christian Education in the Conciliar document 'Gravissimum Educationis' (Abbott 1966). The latter document was content to limit itself to the enunciation of what it called 'certain basic principles of Christian education, especially those relating to formal schooling' (Abbott 1966), and the preamble to the document noted that such principles 'will have to be developed at greater length by a specific post-Conciliar Commission and

applied by episcopal conferences to varying local situations'
(Abbott 1966). Now it was in response to this last sentence
that the Italian Episcopal Conference set in process a detailed
study of the whole nature of religious education at all levels
in Italy. This very broadly based investigation, coordinated
by a catechetical commission under Father James Medica, a
Salesian at Genoa, worked six years in close consultation
with various groups in the community before proposing the
final version of a document called 'Il Rinnovamento della
Catechesi' adopted by the Italian Episcopal Conference in
February 1970. It is this document which has been translated
as 'The Renewal of the Education of Faith'. What lies behind
this new term for catechesis?

If it is accepted that changes in language are often a
reflection of a changed way of viewing something, then I
suggest that there is strong evidence that Catholics may be at
a very important stage of evaluating their position as regards
religious education. Consider, for example, the following list
of terms, all of which have served as subject descriptions over
the past thirty years or so and many of which are currently in
use in English schools — Catechism, Catechetics, Religious
Instruction, Religious Knowledge, Christian Knowledge,
Theology, Divinity, and now, Religious Education. Add the
term Christian Living, which is currently used in many
Catholic schools in Australia, and I think it is evident that
there are not only various degrees of emphasis implied by this
range of terms but perhaps also a certain confusion of aims.
Certainly these are not equivalent terms. Is it fanciful to
suggest that perhaps we are here witnessing a mutation of
some kind? I will argue in this chapter that, in Catholic terms
at least, there is a decided move in the *de facto* situation
away from the explicitly catechetical model related to the
special concept of 'catechesis' and a move towards a broader
concept of 'religious education' within which 'catechesis'
occupies a special and privileged position. As this is a
distinction which I have argued at length elsewhere
(Rummery 1974) I will attempt to clarify the important
distinctions which need to be made between the concept of
'catechesis' itself and some particular forms of catechetical
activity which have been associated since the Reformation
with the idea of catechisms.

## What is catechesis?

Viewed historically, *'catechesis'* is the Greek term adopted by the early Christian Church to describe instruction of those who have been brought to the Church as adult believers. As such, it is a second-stage process which follows the acceptance of the gift of faith. In contrasting senses of the idea of faith, it is the instruction in the faith of the Church of those who have received the 'habitus fidei' conferred in Baptism. If, ideally, this personal faith will grow and develop most naturally through a deeper understanding and liturgical experience of the faith of the Church as a complementary process, it must still be emphasised that faith as the 'donum Dei' — the gift of God — requires acceptance by the individual. It must not be lightly assumed. Such is the clear insistence of the famous baptismal catecheses of the fourth century (Yarnold 1971).

But an inspection of the concept of catechesis at various stages of the history of the Christian Church shows quite clearly that there has never been either a uniform method or content which was essential to the concept; rather, there has been a great diversity arising from the different situations of those being catechised. Part of the dominance of the written word since the days of Gutenberg's first press has been the prevalence of the idea that knowledge has a new authority by being available in a printed form. As a result, generations of Christians (Lutherans, Calvinists, Anglicans and Catholics) have had their doctrinal grounding in Christianity established by the use of catechisms, but it is easy to claim overmuch for what was achieved by such catechisms and the manner of their use. Perhaps the limitations of such an approach were well pointed up on the opening page of Newman's *Apologia* in his remark:

> I was brought up from a child to take great delight in reading the Bible; but I had no formed religious convictions till I was fifteen. Of course I had a perfect knowledge of my catechism (Newman 1903).

In its historical setting, the catechism, from the time of Luther's 'Kleine Katechismus' in 1529, has often been used in a polemical fashion. For Catholics in the late nineteenth century and the early part of the twentieth, the catechism offered a short, clear and easily memorised summary of doctrinal truths, moral obligations and common prayers and devotions. In its unattractive format and use as a class text, it was no better and no worse than similar texts used in other subjects. But we may now be in a better position to see the limited nature of its achievement. An ability to repeat the catechism text often meant very little as regards the more important understanding of the doctrinal truths of the catechism. The precise wording of the catechism which was necessary to safeguard the orthodoxy of what was expressed often made its inherently difficult subject matter even more difficult to understand. After all, a catechism was a compendium of theological statements and such statements were already at one remove from the realities which had inspired such reflection.

This is not to say that it was not possible for most to learn the catechism but rather that such learning was given an exaggerated place of importance. In a strongly knit sociological community where the priest was often a man set apart no less by his relatively high standard of education than by his priesthood, the authoritative approach of the catechism was simply another part of the hierarchy of such a group. One of the results of this approach, especially given the minority of Catholics in most English-speaking countries, was the easy reduction of the broad concept of catechesis to the much narrower idea of catechism teaching. Among the complex factors influencing this confusion, there was also the general tenor of many nineteenth-century Catholic statements which referred to the 'traditional pedagogy of the Church' (St Paul Books 1970) in a way which confused the whole tradition of catechesis properly so called with the particular and more recent development of catechism teaching – and then tended to argue for 'the tradition of the Church' without examining the very limited tradition being commended.

The catechetical movement of the last forty years or so in the Catholic Church has moved away from the use of the catechism as its main text: for example, after the Munich Catechetical Congress of 1928, it is possible to see much more emphasis on children learning rather than on teachers teaching, a movement clearly related to psychological and sociological aspects of learning in the classroom. After the Second World War, the movement resulted in the preparation of better texts, that is texts which were better written for different age levels and more attractively produced and illustrated; but such innovations often encountered opposition on various grounds.

Perhaps, as many commentators have noted, the basic error was in taking as the starting point with children, what was really the end point of an adult investigation. Various compromises — the German Catechism of the 1950s and the two Australian Catechisms of the 1960s — attempted to preserve some aspects (for example, some learning by heart, a comprehensive statement of important matters, and so on) while at the same time regarding the catechism as the end and summary point for an approach which was based both on children's perception of life and on the revelation of God's great saving plan within the events of life. This approach, often reduced to the generally inadequate description of 'Salvation History' was the fruit of the kerygmatic movement which so broadened the catechetical movement in the 1950s following the translation and deeper understanding of Josef Jungmann's great work of 1936, known in English since 1959 as *Handing on the Faith* (Jungmann 1959). This emphasis, however, could never have taken place without the great impetus given to Biblical studies by the Catholic Church in the post-war period. It is not too strong, I suggest, to talk of the Catholic 'discovery' of the Bible, in the sense that the Bible began to occupy a much more important place in the whole catechetical process, in teaching, in prayers and in liturgical functions. But it needs to be said firmly that the various emphases of the post-war catechetical movement — scriptural, kerygmatic, anthropological, life-centred or group-centred as I have characterised them elsewhere (Rummery 1974) — have none of them succeeded in establishing their particular emphasis as anything more than one emphasis among many. However perplexing this state of affairs has become for many teachers, parents and clergy, it may be considered as a clear rejection by practising catechists of any doctrinaire approach which does not take into account the situation of catechesis in a school context.

That is why the translation and commendation of the Italian document already referred to, 'The Renewal of the Education of Faith', points to the importance of catechesis as something not adequately noted in expressions such as 'teaching the faith' or 'preaching the faith'. The description of catechesis as 'the education of faith' is part of what is implied in the expression which arose out of the French catechetical movement *'l'éducation de la foi'*, an expression which safeguards better than its English translation both the personal and the communitarian dimensions of faith because it does not imply that didactic instruction in the faith of the Church is necessarily the same thing as developing that personal faith, that 'habitus fidei' which is conferred in Baptism. Moreover, the document deals with such a wide range of situations that it is possible to see even from the chapter headings the very core of what is being taken as the concept of catechesis, namely faith — personal faith and the common faith of the Church. On this assumption, consider the description of the contents of the document. (I set out the full chapter headings of the first three chapters to indicate the emphasis.)

1 The Church at the Service of the Word of God
  God's Revelation to Mankind
  The Church and the Word of God
  God's Pedagogy and the Church's Pedagogy
  The Journey of Faith
2 The Principal Expressions of the Church's Ministry of the Word
  The Prophetic Mission and the Ministry of the Word
  Evangelization — The Joyful Announcing of God's Love
  Liturgical Preaching, Culminating Point of the Ministry of the Word
  Catechesis for the Journey of Faith
  Catechesis, Liturgical Preaching and the Witness of Life
3 The Aims and Tasks of Catechesis
  The Mentality of Faith
  An Ever Deeper and More Personal Knowledge
  Initiation into the Life of the Church
  A Profoundly Universal Mentality
  Integration between Faith and Life
4 The Message of the Church is Jesus Christ

5  The Exposition of the Entire Message of Christ
6  The Sources of the Church's Teaching
7  Those Who Are Taught
8  Catechesis as the Work of the Local Church
9  Catechetical Method
10  The Teachers.

It is obvious from these headings that catechesis as envisaged here may be described in shorthand terms as *a dialogue of believers* or *a conversation of believers*, in that it presupposes a common faith and proceeds on that assumption.

Now, it seems to me, that it is precisely this better recognition of the demands of catechesis which poses some serious practical problems in the Catholic school today as schools themselves move away from an educational model which was often too much tied to the idea of education as 'transmission'. At one level, it is reflected in the attitude of many young teachers and final-year students in Colleges of Education who ask to be excused from taking lessons in religion with their pupils — a request, I suggest, which may in many cases be based on their correct perception of catechesis as a dialogue of believers, and, as such, a situation which they do not wish to face on conscientious grounds. It is no solution to maintain that the Catholic school constitutes a 'faith community' by the fact of the common Baptism in Christ of all, teachers and pupils. A faith community in the sense of active participation and sharing of the common faith of the Church still requires a great deal more *personal faith and commitment* that one can assume by the mere fact of people being baptised. The assumption that a nominal Catholic is by that fact a believer and one who must accept the responsibilities of catechesis seems to me a doubtful kind of assumption to be sustained in practice, even though I feel that many Catholic schools which I visited in 1971–1972 were claiming this special character of the Catholic school as their justification for not having a separate Religious Education department. At another level, I wonder whether the increasing difficulties with regard to teaching religion in Catholic secondary schools are not also related to this too easy assumption of the Catholic school being a faith community.

To indicate the way in which this kind of question may need to be approached, allow me to ask three questions which I will consider again together at the end of this chapter:

— Firstly, under what conditions may one presume on a context of shared belief, that is, how do we recognise this shared belief?
— Secondly, is belief shared at the sociological level of 'the Faith' the same as that of the individual's growth in personal faith through progressive commitment to his status as a Christian baptised and redeemed in Christ?
— Thirdly, is your major relationship with your pupils in a school context what can be called, in strict use of terms, a 'catechetical' one, that is, a dialogue or conversation of believers?

### Religious Education in schools
In the same year as the Italian Episcopal Conference published the document we have been considering, the Durham Report on Religious Education *The Fourth R* was published. Space does not permit me to do more than note the much more practical bias of the Durham Report, commissioned as it was for a specific investigation, but some of the recommendations made are relevant in establishing the rather different concept of religious education which it envisaged. The first two recommendations were as follows:

1 The term 'religious instruction' should be replaced forthwith by the term 'religious education'. What we understand by 'religious education' in the context of this report is fully set out in Chapter 4.
2 Religious education, including participation in school worship, should form part of the general education received by all school pupils. (Durham Report 1970.)

The reference to what the framers of the Report saw as religious education seems to me to be indicated in the following section of Chapter 4 par. 191:

We recognise that 'religious education' in the schools of

England and Wales has two essential components:

1 Religious teaching i.e. what pupils learn about the subject through curricular and extra-curricular study and activity.
2 Worship, i.e. what pupils experience through participation in acts of worship in school. We recognise the many complex problems connected with school worship require separate treatment (Durham Report 1970).

It seems important to note the significance of the first recommendation, the proposed change from the 'religious instruction' of the 1944 Act to the term 'religious education'. A survey of the evolution of various kinds of Local Authority syllabuses since 1944 shows that the kind of change recommended is already implicit in the changing emphasis on a more open approach, so that the recommendation itself is really a commendation of what had already taken place. This is recognisable in other ways, most noticeably in the changing models of some of the schemes of work being evolved in the 1960s, so that it seems possible to characterise the habitual stance or attitude taken by the teacher around the following sequence of ideas:

First, there is the traditional 'Agreed Syllabus' approach which in the majority of cases is best described as a 'teaching *that*' activity, because it was designed as the giving of instruction in Christianity, especially through the Bible, to pupils who were (or it was implicitly presumed should be) Christians. At the least, as young people growing up in a country with a Christian heritage, they were to have some understanding of Christianity.

Secondly, there has arisen a model which seems best described as a 'teaching *about*' activity, because it set out to neutralise what was thought to be the kind of privileged access or even proselytising activities of the Christian churches among pupils compelled by Act of Parliament to be present at school for educational purposes. The Schools Council Humanities Curriculum Project directed by Lawrence Stenhouse from 1967 to 1972, with its emphasis on 'procedural neutrality', was probably the most influential example of this kind of model.

A third model seems to me to have been developed by

approaching the whole question in a way which can be characterised as 'education *in* religion'. The force of this model has been particularly in recognising the distinct kind of activity which religion is and attempting to strengthen the educational approach at precisely that point where the neutrality model was weakest. It is not accidental that this model has concentrated on exploring the implications of the kinds of philosophical thinking about education which has been the distinctive contribution of the London University Institute of Education under R.S. Peters, Paul Hirst and R.F. Dearden (see Chapters 4 and 8, above).

Fourthly, the contribution of the University of Lancaster Project on Religious Education in Secondary Schools, especially through Schools Council Working Paper No.36, published in 1971, has been to suggest as a basic kind of model the idea of 'teaching *how*' or 'teaching *why*', a model more closely related to the activity of the teacher.

The first model, the 'teaching *that*', was in many ways not unlike the former catechetical model based on the catechism, in that it was authoritative in its claims and was tied like it to a 'transmission' concept of education. The second model, 'teaching *about*', seems to me to have claimed as an absolute the idea of impartiality which is better regarded as a necessary safeguard against indoctrination. From an educational viewpoint, it is difficult to see this kind of activity as having much positive value, and in the long run one must ask seriously whether such an activity is not implicitly commending a secular view of religion.

The third and fourth models, however, seem to me to be extremely valuable approaches to religious education, given the nature of this activity in the County schools of the United Kingdom where one may not necessarily presume on the religious faith of the pupils and where, increasingly, there may be representatives from other religious traditions than the Christian. In examining these models in a comparative way according to ten criteria, I think that it can be established that there are many instances where they appeal to most teachers who are interested in a concept of religious education which attempts to include both *religion in education* and *education in religion*. (This theme is developed by Colin Alves in Chapter 2.)

In a recent article in *The Tablet* (1974) Norman St John-Stevas suggested to Catholic readers 'that I do not think we can escape responsibility for playing some part in influencing what is taught as religion in most English schools.' (The Tablet 1974.) In terms of the kind of analysis this article has attempted, I think there are much stronger lines of convergence than his article suggested. If catechesis is to be regarded as a dialogue of believers, that is, a situation in which one assumes a common faith as a point of departure, the two models of religious education I have just been discussing may not make this assumption of a common faith. But given the approach of 'educating *in*' or 'teaching *how*', I think that it is reasonable to hope that the educational process may help to create the conditions under which the individual may find some development of his personal faith and even some commitment to it. But I think that this approach may not necessarily be restricted to the situation of religious education in the county school.

## Pre-catechesis?

In terms of the open question asked earlier concerning the assumption of faith in the Catholic school, I wish to question the extent to which, in the *de facto* situations they encounter, Catholic teachers may presume on the faith of those they encounter in the classroom. Teachers are sometimes aware that a significant number of their pupils are not what could be called 'practising Catholics', if the usual norms of regular attendance at Sunday Mass and the Sacraments are applied. They are indeed baptised believers but only the most literal belief in the principle of 'ex opere operato' (the idea of the efficacy of a sacrament being related to the intrinsic importance of the action performed) would justify the attitude that the recipient is to be considered as a believer whether he likes it or not. Catechesis as a dialogue of believers can hardly take place because the school or the Church prescribes it or because I, as a teacher, enforce it. In the secondary school in particular, and indeed in many aspects of the primary school, the concept of 'the education of faith' means precisely that we try to make use of our positions as teachers to help our pupils grow in their personal faith. We cannot give them our faith but hopefully we can help to create the conditions under which they may be helped to grow more deeply in the faith of the Church. The fine balancing point in all this is obviously our respect for the freedom of every single pupil we teach and the way in which we endeavour to maintain what Joseph Colomb, the great French catechetical leader, summed up as 'Fidelity to God and Fidelity to Man' (Colomb 1967). Let me emphasise that I do not see any infringement on the liberty of pupils in having them taught and helped to understand the faith of the Church in which they were baptised, but I do question very seriously the basis on any presumption we may make with regard to compulsory prayers or compulsory worship. I am not questioning the value of these activities. What I am saying is that the traditional Christian formula for introducing prayer in common is the invitatory 'Oremus – Let us Pray' which is neither prescriptive nor imperative, and it is so, in my opinion, because our respect for the freedom of the other is one of the basically religious attitudes man has.

In practical terms, I am inclined to believe that the greater part of what goes on in most Catholic schools is more accurately described (as is the more common usage I have noted earlier) by 'religious education' rather than 'catechesis'. By this I mean that there is a process of religious education, meaning *education in religion*, which is valuable in its own right. By its nature, its subject matter, its attempt to probe the questions of ultimate concern, it may well prove to be the means of providing what I have called elsewhere 'platforms towards faith', that is, progressive understanding of and commitment to religious values in a personal sense which allows at the same time for growth in the faith of the Church. But it does not preempt the whole process by assuming as a beginning what hopefully is to be the crown and achievement of the total process of life. For to assign arbitrary end points in religious education seems to me to be a denial of what the religious attitude to life has to be. That is why there is a sense in which some aspects of religious education as I have described it may be thought to be closer to what much recent writing on the catechetical movement has described as 'pre-catechesis.' I would accept this description provided that it is clearly recognised that what is done in religious education is valuable in itself and not simply in view of the final achievement attained. This approach, I suggest, will lead to those privileged situations of catechesis for which the Catholic school offers such special opportunities.

I would like to offer some concluding reflections on the scope and nature of 'The Renewal of the Education of Faith' as it is being offered to English Catholics. At the time of its promulgation in Italy, the Italian Episcopal Conference indicated that it was intended to provide the principles upon which five books or courses would be offered from childhood to adulthood. The Australian Bishops issued their translation to accompany a very up-to-date course for sixteen-year-olds called *Come Alive* a nine-booklet, four-colour approach to a rethinking of their faith by this age group. It seems to me most unfortunate that the English Bishops have not, to my knowledge at least, given any indication of the preparation of courses or texts based on these principles. In particular, I wonder whether the present document speaks sufficiently to the kind of society which the UK is — various Christian groups, apathy and hostility towards religion, other religious traditions than the Christian — in other words, a pluralist society with all its implications. Does your reading of the contents of the Italian document suggest it to be more of an 'intra-Church' document rather than that of a Church seeing itself as squarely inside society, serving that society and deeply concerned with its problems? Such, indeed, was the vision of Pope John XXIII and the Fathers of the Second Vatican Council. If the matters treated by the Durham Report which I have sketched lightly here are important for society in the United Kingdom, are they any less so for Catholics? What should this mean in practical terms?

## References

W.M. Abbott SJ, ed. (1966) *The Documents of Vatican II* Geoffrey Chapman.
Australian Episcopal Conference (1970) *The Renewal of the Education*

of Faith (translation and supplement) E.J. Dwyer, Sydney.

J. Colomb (1967) Le service de l'evangile Desclée, Paris.

Durham Report (1970) The Fourth R National Society and SPCK.

J.A. Jungmann, SJ (1959) Handing on the Faith: a manual of catechetics Burns Oates.

J.H. Newman (1903) Apologia pro vita sua Longman.

R.M. Rummery (1974) Catechesis and Religious Education in a Pluralist Society E.J. Dwyer, Sydney.

G. Sloyan (1964) Modern Catechetics: message and method in religious formation Collier-Macmillan.

St Paul Books (1960) Papal Teachings on Education St Paul Books, Boston.

N. St. J.-Stevas (1974) 'Religious education within the state' The Tablet 24 August.

E. Yarnold, SJ (1971) The Awe Inspiring Rites of Initiation St Paul Publications, Slough.

# 11 Religious education in Primary Schools

JEAN HOLM

The effects of the new approaches in religious education have probably been felt more acutely in the primary school than in any other sector of the education system. There are several reasons for this. In the first place, primary school teachers, faithful attenders at in-service courses, had already encountered developments in other aspects of the curriculum, notably mathematics, and they were therefore more quickly alerted to possible changes than many subject-based teachers working with the older age groups.

Secondly, Dr Ronald Goldman's research, with its accusation of 'too much too soon', was given a great deal more publicity than the earlier research relating more spcifically to the secondary school (Pollard 1961, Hyde 1965, Loukes 1961 and 1965, etcetera) and although there were many headlines like 'Goldman says Bible out in Primary School' and articles and reviews that were unfair to Goldman's position, nevertheless it meant that the issues were discussed much more widely than they might otherwise have been.

Thirdly, in the mid-sixties the 'new' RE, like the 'new' maths, was less recognisable as a subject the lower down the age-group one went, and there was considerable debate as to whether RE any longer qualified to be called religious. It was noticeable that, although most Infant teachers had by then become adept at explaining to anxious parents that 'playing' with containers and water was an essential preliminary stage in mathematical understanding, many of them found it far more difficult to convince either themselves or others that exploring themes like 'Hands' or 'Homes and Families' was an essential preliminary stage in the child's religious education.

The situation was not made easier by the fact that there were two 'revolutions' in religious education within a decade.

The first was part of the whole movement within education which resulted from the much greater awareness of the importance of experience in the child's learning process, and the primary schools were quick to respond to the findings of the educational psychologists. The expression 'child-centred' was contrasted with 'subject-centred' and the emphasis in many aspects of the curriculum was put on the child's own experience. Religious education was no exception. Life-themes multiplied in both Infant and Junior schools.

Life-themes were defined by Ronald Goldman as 'teaching by means of themes based upon the real life experiences of the children' (1965, p.110). However, many of the life-themes which appeared in the second half of the sixties could more accurately be called general primary school topics with Bible stories added. It is not surprising that many people came to identify the religious element in the theme with the biblical material.

Attempts were made to show that the religious significance of themes lay in the exploration of the experience rather than in the added Bible story — for example John Hull, 'Theology of Themes', Albert Leavesley Memorial Lecture, 1970 (Hull 1972); Jean Holm, 'Life Themes — What are They?' (Holm 1969). But expressions like 'hidden theology' and 'theology in non-theological language' only served to underline the fact that the 'new' religious education might involve different content and method but its overall aim had changed little. It was still basically 'confessional.'

A much more radical reorientation was demanded by the second 'revolution' early in the seventies. The lessons which had been learnt in the new approaches of the sixties were not left behind, but now teachers were asked, under the influence of the philosophers of education, to look at the place of each subject in the child's total general education. What was the justification for the subject in the curriculum? As already mentioned in Chapters 4 and 8, one of the most helpful analyses of the general curriculum was provided by the American, Philip Phenix. In his book *Realms of Meaning* (1964) he suggests that there are six main ways in which man comes to terms with and explains his experience, and that religion is significantly involved in two of them. These are the 'Synnoetic' realm, what it means to be a person and to know other people as persons, and the 'Synoptic' realm, the integrative realm which is concerned to make a coherent pattern of the whole of man's experience.

It was in the light of this kind of thinking that the religious education of the seventies was developed. Its aim has been described as to help pupils to understand, by the time they leave secondary school, what religion is and what it would mean to take a religion seriously.

This is, quite explicitly, an aim which cannot be achieved until the end of secondary schooling (if then). What therefore does it mean for the primary school? Religious education in the primary school must be good in its own right for children of that age-group, but it must at the same time be laying the kind of foundations on which teachers in the secondary school can build, if the overall aim is to be achieved by the time the pupils finish their schooling. It will be necessary therefore to look at what the study of religion involves and to see what the appropriate early stages of such a study are.

Religions (and non-religious systems of belief such as Humanism and Marxism) offer answers to the ultimate questions which man asks. These ultimate questions — 'Who am I?' 'What is man?' 'Who is my neighbour?' 'Is death the end?' 'Is there any purpose in life?' 'How do I come to terms with evil and suffering?' — are questions about the meaning of man's existence. A study of the answers given by the major religions and non-religious systems of belief will be an important part of religious education in the secondary school, but this is obviously beyond the capacity of children under thirteen. However, what *is* possible in the primary school is that the children should begin to think about some of these questions, and in particular that they should be aware of the kind of experience that has caused man to ask such questions.

This brings us back to the experiential themes which figured so largely in the RE of the sixties. However, we now have different criteria for our choice of themes and for the way in which we handle them in the classroom. Our aim is not to enable children to develop religious concepts but rather to encourage them to reflect on different aspects of human experience. We can express the criteria in the form of questions: (a) Does what we are doing help the children to understand themselves, other people and the natural world better? (b) Does it help them to understand better their relationship to other people and to the natural world? And (c) does it raise for them questions about what it is to be human experience themes. The children's own development

The experience on which the children are asked to reflect will, of course, be at a level appropriate to their age. Ultimate questions relate fully only to adult experience. It would, for example, be completely wrong to confront young children with the horrors of the suffering of the world, but at their own level the frustrations and disappointments they encounter, the fears and the unfulfilled hopes, stimulate the question 'Why?' just as much as apparently meaningless suffering does at a later stage.

Themes like 'Homes and Families', 'Babies', 'Parties', 'Happiness' and 'Colours', which are already familiar in the Infant school, are appropriate for the youngest children. Junior children will tackle such themes as 'Growing Up', 'Night and Day', 'The School', 'Journeys' and 'Sight'. The themes provide an opportunity for a straightforward exploration of different aspects of human experience. They no longer lead up to Christian teaching as they did in the RE of the sixties, nor are they punctuated by Bible stories. They belong to what is called the 'implicit' element in religious education, in contrast to those aspects which contain explicit references to religious phenomena of one kind or another.

The 'implicit' element, however, involves more than just human experience themes. The children's own development as persons and their ability to enter sympathetically into other people's situations will be influenced largely by their own experience, and in school that means their relationship to their teacher and the relationships which the teacher encourages them to establish with other children.

The use of literature can also play an important part in the child's personal development. It is through the world of the imagination that he is often enabled to come to terms with his own experience and acquire a deeper understanding of other people. The child's personal development will, of course, be of fundamental concern to the teacher, but it is also important for his religious education. The pupil who has not developed the ability to enter imaginatively into someone else's situation is going to find it difficult if not impossible to understand what the beliefs and practices of a religion might mean to an adherent of that religion, and that will be a central element in religious education at the secondary level.

The 'implicit' approach will make up the largest part if not the whole of the Infant school's religious education. It is a most important aspect and it provides the foundation on which much of the religious education of later years is built.

Religion is a highly complex phenomenon. It has a number of different dimensions, and a number of different disciplines are required for its study. So if pupils are to gain any adequate understanding of the nature of religion by the time they leave secondary school they will need to consider in some detail its different aspects or dimensions, and they will need to have learnt how to handle the disciplines needed for its study. And because it is virtually essential to have some knowledge of a religion other than one's own if one is to understand what religion is, the study of world religions will play an important part in religious education.

It will be important at some stage for pupils to learn about one or two religions as a whole, and to see the inter-relation of their beliefs, scriptures, codes of ethics, social institutions, etcetera, but this comes late in the process and it will be preceded by a thematic approach, that is, looking at one or two aspects of religion, such as Sacred Places or Festivals.

Where classes include children who belong to different faiths this kind of theme can obviously be tackled at an earlier age than is possible where all the children come from a Christian background. (I include European children from non-religious homes in the category 'Christian' because Christmas and Easter are important occasions for them and they know something about churches even if their families are technically atheist; their cultural heritage happens to be Christian as opposed to Hindu or Muslim.) The relationship of religion and culture is very close. There is no such thing as a religion existing in a cultural vacuum, and part of the understanding of religion involves the apprehension of this interdependence. This is very much to the advantage of the primary school teacher. What people do rather than what they believe is not only of much greater interest to children, it can be within their experience and within their capacity to understand.

In a class which has representatives of different faiths those particular religions will play a part from the very beginning, even in the nursery school. This is not because world religions are expected to figure in the curriculum but because festivals and parties and clothes and food are part of the child's life and what is important to the child must be acknowledged as important by the teacher. This will mean encouraging the children to talk about special occasions, to show presents they have received or new clothes they have been given. It will not mean trying to set the custom or the festival in any context of belief, nor will it mean trying to teach the meaning of the festival to the other children in the class. The task is primarily a psychological one — assuring the children of their significance and helping the class as a whole to accept different ways of doing things as interesting and important.

Where a school does not include children of other faiths among its members, nine is probably the earliest age for undertaking any thematic study of other religions. This is the stage at which children are interested in classifying and comparing, though it must be at a concrete level — and obviously no value judgments will be involved in the comparisons they make. The study of the significance of worship belongs to the secondary stage but its preparatory studies — Sacred Places and Festivals — are appropriate in the middle years of schooling.

Among the other phenomena of religion which should appear in the secondary school religious education syllabus are Sacred Writings. Pupils who have made some study of Sacred Places will already have come across the importance of the scriptures of Islam, Sikhism, Judaism and Christianity, and the part played by these scriptures in the services of worship; and children whose families belong to one of the religious communities will know something about the sacred writings of that community. But it is also possible to do quite a lot in the primary school about the scriptures which have been so influential in our own predominantly Christian culture.

Now the Bible is without doubt an adult book, and it would be quite wrong to try to give young children the kind of understanding that is possible only at a much later stage;

but there are a number of things we can do, once we are sure that real interest has been aroused.

First, we can let the children learn about life in Bible times, as we let them learn about the way people lived in other lands in other ages. We can do this in a straightforward study of the way of life of people at a particular time, for example, in Palestine at the time of Jesus. The selection of material will be influenced by the age of the children: for seven-year-olds it is likely to be home-centred, what life would have been like, say, for a seven-year-old; for nine to eleven-year-olds it will range more widely and will include much more detailed information about such things as Synagogue, Temple, Sabbath and Festivals. For both age-groups it will mean some emphasis on the Jewish Scriptures. No study of Judaism would be authentic which omitted this element, and it is part of the process of helping the pupils to realise that the Old Testament of the Christian Scriptures is also the Bible of another world faith.

Biblical background can also be tackled thematically, taking themes such as Shepherds (for the seven to nines) or Bread or Water (for the nines to elevens). These are among the great images of the Bible and the purpose of the themes is to explore the way of life that produced the image. What, for example, was the life of the shepherd like that it came to evoke so powerfully a relationship of trust and caring?

Work on biblical archaeology is particularly suitable for the middle school years. Possible topics are Massada, Qumran (the Dead Sea Scrolls finds), Egyptian and Mesopotamian discoveries which throw light on the times of the Patriarchs, and the discoveries which bring the age of Solomon to life. These studies should not only give the pupils knowledge of what archaeologists have found, it should also help them to understand how archaeologists make their discoveries and how they reach their conclusions.

Another approach to the Bible is by way of its transmission and its translation. This again belongs in the middle years of schooling. Children are fascinated by the story of the discovery of biblical manuscripts — and the nature of the work, which often involves the piecing together of fragments. Learning about the work of scholars in connection with biblical manuscripts and the translation of the Bible down the centuries is an effective way of demonstrating to children the important part the Bible has played — and continues to play — in the Christian religion. Why should scholars devote their lives to translating the Christian Scriptures? And why should men be prepared to suffer great hardship — even death in the case of William Tyndale — in order to put the Bible into a language that ordinary people could read?

Traditional religious education concentrated on teaching children the content of the Bible, or at least that part of the content which was in story form. But the Bible is made up of many different types of literature and one's understanding of the content is to a large extent dependent on one's ability to distinguish the nature of the writing which carries it. Some of the content will obviously have been included in the kind of schemes suggested above, but the emphasis will have been on what the material tells us about life in Palestine in the first century, or what kind of stories Jewish children learnt from their mothers, or what certain passages look like in different English versions. In addition to this, children need help in learning to recognise different kinds of writing in the Bible. This can begin in the Junior school as the children find out about the synagogue school at the time that Jesus was growing up in Palestine. As they meet examples from the Jewish Scriptures of the poetry, stories about the nation's ancestors, laws, etcetera, that would have been studied, they will be helped to see that the biblical material came into being at different times and was written for different purposes. In the middle school years it is possible to look at two or three of the biblical books in greater detail to find out what can be known of their origin and purpose.

Stories about Jesus have traditionally been an important part of religious education; in fact teaching about Jesus and the teaching of Jesus have been the focal point of all Agreed Syllabuses. This is therefore the area in which the recent changes in the subject will be most marked. If religious education is no longer 'confessional', that is, if our aim is no longer the establishment and building up of the children's religious faith, then we can no longer teach about Jesus as if the school were an extension of the Christian Church.

This does not mean that we discount Christian beliefs about Jesus. Indeed at secondary level this will be a very significant part of the pupils' study. But it does mean that we cannot just apply titles like 'Son of God' and 'Saviour', which are expressions of Christian theology and faith, as if they were factual descriptions.

How then is the primary school teacher to teach about Jesus? There are four aims which are consistent with the purpose of helping the pupils to understand the nature of religion. The first is to teach about Jesus in his Jewish setting. This will be done in some of the biblical background schemes, for example, the home life of a Jewish child at the time of Jesus. Such a recognition of Jesus as a Jew, growing up in a Jewish environment, is an essential prerequisite for understanding Jesus' later actions and teaching.

The second is to present Jesus as a man, as human. This is not untrue to Christian theology which has always maintained that Jesus was fully human. Children are not able to hold in their minds both the humanity and the divinity, and once they have heard of Jesus as divine they will no longer be able to think of him as fully human.

The third is to encourage the children to think about what kind of a man Jesus must have been if he could compel the loyalty of such tough men as the fishermen and tax-collectors, and yet could also arouse intense hostility. The children will discover that Jesus was a person about whom people felt strongly — not the 'meek and mild' figure of traditional teaching.

The fourth is to allow the children to see the consistency between what Jesus did and what he said. This will not mean putting emphasis on his teaching, but rather linking it up incidentally with accounts of his relationships with people.

If these four approaches have been followed in the primary school then it will be possible at secondary level to undertake the kind of study which seeks to answer such questions as: What was it that made the first Christians want to say more about Jesus than that he was just a man? What was it that made them apply to him titles like 'Son of God' and 'Saviour'?

Much of the explicit element in religious education involves the pupils in learning factual material. There is nothing wrong with this. One of the outstanding characteristics of Junior pupils is their insatiable curiosity and their enthusiasm for finding out things. And the factual material they will learn in the schemes referred to above helps them to build up their understanding of what religion is. However, there are other aspects of religion, and religious education must also be concerned with these. We have already dealt with one of them in discussing human experience themes. Religions offer answers to man's questions about the meaning of existence and therefore an exploration of and reflection upon human experience are the necessary prerequisite of any direct study of such answers.

Another element in religion is myth. There is a link between myth and human experience themes because the former is one of the ways in which man expresses what is most profoundly significant in his experience. The study of the role of myth in religion belongs in the secondary school but an important preparation for that study is meeting myths from many lands and this is appropriate at the Junior school stage. Some of the creation myths are particularly good for helping children to discover that certain motifs — such as order out of chaos or the conflict between good and evil — express a universal human awareness of the nature of the universe. Myths also help children to discover new depths in the word 'true' because although the events which they describe are not 'true' in the sense of having happened like that, they do express something that is 'true to man's experience'.

Symbolism is another important element in religion. This involves an event, an act, an expression or a sign pointing beyond itself to something which contains a meaning deeper than the actual symbol. There are two ways in which the primary school can prepare children for a later understanding of religious symbolism. The first is by encouraging confidence in the handling of language and, in the Junior school, by allowing children to explore the different ways in which we use words. The assumption that words are to be interpreted only according to their literal meaning is one of the barriers to understanding religious symbolism.

The second approach is by directing the children's attention to the manifold use of signs and symbols in the world around them — from road signs and the conventional signs used in maps to the characteristic symbols of the different religions. Classes which tackle a study of Sacred Places will come across such religious symbols on the places of worship they learn about, but there is also a place for a scheme devoted entirely to Signs and Symbols at some stage during the last two Junior school years.

The various elements of religious education which have been outlined in this chapter (for fuller treatment see Holm 1975) may appear at first sight to be a rather motley collection. However, their place in the pupils' total religious education can be seen only in relation to the work at secondary level. This is not in any sense to depreciate the subject at primary level. It is rather to recognise the unity of the subject. It is also to recognise that it is the same pupil who moves through the age-groups, and teachers at each level will be concerned with the gradual building up of his understanding of the nature of religion. The integration of the apparently diverse aspects at the primary stage will be provided by the teacher, who will know what the whole looks like even though he is dealing only with a part.

Finally a word about assembly. Many primary schools long ago gave up the formal service of worship with its conventional ingredients — Bible story, hymn and prayer. There has been great variation in the form of assembly that has replaced the traditional pattern but three particular features have been adopted by so many schools that it is reasonable to describe them as the basis of the new pattern.

The first is that in these schools the assembly is prepared and conducted by the children, often on a class basis. The second is that the theme arises out of the children's own experience — a school journey or something they have been learning about in class. The third is that what the children want to share with the rest of the school is expressed in a variety of ways, including dance, drama, art and music (the latter often created by the children themselves).

It should not surprise us that the revolution in the approach to assembly has been most extensive in the primary school, for primary teachers work so closely with the children *as children* that they are particularly sensitive to those activities which provide a creative experience for their pupils.

It is for the same reason that a number of primary schools

have decided that the whole school is too large a unit for effective assemblies and have organised at least some of them on the basis of smaller units.

Many schools, however, still regard the new type of assembly as an act of worship and they set it within an explicitly religious framework, even though this may be apparent only in a brief closing prayer that has been written by the children. Other schools have become uneasy about putting children into a position of religious commitment. Some of the families represented in the school may belong to other faiths, some will certainly be Humanists or agnostic, and if it is not appropriate to teach for belief in religious education then it is hardly likely to become appropriate just because the children have moved from the classroom to the school hall!

This does not mean that when prayers explicitly directed to the God whom Christians worship are no longer part of the assembly it ceases to have any importance for religious education. Far from it, for assembly can now be seen to be making a profoundly important contribution to the 'implicit' element of the subject. And it becomes much easier for assembly to be the focus of that unity of all members of the community — children and teachers, which is such a notable characteristic of the good primary school.

### References

R.J. Goldman (1965) *Readiness for Religion* Routledge.
J. Holm (1969) 'Life Themes — what are they?' *Learning for Living* vol.9 SCM Press.
  (1975) *Teaching Religion in School* OUP.
J. Hull (1972) 'The Theology of Themes' *Scottish Journal of Theology* vol.25 no.1, CUP.
K.E. Hyde (1965) *Religious Learning in Adolescence* Oliver & Boyd.
H. Loukes (1961) *Teenage Religion* SCM Press.
  (1965) *New Ground in Christian Education* SCM Press.
P. Phenix (1964) *Realms of Meaning*, McGraw-Hill.
H.M. Pollard ed. (1961) *Religious Education in Secondary Schools* Nelson.

# 12 Religious education in Secondary Schools

DONALD HORDER

Every chapter in this book, including even the previous one, has a bearing on religious education in secondary schools. I want, in this chapter, to pull together some of the threads and show some of their implications for work in the classroom.

Few subjects on the time-table have been so deeply disturbed by changes in educational thinking, and few have been, in certain quarters (including most Examination Boards) so resistant to change. There have been some exceptions, but in most schools this has been an unpopular subject with the pupils (Loukes 1961) and teachers themselves have sometimes spoken of it as 'sticking out on the time-table like a sore thumb', because it was not taught like other subjects, and its aims and methods were different.

Those who in 1944 so enthusiastically supported the religious clauses of the new Education Act could not have foreseen that a quarter of a century later these very clauses would be regarded by many teachers as a dead hand upon the subject, fixing not only its aims and objectives, but even to some extent its methods and the concept of the subject itself, in accordance with the educational thinking of thirty years before. It is not perhaps surprising that there is widespread vagueness and confusion concerning this subject in secondary schools. Much that goes on under the name of RE is not really religious education. It may be moral education, social education, aesthetic education, useful social service, pastoral counselling, but it is not necessarily religious education. To deserve that name it must contribute to the religious development of the pupils and to their growth in understanding the religious heritage of mankind.

If the kind of religious education envisaged in 1944, and in most of the Agreed Syllabuses, was found to be no longer effective or appropriate, it was natural that sensitive teachers should explore alternatives; but this pragmatic approach needed the guidance and corrective of educational theory, and this was not always realised. Fortunately, there is evidence that in the last few years a considerable number of secondary school teachers have been seeing more clearly the real task of the school in RE today (see, for example, Hassall 1974). In this new movement teachers have been encouraged by LEA Advisory Councils (see Chapter 7) and even by a few of the Examination Boards. Courses organised by HMIs and by LEA Advisers have also assisted this development, and the Schools Council Project based on the University of Lancaster served as a focus for this general movement to find a 'new RE'. The breakthrough came where teachers, either by instinct or design, turned back to the first principles of teaching, basing their work on the consideration of three factors:

1  the psychological capacity of the pupils, their interests and needs;
2  the social setting in which they and their pupils were working, and the needs and possibilities of that situation;
3  the nature of the subject-matter and the types of learning that can arise from it.

These three form a triangle within which effective curriculum planning is possible. None of the three sides may be ignored — interest, relevance, subject-matter — or the work will fail. The old style of RE failed chiefly because it ignored the first two factors. Many of the new substitutes fail because they ignore the third. They reject undue concentration on scripture or doctrine as too narrow a concept of the subject-matter, but they have no clear concept to put in its place.

The two words 'religious education' can mean a number of different things to different people. In schools they have been interpreted in four different ways.

1    The commonest, the 'received tradition', assumes that the object of religious education is to pass on the beliefs of the teachers — or the religious community they represent — to the rising generation. This has been called the *confessional* approach.

2    At the other extreme is the view that, although pupils should know what religious people say and do, care should be

taken to limit this to an objective, dispassionate giving of information. The subjective aspects of religion are to be avoided. This has been called the *anti-dogmatic* approach.

3    A third view, associated particularly with the names of Harold Loukes and J.W.D. Smith, sees religious education as a means whereby 'each society and each age' seeks to 'find its appropriate "form of reverence",' (Erikson 1965). In this quest for meaning and purpose in life – and death – all secular experience has a 'religious' dimension, or a dimension of depth. To quote J.W.D. Smith:

> Men may be Christian or non-Christian, religious, agnostic or atheist, but all men are human. True human life begins in the awareness of death. Death symbolises the mystery, and the menace, of conscious finite existence. At some stage – and especially perhaps in contemporary adolescence – we are all 'grazed' by the mystery of being and non-being. We may seek to escape from it. We may rebel against it. We can only become mature, whole and free human beings by learning to live with our finitude. This task reaches the level of conscious response and decision in adolescence. It remains an uncompleted task throughout our mortal lives. Religious education should provide help in this task (Smith 1969).

This quest for meaning and purpose has been called the *implicit religion* approach.

4    Another view stresses that schools exist to help pupils understand the world in which they live. Since in that world there are a number of religions and religious denominations which have played, and still do play, an important part in the life of society, the pupils should be given a chance to explore them, beginning with the phenomena that they may already have noticed. This has been called the *phenomenological* or *explicit religion* approach.

Only two of these four approaches seem satisfactory for use in secondary schools today. The *confessional* approach may be the proper stance for a believing community, like a Church or Sunday school. It is not an approach that can be adopted by a publicly maintained school in a multi-belief society. Moreover, in most secondary schools, it is resented by pupils and 'does not work'. The *anti-dogmatic* approach is unsatisfactory because it excludes consideration of motives or any other subjective elements. Yet what religious people say or do notoriously looks like nonsense to those outside. This is too narrow a concept of objectivity. (For a fuller discussion see *Schools Council Working Paper 36,* pp.24–8).

But the other two interpretations of the term 'religious education' – the quest for meaning and purpose and the quest for understanding of religion and religions (the *implicit religion* approach and the *explicit religion* approach) – are both right and proper activities in schools. In fact, it can be shown that they belong together, like two foci of an ellipse or two overlapping circles. Ninian Smart sums up this fresh understanding of the task of the school as he sees it:

> First, religious education must transcend the informative. Second, it should do so not in the direction of evangelising, but in the direction of initiation into under-standing the meaning of, and into questions about the truth and worth of, religion. Third, religious studies do not exclude the committed approach, provided that it is open, and so does not artificially restrict understanding and choice. Fourth, religious studies should provide a service in helping people to understand history and other cultures than our own. It can thus play a vital role in breaking the limits of European cultural tribalism. Fifth, religious studies should . . . enter into dialogue with the parahistorical claims of religions and anti-religious outlooks (Smart 1968, pp.105–6).

This can be set alongside another quotation from J.W.D. Smith:

> Secondary school classrooms contain boys and girls at many stages of development towards personal maturity. They all need help but they need different kinds of help. The help they need most does not depend primarily on growth in religious knowledge or understanding at the intellectual level. The most important needs of adolescence, as of early childhood, lie below the level of consciousness (Smith 1969, p.98).

Both emphases are needed. Smith begins at the end of personal need and relevance; Smart begins with the subject-matter. Any scheme of work at secondary level is likely to be dealing with both — if it is really contributing to the pupils' *religious* education.

How does the new concept of religious education in secondary schools work out in practice? Where should the teacher begin? There is so much excellent material that might be included but, even when a fair share of the time-table is devoted to RE, he cannot use it all. How should he choose? He should choose by reference to the three factors discussed earlier in this chapter

- the capacity, interests, and needs of the pupils,
- the social setting in which he is working,
- the nature of the subject-matter and the various ways in which it may be apprehended.

The actual process of curriculum planning is outlined in Chapter 8. The real key to this process is the selection of the right educational objectives. Objectives, if they are specific enough, show what 'learning experiences' the pupils must be given, that is, what methods and content are needed. In Chapter 10 Dr Rummery suggests that the task of the RE teacher is not to teach *that,* nor even to teach *about* religion, but to teach *how* to understand the beliefs of others, and *why* they feel and act as they do. This process of education should be accompanied by — indeed should be part of — what he calls 'education *in*' religious understanding. We ought not, therefore, to think of educational objectives in terms of subject-matter alone, but in terms of the skills to be developed, the insights to be gained, and the sentiments or attitudes which may result.

The 'knowledge explosion' has made it impossible to think of religious education today in terms of 'communicating a body of knowledge'. Nevertheless, there will always be a 'minimum body of knowledge' required by all pupils growing up in a limited area, like the United Kingdom. All boys and girls growing up in Britain need to understand Christianity, its influence in the past and today. They need to know about some of the religious groups in their own neighbourhood, and the part these play in the life of the community, as well as their links with co-religionists overseas. They also need to be aware of the views and life-style of others in the community who consciously choose a non-religious stance, and the implications of this. In John Macquarrie's phrase: ' . . . exercising our freedom in finitude in all the light that we can get, we decide to take either the risk of faith, or the risk of unfaith' (Macquarrie 1966).

This 'minimum body of knowledge' is required by all pupils, whether they are natives of this country or immigrants from overseas. But beyond this the programme may branch out in ways congenial to the class and to the teacher, in all kinds of fields. The main thing is to ensure that, as far as possible, the specific educational objectives are achieved, so that by the end of their years in secondary school, when pupils are confronted with aspects of life calling for religious perception, sensitivity and skill, they are able to cope. This calls for much more professional skill than the old style of RE which followed an Agreed Syllabus. The teacher cannot hand over responsibility for curriculum planning to some committee, meeting far away from his classroom at some date long before his class was even formed. He knows the needs of his situation, and of his pupils, far better than any Agreed Syllabus Conference – and he must use this knowledge. The class teacher is the best architect of the syllabus, the principal agent in curriculum development.

At the same time it is possible to offer him suggestions as to the sort of thing that may be appropriate at each stage, and the 'Handbooks of Suggestions' that now supplement some of the Agreed Syllabuses may be helpful here. The Schools Council Project on Religious Education in secondary schools is publishing a whole range of teaching materials developed by serving teachers, together with an *Introductory Teachers' Handbook* (Horder 1975). This Handbook contains a section entitled 'An outline programme for the years 11 to 16', which may be summarised as follows:

*The years 11 and 12*
Here most of the topics described as the 'minimum body of knowledge' are introduced, though some of them will need further exploration later. Also at this stage, it is suggested, pupils need to discover what is meant by a 'religious' question or a 'religious issue'. They also need to understand

the language people use to express their religious beliefs — signs and symbols, metaphors, myths, poetry, truth embodied in a tale, etcetera. 'Children of this age', says one of the Agreed Syllabuses, 'need two things — something to think about, and something to think with' (Lancashire 1968). The following teaching units are offered for this age range:

The Man from Nazareth as they saw Him.
Religion in Britain today.
Islam and the Muslim way of life.
Signs and symbols — the language of religion.
Pilgrimages.
An introduction to the first Christian writings.
The Faith that sings.
Who am I?
Creation (a study of myths and myth making).
Religious response.

## The years 13 to 16

After two or three years in the secondary school, it is suggested, pupils should be given a chance to choose the units they wish to explore. This is the age when young people are most critical of RE, and suspicious of being 'got at'. By introducing an element of 'opting in' some of this can be allayed, providing there is real choice and a wide enough selection. This means, of course, that there must be more in the way of study boxes and work cards, for individual and group work, with careful planning beforehand to allow for variety of methods as well as content.

Young people have different needs and interests. They differ in temperament, gifts, previous experience and home background. Nowhere are these differences so significant, for good or ill, as they are in religious education. By providing for this variety we avoid both the fallacy of proceeding as if all pupils had the same religious background and the fallacy of acting as if they were all secularists. Britain today is a multi-belief society not a secular society. Teaching units offered for these years include the following (amongst others):

Exploring Belief.

The Making and Meaning of the Bible.
How others see Life.
Science and Religion.
What is the Christian Church?
Freedom and responsibility.
Worship.
Why do men suffer?
Religion through culture — Judaism.
Race and Creed.
The Hindu Way.
Humanism.
The Religion of the Sikhs.
Building a Church today.

The Project team emphasise that these units are only a beginning — examples of the way teachers have been developing the new RE in secondary schools. More units are needed, particularly on Christian themes, but the present list provides some choice for both teachers and pupils.

It is difficult in a short space to give an adequate impression of these new teaching units. However, a few extracts from the Introduction and Specific Educational objectives of two of them will show how the writers see their task:

*The Man from Nazareth as they saw him: age range 11—12 years*

INTRODUCTION

One of the long-term aims of religious education in Britain is to see that all children understand the nature and spirit of Christianity. Whether a child is born in Bristol, in Bengal or in Benares, if he is to live in this country and to understand the British way of life he needs this knowledge and insight. Consequently courses offered in secondary schools should include several designed to develop and increase this understanding.

Central to a child's view of Christianity is his impression of Jesus. During the years preceding secondary schooling children hear many stories, usually including some stories of Jesus. By the age of 11 they are aware that many stories are not to be taken literally, and there is a tendency to dismiss stories of Jesus as 'just stories' — part of 'Noddy-land', unhistorical. This course is designed to establish Jesus in the children's minds as an historical figure, living in this real world. At the same time by exercising some reserve about the central figure, it avoids trivialising him and allows the children to make their own approach to his uniqueness.

This unit calls for exceptional sensitivity and restraint on the part of the teacher in three respects. In the first place, he must remember that, although some children have a Church background, many — perhaps the majority, — have not. It may be best to assume little or no knowledge of Jesus, and no positive disposition towards him. In the second place, the teacher must resist the temptation simply to pass on his view of Jesus. The course is intended to give children an opportunity to begin forming their own impressions and opinions. This process ought not to be short-circuited. If their views seem at times woefully inadequate, further information and evidence is called for, not preaching or dogmatism. The third matter calling for restraint is the selection and use of resources. Most religious education teachers have at their finger-tips far more material on this subject than the children need at this stage. Care should be taken not to overload the course. Any additions to the outline suggested here should be carefully structured and limited to material that will promote the specific educational objectives.

## SPECIFIC EDUCATIONAL OBJECTIVES

1  To recognise that Jesus was a real man, living in this world, and to become familiar with some aspects of the society in which he lived.
2  To begin to discover how to enquire into the origins of Christianity, and to become aware that there has been a great deal of scholarly research of this kind.
3  To appreciate that the Gospels are not histories or biographies in the modern sense, but that they express the beliefs of four of the earliest centres of Christianity.
4  To see what the Gospels have to say about Jesus'

dealings with individuals and with some of the main social, political and religious issues of his day.

5 To note how different individuals and groups appear to have reacted to him, and from this to try to sense what he was like.

6 To see something of the difference his coming has made, and some of the reasons for his continuing influence.

(Horder 1975)

*How others see life: age range, 14 and over*

INTRODUCTION

There is widespread ignorance concerning the religions of the East, and ignorance is the breeding ground for prejudice. This unit of work attempts to make pupils more familiar with some of the practices and ideas of six world religions. It cannot attempt to give a full introduction to any one of these, but by enquiring into some of the 'rites of passage', and other details likely to be of interest to young people, it may prepare for fuller study at a later stage.

Most young people are interested in what different cultures believe. Initially it is the 'strangeness' to them of some of the ideas and customs they meet which intrigues them. If presented, with a little imagination this topic is immediately fascinating to a lot of teenage pupils. They are at an age when they are exploring alternative views of life. The other great world faiths have thus a direct appeal.

At the same time it is impossible in one term (or even in two) to give more than a hint of the rich heritage and on-going life of six major religions. The intention of this unit is to convey something of the 'feel' of these great faiths rather than a multitude of facts. The religions of mankind are distinguished as much by their differing attitudes as by their doctrines. These attitudes become apparent not only in what people say but in what they do. The main emphasis of this unit is therefore on what is done.

The unit will have obvious relevance in areas where there are communities of non-Christian immigrants or Jews -- and full use should be made of local resources (e.g.

visit to, or visit from, local synagogue, mosque, gurdwara, temple, etc.). It should be remembered that in most of these groups the influence of religion pervades the whole of life and no sharp distinction is drawn between religion and general culture. In Britain today religion affects only a part of the lives of practising Christians, who, if the term is restricted to regular church-goers, are only a minority of the population anyway. But to most of the Muslims, Sikhs or Hindus religion is far more all-embracing. It is the central feature of their culture: their social customs are justified in terms of it, and it is one of the most important bonds in the maintenance of the group's social solidarity and cultural unity.

The unit has another value where many children come from a convinced Christian home background. One teacher writes: 'Our school happens to have quite a number of such children. There is great value in introducing them to differing ways of viewing life followed by millions with devotion equal to, and often greater than, their own. This is an education to them! Probably for us this was one of the most useful aspects of the course.'

## SPECIFIC EDUCATIONAL OBJECTIVES

1 To be able to identify and name some of the main ceremonies and festivals of two or more world religions.
2 To be aware of the belief dimension in these practices and to be able to suggest their importance for believers.
3 To recognize that in the crises of human life religion can play an important part.
4 To be able to specify what difference it makes to view these crises from a religious standpoint.
5 To acknowledge the sincerity of those who engage in these religious rituals and ceremonies, and to have a sympathetic attitude towards them.
6 To develop an open and unprejudiced attitude to the beliefs, practices and values of others, especially those of non-Christian immigrant groups.

(Horder 1975)

*The years 16 to 19*
This age range was outside the 'brief' of the Lancaster

Project, but clearly the principle of choice and the encouragement of individual and group study should continue into the sixth form. Group discussion, which has played a large part in most of the teaching units, will continue also, but by now it should be less random and better structured, promoting the growth of the young people towards intellectual and emotional maturity. Here the teacher needs to show great restraint. If the objective is to get young people to do their own thinking he must leave them free to do so. Many former pupils have said to me, 'When we got to the sixth form we had lots of discussion and this was fine — except when Mr X or Miss Y took it (usually the Head Teacher). They would allow no opinion to prevail except their own; so there could be no discussion.'

External examinations play a large part in most schools at this stage. Should there be external examinations in RE? Opinions are fairly evenly divided. There are those who point out that conventional examinations are based on an outmoded conception of the educational process — communicating a body of knowledge. True religious education, as we have seen, is not of this kind; but can one measure — ought one to measure — progress in the deeper kinds of religious understanding? Others point out that, in a school where every other subject is examined, religious education will not be taken seriously or be regarded as academically respectable unless it is also an examination subject. Some schools manage to strike a balance between these two points of view. RE is offered as a subject for external examinations, and some pupils opt to take it, realising full well that only certain aspects of the subject are examinable. But, having secured the status of the subject in that direction, most of the RE is broader in concept, though no less rigorous.

However, if RE is to be set free from the pressure of external examinations which distorts and cripples the subject in far too many schools, several changes are needed. First and foremost, Examination Boards must begin by considering specific educational objectives. Secondly, they must take into account the wider concept of the subject as seen in schools today. (Some GCE Boards have already made significant strides in this direction, with new alternative syllabuses for O and A level examinations.) Thirdly, if examinations are to cease distorting the whole process of curriculum planning, they must do more than sample factual knowledge. Other aspects of RE can be assessed, but by different methods. Perhaps we need to consider again the possibility of giving real weight to some forms of continuous assessment and course work, as well as to written papers. (For further discussion of this subject see *Schools Council Working Paper 36*, pp.101–103.)

## References

E. Erikson (1965) *Childhood and Society* Penguin Books.

D. Hassall (1974) 'Non-Examination Religious Education in Bradford Upper Schools', MA Dissertation, University of Lancaster.

D. Horder, ed. (1975) *Journeys into Religion* teaching units and introductory handbook, Hart-Davis Educational.

Lancashire (1968) *Religion and Life* Lancashire Education Committee.

H. Loukes (1961) *Teenage Religion* SCM Press.

J. Macquarrie (1966) *Studies in Christian Existentialism* SGM Press.

Schools Council (1971) Working Paper 36 *Religious Education in Secondary Schools* Evans/Methuen.

N. Smart (1968) *Secular Education and the Logic of Religion* Faber.

J.W.D. Smith (1969) *Religious Education in a Secular Setting* SCM Press.

# ASPECTS AND ATTITUDES

# 13 The one and the many

ERIC J. SHARPE

I assume, first of all, that most people have a fairly good idea about what is meant by comparative religion or the study of world religions. Whatever this expression may or may not have meant in the past (on this subject see my article 'The Comparative Study of Religion in Historical Perspective', Hinnells 1969) it now means something like the serious, sympathetic and 'non-confessional' study, along historical and analytical lines, of the religions of the world as phenomena in their own right. Admittedly there are considerable problems of method connected with this study. The potential range of material is so vast that no one simple method will work for more than part of the time. We are studying existential, intellectual, social and ethical questions, rational and irrational, conscious and unconscious attitudes, the spontaneous and the institutional together, in reaction and interplay, and there is still no instrument (save perhaps the trained mind) sufficiently sensitive to be able to measure, weigh and balance these and other factors singly and in combination. Indeed, the undertaking is so complicated that doubts have sometimes been expressed as to whether the comparative study of religions is a subject at all, or whether it might not be just a conglomerate of ill-assorted fragments of other subjects (history, philosophy, sociology, psychology and so on) stitched together into a sort of crazy academic patchwork quilt.

However, the impression has certainly persisted in other quarters that something like 'comparative religion' is necessary today in order to begin to approach religious problems with any measure of understanding. It might be argued that the complexities of methodology in comparative religion correspond very closely indeed to the complexity of the phenomenon which is being studied; it might be further argued that it would be silly to expect a simplistic method to give worthwhile results in this area.

The comparative study of religion is acknowledged to be a fairly popular pastime these days. This was not always so, and I wonder sometimes whether we realise just how recently popular opinion has swung in its favour. If I might give a personal reminiscence, twenty years or so ago, when I first began to attend lectures in comparative religion at Manchester University, the second-year class (first-year students were not regarded, and at Manchester are perhaps still not regarded, as sufficiently mature to tackle the subject) consisted of about ten wary and occasionally hostile theological students, who were taking 'comp. relig.' because they had to. A year later, when I passed into the third-year class, we were, I seem to remember, three in number, and before the year was out, one-third of the class had fallen by the wayside. Recently, I believe that those same classes had eighty and forty students respectively. Twenty years ago, the student of comparative religion was still regarded, as he had been regarded sixty years ago, as an oddity at best, and a dangerous heretic at worst. Today he may still be regarded as an oddity, but an interesting one, and one who is well worth listening to. Students in particular are more than willing to give comparative religion a hearing, and it does not appear to be too much of an overstatement to claim that what was once very much a fringe activity now appears to occupy a position fairly near the centre of religious study. People are seriously saying that if the study of religion is to have a future, that future lies with comparative religion, or with the approach – cool, undogmatic, uncommitted, 'objective' – which the comparative religionist is popularly supposed to exemplify.

And yet I am slightly disturbed by this professionally optimistic situation. The reasons for my uneasiness will perhaps become clearer as we proceed, but I may say straight away that I wonder whether what the professional scholar does in this field, and what the public imagines that he does and expects him to do, are the same thing at all.

What *does* the public expect of a person claiming to teach or study comparative religion? We must beware of abstractions, of course, like 'the public' or 'society': abstractions expect nothing, because they are nothing except words, and most people are as unaware of the existence of comparative religion as they are of the existence of the ruins of Mohenjo-daro. But from time to time cultured people say things which are tolerably representative of a climate of opinion. G.K. Chesterton was once such a man, the spokes-man of the common man, the apotheosis of normality. In his book *The Everlasting Man* (1926) he wrote that

> Comparative religion is very comparative indeed. That is, it is so much a matter of degree and distance and difference that it is only comparatively successful when it tries to compare. When we come to look at it closely we find it comparing things that are really quite uncomparable. We are accustomed to see a table or catalogue of the world's great religions in parallel columns, until we fancy they are really parallel. We are accustomed to see the names of the great religious founders all in a row: Christ; Mahomet; Buddha; Confucius. But in truth this is only a trick ... (p.97).

This was written in 1925, by which time comparative religion had been an accepted idea for about half a century. And certainly there had been comparative religionists around who had done precisely what Chesterton and others thought they were doing: setting out the names and histories of religious founders all in a row, and trying to deduce from them what they all had in common – and incidentally, how unlikely it was that God was at work anywhere in the process.

Today, it is possible that little enough of this survives. But I am fairly sure that the student of the world's religions is still expected to be a thoroughgoing relativist. Like some of the founding fathers of the discipline, he is expected to do his work in a spirit of carefree eclecticism, as though he were attempting to build up a synthetic religion out of the component parts (or perhaps it would be better to say the dismembered limbs) of Hinduism, Buddhism, Islam and the rest. It may be that the occasional student assumes that Christianity (in one or another form) is the highest and most sublime of religions, but a religion different only in degree from the other religions of the world. This may involve a quite remarkable degree of naivety. Take, for instance, these words, written in 1936 by a once-famous Anglican scholar, B.H. Streeter:

> If a committee of students of Comparative Religion were to sit down to compile a synthetic system, carefully choosing the highest elements from each of the greater religions, they might produce something like Christianity.

They wouldn't, of course. They would produce only a monstrosity. But this isn't really the point. The point is that comparative religion as a whole has inherited this image – of a curious, rationalist, eclectic discipline (if this is the right word), dedicated to the devaluation and relativisation of all absolutes, the slaughter of all sacred cows, and the humanisation of all religions.

There are well known reasons why such a position should be not only acceptable, but distinctly popular, today. Sacred cows have never been fairer game for any and every hunter; absolutes have never been regarded with deeper suspicion. And when this particular aspect of the image of comparative religion is linked with another, which decrees that anything emanating from East of Suez should be regarded with unqualified reverence, the comparative religionist who is also an Orientalist finds himself presiding over a seller's market.

But there is more to be said than this. After all, this is very largely a caricature of the work of the comparative religionist. The saying that a much-loved child has many names is eminently applicable to my own field of study: it can be, and has been called, the history of religion, the history of religions, the comparative study of religion, the comparative study of religions, the science of religion, the science of religions, *Religionswissenschaft*, and so on. Now amid this welter of names, one odd circumstance emerges – that students seem unsure whether they are studying religion in the singular or religions in the plural; or (to put it slightly differently) whether the subject of their study is one or many. I shall return to this question more fully very soon. But there is another aspect of popular image-making involved here.

There is no lack of evidence that if religion in one form is suppressed or (more likely) repressed, it will pop up to the surface in another form. Abolish one form of public ritual, and another soon arises to take its place; devalue one set of absolutes, and others, no less absolute though commonly less credible, take over. In an age of declining formal, specific religion, there is perhaps more informal, anonymous religion than ever before.

Now if it should prove to be the case that the comparative religionist, by reason of the many systems of religious belief and practice which pass under his gaze, is expected to demonstrate the relative unimportance of creeds and authorities, priests and sacraments, hassocks and hymnbooks, and to demonstrate what the Hindu, and increasingly some Christians too, would call the transcendental unity of all religions (or rather all religion), then we have another reason for his current popularity.

In point of fact, the search for the genus, religion, of which the actual historical religions are species, is one which has been prosecuted throughout the history of my subject. This aim was expressed in many different ways in the early years of the discipline, and since one example is as good as another, here are a few lines from a book first published in 1895, Allan Menzies' *History of Religion*:

> What everyone with any interest in the subject is striving after, is a knowledge of the religions of the world not as isolated systems which, though having many points of resemblance, may yet, for all we know, be of separate and independent growth, but as connected with each other and as forming parts of one whole. Our science, in fact, is seeking to grasp the religions of the world as mani-festations of the religion of the world.

And lest it should be thought that this is now an outdated ideal, let me point out that the tendency today in America at least is to follow Joachim Wach (*The Comparative Study of Religions* 1961) in calling for some 'integral understanding' of the phenomenon of religion as a whole, and that two recently-published books in this country bear the titles *A History of Religion East and West*, and *The Religious Experience of Mankind* — both of which clearly suggest that there is some unitary dimension of religion which a serious comparative study can disclose. It might also be worth mentioning that the field now called the phenomenology of religion is striving to reach this same goal.

So on the face of it, the popular conception of comparative religion as a mode of study dedicated to revealing a core of religiousness within the various manifestations of religion in world history is not far wrong. Comparative religion *does* appear to seek for the one behind or within the many, the universal behind the specific, and in so doing to devalue the specific. And this is where the trouble starts.

The trouble starts here not because religions (the many) are so alike but they are so different. And every conscientious student of comparative religion knows this. (I say every conscientious student, because there are dilettantes and surface-scratchers who seem never to have found out one or two of the facts of religious life.) He knows it because the facts have been forced upon him: because he has been faced, constantly and mercilessly, with differences of world-view, opinion, practice, belief, and so on, which simply cannot be subsumed under a rapid formula. (That is why any attempt to estimate one religion in terms of another misses so much. That is why 'anonymous Christianity' and Radhakrishnan's version of Christianity are both untrue.) I may illustrate this by asking a question: When a student wants to begin the serious study of a religious tradition, what does he do?

First of all, he learns a language. It may be as they say 'dead', though it is questionable whether a language is ever dead: it may be very much alive. But whichever it is, Sanskrit or Swahili, Greek or German, Icelandic or Ibo, the first great day in the student's life comes when he discovers that a text written in that language conveys a far different atmosphere from the best translation he has ever come across, and when he suddenly realizes that Söderblom was right when he said that philology is the needle's eye through which the theological camel has to pass in order to enter the heaven of knowledge. This stage passed, he immerses himself in the literature, iconography, art, architecture, music of his area. To the best of his ability he becomes in imagination a Brahmin, a Viking or a Bushman, a Quaker or a Catholic Modernist. Given the opportunity, he travels, either to examine monuments or to live with the people he is studying. And gradually, he should come to know intuitively what the place of religion is in his chosen culture. Of course, it need not be a remote culture, either in place or time. It may be as near at hand as the church on the corner. But whatever the field, understanding does not come easily or cheaply. To know a religious tradition in this way involves a life sentence, but it is a life sentence willingly accepted.

Of course, this is the scholar's ideal, but it is an ideal which simply has to be followed by anyone who is seeking understanding as opposed to acquaintance, to know a religion as it is to those who live in it as opposed to the impression it is making on his own mind. And I must emphasize that every comparative religionist worth his salt has one such field of specialization, linguistic and cultural – a home base to which he returns with relief after excursions into other less familiar areas. In this area he speaks with conviction, not on hearsay.

Yes, he may well compare; indeed, he must compare, particularly within well recognized limits. But he does so with extreme care. One of the fruits of his language study will have been that he is able to recognize linguistic problems in an unfamiliar language when he comes across them, and he will have learned to discriminate between first, second and third-hand sources. He may well read widely – though without megalomania or the desire to appear to be an encyclopaedic genius. He will also have learned to say 'I don't know' – though he may well have learned how to find out when the need arises.

This ideal picture which I have been trying to paint of the present-day comparative religionist differs somewhat from the kind of ideal which was common around the turn of the century, for one very simple reason – the accumulation of material. In the heyday of evolutionism, it seemed altogether reasonable, to quote Allan Menzies again, for a science 'to seek to show the unity of law amid the multiplicity of the phenomena with which it has to deal, to gather up the many into one, or rather to show how the one has given rise to the many'. Nowadays not only are we less convinced of the possibility of such a procedure, but the vast range of material more or less forbids it. Life just isn't long enough!

It sounds, doesn't it, as though I am saying that somebody

somewhere has made a serious mistake in trying to reduce the multiplicity of religion to general principles. Not so. The objective is an entirely worthy one, and I do believe that there is a dimension of human behaviour rightly called religion, in which man expresses, singly and collectively, his sense of dependence on unseen powers, and his attempts to find meaning in life. But what I *am* saying is that we must reject the rather naive idea that if you put all the religions of the world in parallel columns, and cancel out the differences, *what is left* will be 'religion'. That is nonsense. The essence of religion (if there be such a thing) is not to be measured in terms of highest common factors. Even less is it to be measured in terms of rungs on the ladder of evolutionary development. I must also record my belief that there is a distinctive difference between the approach of the student of world religions and the approach of the Christian theologian or the philosopher who is bent on interpreting religion in his own special categories. I do not seek to anathematize the latter; merely to state that this is not the comparative study of religion, which seeks to understand, say, the Hindu *as a Hindu*, against the background of all the complexities of Hindu culture, rather than as a reflex of Christian self-understanding.

Suppose, then, that we assume for a moment that religion consists essentially in man's search for meaning in the universe, seen and unseen (and I know that this begs important questions), I want to maintain, as against the old evolutionary view, that its essence is better revealed in the total impact of religious modes of behaviour on a specific community or a couple of communities than in the arbitrary isolation of certain factors in many such communities. Or, in slightly sharper terms, that to know one religious tradition well is more illuminating than to know several slightly. Best of all is to know more than one reasonably well — for I have already said that I doubt the capacity of any mortal to achieve total mastery of more than one tradition. For the Christian by inheritance to attempt to master the cumulative tradition of even part of Hinduism, Buddhism or Islam is salutary in the extreme; but it is better to know, say, Methodism well than to have a smattering of inaccurate knowledge of Christianity and Hinduism and Buddhism together.

In the last resort, I believe the comparative study of religion to be a state of mind. It does not consist in freedom from presuppositions, but recognizing one's presuppositions for what they are. It does not consist in being totally uncommitted, but in refusing to allow one's commitment (to Christianity or Marxism or Theosophy or whatever) to interfere with the desire to achieve scholarly accuracy, even when engaged in what may be a highly necessary work of popularisation. It has no natural limits whatsoever, other than those dictated by the scholar's own capacity for mastering material.

I mentioned just now the highly necessary work of popularisation. Some scholars, needless to say, will have none of it. But for someone engaged in school or undergraduate teaching, the need to project a recognisable picture of an unfamiliar religious tradition may well be a constant spur, and a constant headache. And so it should be. Scholars ought all be forced at some time or other to try to present their work in broad outline to totally innocent audiences. Not only will it be good for them; it will prevent the same thing being done in an infinitely worse way by amateurs. Standards ought, if anything, to be higher than ever on these occasions. I do not mean that everything that is said ought to die the death of a thousand qualifications. But that the choice of significant detail ought to be so sensitively made that an accurate outline is given of, say, Hinduism, even when there is no opportunity to fill in every tiny detail.

This brings us, albeit somewhat obliquely, to another question of what I hope will be general interest, not unrelated to what has gone before. It concerns the choice of areas of comparative religious study in schools and colleges of education.

In the first place, I am under no illusions about the amount of material that can be presented in either of these institutions at any level. When we have little enough time in our universities to deal in depth with any given religious tradition, it is plainly out of the question to hope for anything save a very cursory examination of a couple of such areas in a school or college course. But why do we need to do this at all? Of late by far the commonest motivation for

comparative religion in schools has been the undeniable fact
that we have in our midst sizeable immigrant communities —
Muslims, Sikhs and Hindus. Comparative religion is thus
being made into an instrument of race relations. All well and
good. But we must not imagine that this is the only reason,
or even the best reason, for advocating such a study in these
days. In some parts of the country it is at the moment a good
reason, but I would not want to say any more than that. And
when it leads (as I suspect it has led in some quarters) to a
neurotic desire to be fair to Islam, Hinduism and the rest,
existing alongside a pathetic inability to discern and
communicate the role of Christianity in Western society, then
something has gone seriously wrong somewhere. That is the
kind of thing that happens, though, when utilitarianism,
romanticism and inadequate knowledge join forces under the
umbrella of educational theory.

I have said that the comparative study of religion is as
much a state of mind as anything else. And I believe that the
sooner that state of mind communicates itself to the teaching
of Christianity in this country, the better. Failure is nothing
whatsoever to do with teaching the Bible *as such*, but in lack
of insight into the function of the Bible. But that is by the
way. If I am right in supposing that the way to the
understanding of religion is through the sympathetic study of
people behaving religiously, then it does not greatly matter
*which* tradition is made the focus of one's study, at any
educational level. If more than one tradition can be studied,
so much the better, provided that the standards of
impartiality, accuracy and sympathy of which I have spoken,
are inculcated as soon as is practicable. It may sound odd,
but I wonder sometimes why, as soon as the words
'comparative religion' are mentioned, there should be such a
rush to tackle Hinduism — which always seems to stand at
the top of everyone's comparative religion list. But there is
no more difficult subject for study. The field of religion has
no more deceptive labyrinths than those which lie in wait for
the amateur Indologist. The language is excessively difficult,
the history is excessively complicated, the mental processes
involved are far different from our own. Perhaps the appeal is
largely romantic. Be that as it may, while it is desirable to
know something of the religious traditions of India, it is

equally desirable to know something of Africa, of Japan — and of Europe. Not least Europe.

Why no study of 'religion in Britain'?

I have already suggested that one task of comparative religion is to teach something about religion within, and across the boundaries of, the religions. And I have also suggested that there has been a widespread failure to communicate any but the most rudimentary understanding of the role of religion in the society of which we are all part. Now I happen to believe, with Collingwood, that the historian (and the comparative religionist is above all a historian) cannot understand a piece of material under his hand if he approaches it with the wrong question — or with no question at all — in his mind. The question you ask determines to a very large extent the answer you will get.

Clearly there are very many possible questions to ask of a field of study like comparative religion. Questions like: 'In what order did things happen?' This was the evolutionary question *par excellence*, and still seems in many quarters to be the only question some historians are able to ask. Today it is being widely replaced by the question 'What does this mean to me?' This is part of the quest for self-identity in which so many young people appear to be engaged: subjective, uncritical, romantic, concerned more with 'good vibrations' (whatever they may be) than with genuine understanding. Let me give you an example. There are signs that the oriental craze may be on the wane in some quarters today, and that it is being replaced by an intense personal interest in Celtic religion, Druids and so forth. You perhaps recall a recent hippie festival a couple of years ago at Glastonbury, with the steel-and-perspex pyramid that they put up as a focus for 'cosmic forces'. I have been told that increasingly 'gurus are out; Druids are in'. The trend has been westward: from Zen to Hinduism and now to Celtic religion — all legitimate fields of interest within comparative religion, of course, but all in the interests of subjective self-understanding. To my mind, though, this is the kind of question that it is practically impossible to ask in the context of education. It makes nonsense of evidence, it makes a mockery of history. The only thing it does is to teach you something about a corner of the twentieth-century mind.

And all as a result of approaching a subject and asking what, as far as I am concerned, are irrelevant questions. The real questions are about the role and place of religion in Japanese, Hindu and Celtic culture, and can only be answered on the basis of an overall study of that culture.

No one is claiming that such a study is easy. We call it a discipline because it requires precisely that: discipline and commitment. And something of that discipline and commitment must be required of anyone who would attempt to teach the subject, at whatever level.

The search for the one – religion – behind and within the many – the religious traditions of mankind – is thus not to be undertaken lightly, and not (as far as the teacher is concerned) without some form of professional training. And that touches upon a slightly sore point. If, as I have been suggesting, the meaning of the one – religion – is to be discerned most clearly through observing its total impact upon specific communities, rather than through distilling its essence out of the generalities of the religious experience of mankind, or whatever, how is it most successfully to be taught?

As long as comparative religion is thought of in sufficiently vague terms, then vague qualifications will probably suffice for its further propagation. But I do not think of it in those terms, and I do not accept that just anyone can set himself or herself up as an expert on the strength of being observably comparatively religious, with a taste for, shall we say, mysticism or the occult. If I thought that were all that was needed for the study of this subject, I do not think that I should want to have anything more to do with it. No. Since the comparative study of religion admittedly involves out-of-the way knowledge, and since the comparative religionist is constantly teetering on the brink of obscurantism and meaninglessness, it seems to follow that only the best available training – mediated along the academic grapevine from the universities to the colleges to the schools – will do. The onus is on the departments to train specialists in non-Christian and Christian religious traditions like who will be able to apply trained and sympathetic minds to the problems we have been facing.

## References

G.K. Chesterton (1926) *The Everlasting Man* Bodley Head.

J.R. Hinnells, ed. (1969) *Comparative Religion in Education* Oriel Press/Routledge.

A. Menzies (1895) *History of Religion* Williams & Norgate.

J. Wach (1961) *The Comparative Study of Religions* Columbia University Press.

# 14 World religions: practical considerations

an allegory by PETER WOODWARD

*Have mercy on me, O Beneficent One — I was angered for I had no shoes; then I met a man who had no feet.*

Any modern bird flying over the territory known as Reled must find the variety of valley and hill, plain and upland, both striking and strangely comforting. From the rock-strewn coastline the land rises through gently curving valleys until, somewhere near the central area, there emerges an extensive plateau, divided into a number of distinctive regions by the rivers that find their origins there. The plateau is known locally as the Worrel and contains some remarkably fertile soil, laid deep over the oldest rock formations in the country. There are those who — mistakenly — have called the whole land by the plateau's name, but in reality the Worrel is one piece with the rest and merely leads, as a gateway, up to a series of exciting, snowbound passes that the traveller must penetrate *en route* for the towering mountains that lie at the heart of the country. From the edges of the plateau there are sweeping vistas both down to the sea and up to the mountains; but because of the river valleys that cut deep rifts in its surface, the twisting roadway through it is often tricky and occasionally dangerous. It is, however, never dull.

In any study of the Worrel this factor must be dominant. Perhaps the Jewish community has a lesson to teach us here. I remember vividly a visit paid on a stiflingly hot day in August 1972 to a synagogue in Toronto. The rabbi regaled us with a sequence of perceptive anecdotes, mostly anti-Jewish in flavour, that won both our sympathy and our attention. In particular his description of how one distinguishes between Orthodox, Conservative and Reform Jews was a masterpiece of innuendo. The Reform Jew is not over-bothered with legalistic details of Sabbath Observance and behaviour, and quite happily drives his limousine to Sabbath day services and parks in the synagogue car park. The Orthodox by contrast shuns not only the use of his own car but public transport as well and purchases a house within walking distance of the synagogue — or builds a synagogue within walking distance of his house! The Conservative chooses a middle path, gets his car out of the garage and publicly drives to the synagogue area, but gains the best of both worlds by walking up to the synagogue after leaving his vehicle unnoticed in a nearby parking lot.

It follows then that this world of Religions, the Worrel, is fun to live in and fascinating to study. Any field that can produce such stories as those of the Hodja, the Turkish trickster of six hundred years ago, who was made famous through the writings of Turgay Yagan, will never be dull. One day, when the Hodja was working on his farm, a thorn penetrated his foot. 'Dear God,' he said, 'thank you so much; what a blessing I didn't wear my new shoes.' In similar vein *The Exploits of the Incomparable Mulla Nasrudin* (Idries Shah 1966) offers scope for many a wry smile.

But interesting places have their perils, and the pathway across the plateau may prove the more dangerous through the distracting effect of such entrancing scenery. The wary pilgrim will keep a watchful eye open for the following hazards. There will be no warning signs!

The first peril lurks in a ford where the stream, usually gently enough, meanders lazily across the road until the rains come. Then it grows suddenly deep enough to trap the careless traveller. Its name is Commitment, and for much of his week the RE teacher will be able to ignore the issues to which it gives rise. Every so often, however, a chance question, a vivid illustration or the nature of his material, will raise the issue in stark form: how far does the RE teacher need to be committed to his material? Can a teacher introduce his pupils to doctrines, facts, scriptures, experiences, etcetera, in which he does not himself share?

A full debate on this issue is prohibited here by space, and in any case the matter has been dealt with elsewhere at various levels (see, for example, *Learning for Living*, March 1971 and March 1973). In brief, few teachers will object in principle to the presentation of either historical data or scriptural and factual material from traditions other than their own, though some will have reservations on the grounds of the time element involved in such studies. The issue becomes alive when either doctrines or experiences are the centre of focus. Can a teacher imaginatively enter into the experience of thinking and feeling like a Buddhist if he or she is not one? Can he share such an experience with his pupils? What does it mean to become a monk, to shave one's head, to live under discipline, to lose oneself in meditation and contemplation? Can one simulate, or only emulate?

A useful exercise is to relate the question to Voodoo or witchcraft. The scene is a multi-cultural concert. The West Indian musician describes the piece he proposes to play, explains its Voodoo history and background, and then invites his audience to join in the ritual dance. Can the RE teacher, committed as he often is to a conflicting position, involve himself in such a ritual, or does he compromise himself by participating, even though he may believe there is no external power behind the ritual?

The waters here are deep and will affect different travellers in various ways — but the experience of passing through such doubts and uncertainties about his role is an essential part of the RE teacher's preparation for the encounters he will face in the classroom. The fact that a growing number of teachers of all age groups are willing to engage in such experiments both for themselves and in specific teaching situations is a happy indication of the positive approach we are finding in many cities today. And as teachers discover, often to their surprise, that they can empathise with the Hindu in his patient search for the unity of all things, or with the Sikh in his obedient reverence for his scriptures, so the spell of the Worrel is cast upon more and more pilgrims.

Further along our road the pathway over the river crosses a timber-framed bridge. The waters here have rotted the timbers, causing it to sag, and only half of the original causeway is safe to use. The bridge is known as Stereotype, built by old Superficiality. It is a dangerous place because it seems to offer good footing — only through a close examination does the traveller's real peril stand revealed.

The dangers of stereotyping emerge most clearly when describing minority faiths, represented in this country by immigrant groups. Because these are *living* religions with real followers, it is easy for the RE teacher in these areas to make contact either with the leaders of such a group or with members who are more on the fringe of its religious life. The danger takes many different forms: it may lie in assuming that all other members of a particular synagogue are as knowledgeable, or as persuasive, or as upright as the rabbi one has just met; or that Hindus in India all wear the same dress or practise the identical wedding customs that one has encountered in a temple in Birmingham or in the East End of London; or that the Sikh community, because in Britain it holds its weekly satsang at the gurdwara on Sundays (as it does in the Punjab), therefore has special religious reasons for meeting on that day — whereas in fact, as Alan James points out in his recent essay *Sikh Children in Britain* (A. James 1974), 'Gurdwaras in the Persian Gulf States hold their *Sangats* on Friday, the local holiday'; again the danger may stem from meeting a member of a somewhat unorthodox sect and then generalising from his rather esoteric point of view as to the beliefs of the larger, orthodox community. This has been known to happen in glamorous cases such as the Hare Krishna movement and, in a different way, with the Guru Maharaj Ji. It may also occur with more serious alternatives such as the Muslim Ahmadiyya movement or the Church of England. It is only by reading widely and selectively — for example *Man and his Gods* (Parrinder 1971) — by meeting again and again a broad range of representatative spokesmen of differing viewpoints, or by cultivating an approach that is as critical as it is friendly, that the teacher can have confidence that he is not likely to upset local opinion by teaching as universal facts what are in reality simple items of local colour.

In a different way there is an equal danger in describing the practices and beliefs of religions that are not active in this country today. Many teachers are not well read in other religions and tend to pick up books that present all the religions of the world in a few easy chapters (for example Ballard 1971). Such books oversimplify themes that deserve a lifetime's study. Teachers should always leave pupils with the impression that a given religion matters profoundly to those who follow it, and that there is very much more still to be discovered if they really want to understand. It is good to go back to the original writings of the faith, as far as these are available, and to teach as true description only those doctrines and practices that are in harmony with the spirit of such classical writings. In this way a bridge with the past will be provided that should prove reliable enough to prevent the formation of exaggerated stereotypes.

A third hazard on the road takes the form of a dangerous bend that leads through a blind corner to a dead end. It is the line of thought that sees the clear relevance of the Worrel to a multi-racial, multi-faith situation, and therefore relates the teaching of non-Christian faiths to the presence of 'immigrant' groups. This leads on to the conclusion that multi-faith Religious Education is justifiable when there are immigrants present – and not justifiable in other situations . . .

This argument is suspect for a number of reasons. First, it takes to absurd lengths, and then reverses, the belief that people learn best by the development of their existing experience: that experiential teaching is valuable must be unquestioned: that it is the only acceptable form of teaching is a non-starter – what a nonsense this would make of most history and geography, let alone current affairs and simulation exercises. No, the study of the Worrel is aided and modified by the presence of immigrant groups, but it is not dependent upon them. In fact their very presence can increase the danger of stereotype, for in many cases the Muslim pupil's knowledge of Islam is (nearly) as limited as the white British child's information about Christianity! In the second place we live in a mobile society where pupils, teachers, students and workers in all walks of life are moving around the country more and more; many indeed are travelling around the world. To place arbitrary limits on their knowledge so that the absence of Buddhists from Lincolnshire or of Sikhs from Cornwall prevents any local study of those faiths may please the protagonists of environmental studies but cannot be regarded as fitting young people for the adult world they are preparing to enter and in which they will travel – both in person and through the medium of television – far more widely than ever we have.

This is not to say that where immigrant communities are

present the school will not make full use of the assets they represent. Carefully prepared excursions to Sikh gurdwaras, talks on specific topics from Hindu swamis, descriptions by Muslim pupils of when, why and how they pray (preferably in that order), opportunities to examine a Jewish scroll, tephillin or mezuzah, all these enrich and influence the approach one adopts to teaching. *Religion in Birmingham* (Tiptaft 1972) shows something of the full range available in a not untypical city setting. But such is the range of visual and aural aids and religious objects now becoming available that the crofter in Scotland or the gypsy in Kent are equally within reach of the Tantric sound and the Parsee festival.

Two further hazards on the journey through the Worrel may be dealt with rather more briefly. The first lies in the plain of Quantality where the road suddenly narrows (or opens out, depending upon the direction one is taking). The issue is of depth v breadth. Does the school or college curriculum best serve the interests of the students by a study of one religion, or of two or three, or seven or eleven? Is a familiarising 'canter round the kingdoms' — as in one of the better examples (Parrinder 1965) — a better way of starting than a depth study of two religions in their (comparative) fullness or three religions through selected themes? Each traveller will find his own speed at this point, but in my experience the longer one lives in the Worrel, the greater the emphasis one tends to lay upon doing a little well and looking for response rather than seeking a superficial knowledge of facts. Certainly it is much easier for the newly arrived teacher (and his pupils) if his own ·study and preparation can be limited to a smaller area where a concentration of effort will encourage accurate and sympathetic treatment. The use of themes (and comparisons?) will of course require the greatest care. These constitute a high-class tool in the hands of the much-travelled or the widely-read, but they require a sophisticated type of skill which rarely comes without much experience.

Some miles further on the road runs suspended on the lip of a precipice named Syncretism. It is a place to hurry by swiftly, with one's attention firmly on the way one is taking. The temptation to dally for united acts of worship or cooperative activity is natural and healthy, but when this

leads so many (as it has) not to an enrichment of their own
tradition and commitment but to a watering down process
that seeks a shallow unity where none is evident, then it is a
dangerous place. In spite of her fears, Constance Padwick's
*Muslim Devotions* (1961) is an invaluable signpost here,
showing one way to genuine understanding of the depths of
religious traditions without obscuring the vision. Nearly as
useful is Kenneth Cragg's *Alive to God — Muslim and
Christian Prayer* (1970); and the *Christian Presence* series,
edited for SCM by Dr Max Warren, offers a very useful
corrective to the dangers of over-simplification. Sid Hedges'
*With One Voice* (1970), from which the quotation at the
head of this chapter is taken (though it also appears over the
doorway of a Dorset bar) is another mine of useful titbits,
although it could be dangerously superficial in the hands of
the inexperienced.

Not far from this precipice the road forks in a most
confusing fashion, with neither track clearly indicating that it
is the main thoroughfare. In one direction there are gentle,
open vistas with sunlight streaming through the varied trees.
In the other the forest is thicker and the light barely reaches
the road, so close are the overhanging branches. The former
route offers a succession of distant cameos of the scenery
typical of the Worrel, but always separated by streams and
vales, and somewhat remote. Here one sees the exotic
customs of the Muslim festivals, spread out as a fertile valley;
there one glimpses the lofty peaks of Buddhist con-
templatives, 'seated reflectively 'neath their meditating trees'.
The Christian year has left its imprint on the stunted rock
formations of these everlasting hills; the backcloth to much
of the scenic beauty is the Jewish flair for celebrating the
regular events of life in the ceremonies of the home. This is
the pathway of *Teaching About Religion*, a pleasant enough
road for the amateur (and the dilettante) and one that seems
at first sight to offer entrancing delights. Its descriptive
approach to teaching about World Faiths is colourful and
interesting, with an ample supply of details to digest and
customs to encounter. For those with time to spare it is
indeed a pleasant detour. Its defect is that it twists and turns,
always on the same level, and eventually brings one back to
nearly the same point where one began. The other route

plunges upwards into dark crevices between the hills, with overhanging trees nearly meeting overhead. It is a route more interesting and adventurous than artistic or attractive. Always there is some new feature of the landscape developing around the next bend. It is the road of *Teaching Religion*, and offers space for experiencing in depth the nature of religious studies. It seeks to find out what it feels like to live as a member of a Muslim family, to enter into the experience of a Sikh youngster as he reads the Guru Granth Sahib, to share with the Hindu the carefree joys of Holi or the lingering beauty of the ubiquitous lamps at Divali. Even a small paperback like Ninian Smart's recent study of *Mao* (1974) can help us to get *inside* the experience of what it is like to be a guerilla commander, a meditative poet and a spiritual force, all in one, while at the same time opening up (and answering?) the question of the inclusion of 'non-religious stances for living' in the field of Religious Education. In short this route uses not only the intellect but the emotional element within us all, to offer the pupil insights, first into the nature of specific religious experiences and then, by transfer, into the nature of larger religious issues as they emerge from his own tradition, or in more general terms.

An example may help. A secondary school in Surrey invited a class of girls to bring to school the following week one lamb chop each. This became the basis for a description first of the Passover festival in Biblical days, then of the Seder service in the modern Jewish home, and finally the class together ate their (pre-cooked) lamb chops in sympathy for those Jews to whom the wish 'next year in Jerusalem' would be always an unfulfilled hope. In this way a description led to an insight and so into pretty fair progress in getting alongside the thoughts and feelings of Jews. This approach transcends the purely descriptive and yet does not demand marked conceptual ability, though where that is present it may on occasion be possible to verbalise the experience, if this is desirable, or to relate it to relevant theological beliefs. The danger of overmuch analysis is that one may lose the mystery, which is of more significance than the theology. The purist may well argue that the girls quoted above did not and could not enter into a Jewish experience of Passover. This, of course, is true, and any opportunity to complement such a study by visiting a synagogue for a model Seder, or by sharing in the festival with Jewish friends in their home, is very much to be welcomed — or engineered. But the experience was still a religious experience, leading to genuine religious insights and sympathy. This road will be steep and it will not always be clear where it is leading, but it is still the most direct road that climbs up to the hills.

The final features of the journey through the Worrel are not really hazards at all, though any such characteristics can be dangerous to the traveller who is in too much of a hurry. Rather they are striking features of the countryside that show off to best advantage its limitless possibilities. The first offers a marked contrast to the overhanging trees and rocky screes one has just passed. It is one of those rare spots where the road emerges on the side of a hill to offer a panoramic view of the country one has just traversed, spread out below as on a relief map. It shows a landscape full of people coming and going, with colourful processions and gay festivals, interspersed with solemn rituals and silent groups immersed in serious thought. For the life of the Worrel lies not in its natural beauty, or its architectural elegance, or its systematic theology, but in its people. It is in meeting the people as individuals and in groups, in playing with their children, studying with their students, sharing their festival days, joining them on visits to their places of worship and then inviting them back to speak in homes, schools, churches, and so on, that the true nature of their communal life is best seen. Serena Fass has completely caught the spirit of this in her recent mixture of peoples and poems entitled *Faces of India* (1974). Such encounter is of course much easier to arrange in those areas of this country where there is a high level of Asian immigration, but, as we saw above, it is not only appropriate there. It is an approach which can be used with any communities that have religious loyalties, whether they be orthodox Christian denominations or less significant minorities of the sort described in Horton Davies' *Christian Deviations* (1954). In a wider multi-faith context (see, for example, Needleman 1970), it is also an approach which can be pursued at second-hand, either by the teacher travelling to the nearest city to make such visits himself, which he then 'takes back' to his classroom through the medium of his own sets of slides, tape recordings, 8 mm cine film, or whatever; or, such is the development in prepacked visual and aural aids, he may be able to purchase for himself (what approach could be more truly professional?) or for his school, or to persuade his Adviser to obtain for the Authority, such a range of filmstrip, slide, tape, cassette, religious object, picture, pamphlet, etcetera, that his contact with the communities may come alive in the classroom through such media.

The two RE Resource Centres at Borough Road College, Isleworth, Middlesex, and at Westhill College, Selly Oak, Birmingham, are able to demonstrate and advise here on materials that are appropriate to help achieve this in the classroom, and the Director of the Borough Road Centre has plans for producing a revised, annotated list of such aids. This will supplement the unannotated list in the Shap Working Party Community Relations Commission production, *World Religions – Aids for Teachers* (Shap 1972). The latter includes a set of bibliographies, addresses, and other articles, and has proved useful to many teachers as an informative medley of information. The CRC also distributed thirty thousand copies of an *Annual Calendar of Festivals* in 1974 and this will prove a useful aid in many schools, not least for those whose responsibility is the conduct of school assemblies. Also of value for its intriguing mixture of stories and lists is the Yorkshire CCR production, *Religion in the Multi-Faith School,* edited by W.O. Cole (1973).

It may be useful here to draw attention to a few of the more lively items such as the Unilever film, available on free loan, *Four Men of India*. This is a colourful and varied survey of life in different areas of India, with reference to birth, marriage and death, and various modes of employment. It is particularly useful in its vivid juxtaposition of town and country. A boxed kit containing two filmstrips, two cassettes and other items is available from ESL, Bristol (former Gateway) under the title *Islam and Europe*. Many teachers have found this useful with ten, eleven and twelve-year-old pupils as providing clear historical background to the development of Islam. It is intended that this will be the first of a series of such aids, with Hinduism next in line. A unique source of slide material is a professional photographer, Bury

Peerless, of 22 King's Avenue, Minnis Bay, Birchington, Kent, who can supply a catalogue of his various packs of slides — the visual quality is superb — or will produce sets to the customer's specification. Somewhat more expensive are the Time/Life series of boxed kits on six world religions, which contain a great deal of useful material (Time/Life 1973). Smaller specific kits on Hindu Puja and Sikh Amrit (from Educational Productions) may point the way ahead for the techniques of the future, and there is of course a full range of multi-faith/multi-cultural filmstrips on the market, of which the BBC Radiovision and Concordia series are the most popular. These then are some of the aids to help the traveller explore this magnificent panorama, the setting for a steadily unfolding drama; but it is only *the people* whose stories are recorded there who can truly bring it to life.

The next feature of the road lies unexpectedly round a further corner where children are often found at play, usually racing down the hillside on home-made trolleys, or sledging down the slopes in the snowy weather. They are of many different age groups, and it is interesting to ask oneself which one is most at home in the Worrel. Is multi-faith education more relevant to pre-school babes, infants, juniors, adolescents or teenagers? Is it relevant to each age range in a different way? Is there an optimum age for different forms of teaching, and can a syllabus be devised that will relate multi-faith teaching to developmental education? Clearly doctrines and systems of belief cannot be studied until later years in the secondary school, but religions are about people — what they do, what they enjoy, what they care about — and much of this can be understood in primary school — stories, music, festivals, parties, processions and much else.

There is much that might be drawn upon as occasion arises. Here are some suggestions:

Nursery level:
> *Stories*: games and songs from the backgrounds represented by the children present.

Infant level:
> *Stories:* Maya of Mohenjo-daro; Chendru;
> *Customs* (often through story): Ag and the birds;

    *Food*: chapattis, sweetmeats, etc.
    *Clothes*: sari, shalwar kameeze, etc.
    *Animals*: slides, pictures and stories.

Lower Junior level:
    *Stories:* The Station Master of Guntakal;
    *Customs* (through story): Bell Ears and Shiva;
    *Names* and their meanings;
    *Birthdays*: own, others and famous;
    *Festivals*: Divali, Hannukah, Christmas;
    *Birth, Marriage and Death*: through stories and pictures;
    *Buildings*: Patterns and Shapes, Islamic and Hindu.

Upper Junior level:
    *Names* and their power;
    *Birthdays and anniversaries*;
    *Festivals*: Dussehra, Tabernacles, Eid;
    *People*: Gautama and Jesus, Moses and Nanak,
        Muhammad and Zarathustra;
    *Birth, Marriage and Death*: through pictures and slides;
    *Scriptures*: Qur'an, Ramayana, Japji;
    *Clothes*: turban, shoes hats;
    *Food*: see *Samosa, Indian Cook Book*, etc.;
    *Buildings* and their uses.

Lower Secondary:
    *Festivals*: Feast of Weeks; Baisakhi, Pentecost;
    *Mythology*: Creation and evil in various traditions;
    *Scriptures*: Prophetic books, gospels, Mahabharata;
    *Buildings* and their symbolic architecture;
    *People*: cantor, imam, swami;
    *Places*: Jerusalem, Benares, Amritsar, Mecca;
    *Initiation ceremonies*: Hindu, Parsee, Sikh, Christian,
        Jewish.

Upper Secondary:
    *Festivals*: Passover, Wesak, Holi;
    *Man*: African, Buddhist, Jewish;
    *Morality*: Hindu, Sikh, Christian;
    *The Future*: Buddhist, Christian, Muslim.

(For further ideas, see Hinnells and Sharpe 1972, Cole 1973, Bridger 1969, Ward Lock 1971–74, Trudgian 1971–74, Domnitz 1974, James 1971, Boyce 1972, and Zinkin 1968.)

Such material could be used in a continuous process or interspersed with more traditional teaching. Alternatively it could be taught through a systematic study of particular religious traditions in, say, the second term of the first, third and fifth secondary years, though the material would still be better selected to relate to the child's developing ability. Many younger teachers find thematic teaching (as outlined above) difficult to cope with until they have first taught a religion 'straight', on account of the demands made in preparation if a formal teaching method is involved. Where discovery methods or work sheets or library periods are used, the thematic method becomes much easier to handle, as every primary teacher knows. Even so there is nothing but study, contact and experience that will make such a demanding approach genuinely effective. Those anxious to try their hand with themes will find useful material in a number of books by Professor E.G. Parrinder, for example, *Worship in the World's Religions* (1961) or his *Book of World Religions* (1965). In the long run, however, the variety of methods used to involve the pupils in learning situations will be equally as important as the material to be studied.

Finally the road we have been following so tortuously leads through a glorious series of hairpin bends to the pass itself that gives onto the mountain range. This series of bends is known as Integration, and it is where the Worrel has closer links than most other areas of the Reled land with parallel fields in Education. Many who take short cuts find it a costly and dangerous slope, but those who can negotiate the tricky bends and find the link roads between their own studies and those parallel fields of History, Geography, English, Languages, Music, Dance and Drama, Art, Craft, Home Economics, Environmental Studies and so on, will find it an exhilarating hill both to climb and to descend. The scope for some form of organised team teaching is wide, and in a day when the RE teacher has to be Jack (or Jill) of so many trades, the strength that each can offer the other is welcome indeed. In the primary field many teachers will, of course, already be integrating their curricula by teaching through themes, but even here some form of team work can be a valuable asset to those whose specialisation is limited. Many teachers will find the 'glossy' books of use here — such as the superb Hamlyn series on Mythology. Others worth considering are: James 1974, Wosian 1974, Duerden 1968 and Deneck 1967.

This then is the Worrel — a fascinating and picturesque country, right from the A level and O level syllabuses that such Boards as AEB, Cambridge, JMB and London have recently approved through to the simplest studies of each other that nursery children can devise. For those who hesitate to walk this way alone, there is an organisation known as the Shap Working Party on World Religions in Education which offers travellers both guidance and comradeship. There are even huts in the mountains to which the weary may turn for sustenance and shelter.

Fuller information may be obtained from the Shap Information and Advisory Officer, Borough Road College, Isleworth, Middlesex.

## References

M. Ballard (1971) *Who am I?* Hutchinson.

R. Boyce (1972) *The Story of Islam* REP.

P. Bridger (1969) *A Hindu Family in Britain* REP.

W.O. Cole (1973) *A Sikh Family in Britain* REP.

W.O. Cole, ed. (1973a) *Religion in the Multi-Faith School* Yorkshire Committee for Community Relations.

K. Cragg (1970) *Alive to God — Muslim and Christian Prayer* OUP.

H. Davies (1954) *Christian Deviations* SCM Press.

M.M. Deneck (1967) *Indian Art* Hamlyn.

M. Domnitz (1974) *Understanding Your Jewish Neighbour* Lutterworth.

D. Duerden (1968) *African Art* Hamlyn.

S. Fass (1974) *Faces of India* Serena Fass.

S. Hedges (1970) *With One Voice* REP.

J. Hinnells and E. Sharpe (1972) *Hinduism* Oriel/Routledge.

A. James (1974) *Sikh Children in Britain* OUP.

D. James (1974) *Islamic Art* Hamlyn.

G. James (1971) *The Bodhi Tree* Chapman.

J. Needleman (1970) *The New Religions* Penguin.

C. Padwick (1961) *Muslim Devotions* SPCK.

E.G. Parrinder (1961) *Worship in the World's Religions* Faber; 2nd edition Sheldon 1974.

E.G. Parrinder (1965) *A Book of World Religions* Hulton.

(1971) *Man and his Gods* Hamlyn.

Idries Shah (1966) *The Exploits of the Incomparable Mulla Nasradin* Picador.

Shap Working Party (1972) *World Religions: Aids for Teachers* Community Relations Commission.

N. Smart (1974) *Mao* Fontana.

N. Tiptaft (1972) *Religion in Birmingham* N. Tiptaft, 3 Warley Croft, Warley, Worcs.

Time/Life (1973) *Six World Religions* (boxed kits), Edward Patterson Associates Ltd, 68 Copers Cope Road, Beckenham, Kent.

R. Trudgian, ed. (1971—74) *Thinking About Religion* series, Lutterworth.

Ward Lock (1971—74) *Living Religion Series* (11 booklets) Ward Lock.

M.G. Wosien (1974) *Sacred Dance-Encounter with the Gods* Thames & Hudson.

T. Zinkin (1968) *The Faithful Parrot* OUP.

# 15 Learning about Christianity

JULIAN FROST

## CHRISTIANITY, SOCIETY AND THE SCHOOL

For centuries it had been taken for granted that our school children should be instructed in the Christian faith. This rested on a widespread belief in the truth of Christianity and acceptance of its teachings. The belief and acceptance was sufficiently widespread for our society to be described as Christian. It is not surprising that a society conceiving of itself as Christian should expect its children to grow up as Christians nor that it should accord to schools the role of nurturing young people in the Christian faith. This nurture was largely in the form of instruction, imparting knowledge of the Bible, the major source book of Christianity, and of the central Christian doctrines. The emphasis was upon factual knowledge of historical origins and doctrines.

Can our society any longer be described as Christian? Some assert that it is 'post-Christian', others, suggesting that the retreat from institutional religion is not necessarily indicative of a lack of interest in religious and spiritual matters, claim that it is 'post-ecclesiastical'. There are many belief and value systems in a state of dynamic interaction where previously there was a fairly static situation with one dominant faith system. Although Christianity continues to exercise a strong influence on society, the presence of members of non-Christian religions and adherents of Humanist and other non-religious stances for living suggest that a 'pluralist society' is the best description. Over the centuries there has been a complicated interaction between Christianity and our culture. Neither has remained autonomous, each has influenced the other in varying degrees at different times. This dialectic continues, but it has been made vastly more complex by the pluralism of today. The resulting cultural synthesis is the background against which education takes place.

Changes in patterns of belief and in the position held by Christianity in our society have led teachers to review the study of Christianity in schools. No longer can the County school be regarded as the agent of the Church, no longer is it an acceptable aim to bring children to Christian commitment and growth in the faith. (Christian teachers may still cherish hopes that their pupils will embrace Christianity, but that is a different matter.) The inclusion in the curriculum of religious education, let alone the study of Christianity, requires educational justification. This is being sought in the theories that religious thinking, comprises a distinct and significant part of the characteristic human activity of seeking patterns of meaning in experience. In other words, religion comprises a distinct form of knowledge, understanding of which is an essential part of a liberal education. (See Phenix 1964 and Hirst 1965.)

In their search for educationally valid aims many teachers find sympathy with *The Fourth R*'s suggestion that the 'aim of religious education should be to explore the place and significance of religion in human life and so to make a distinctive contribution to each pupil's search for a faith by which to live' (Durham 1970). Two points follow from this:

First, an understanding of the place and significance of religion can only be cultivated through an understanding of a religion or religions. For pupils in our schools, learning about Christianity is an important and usually the most appropriate way of gaining this understanding. As the major religion in our society it is the one most pupils are likely to have encountered. This may be through their family upbringing or because Christianity manifests itself in every local community. It is a living religion immediately available for examination. Also, to be a member of our society is to be familiar with many of the underlying assumptions, ideas and beliefs of Christianity.

Second, religions invite acceptance and encourage commitment. It is inevitable that pupils will measure the beliefs and practices studied against their own developing understanding and commitments. Acceptance or rejection may be involved, certainly discrimination and judgment will be called into play. The school is caught up in this search for personal identity and an acceptable life style. It can aid or hinder it.

Helping pupils to discover 'a faith by which to live' is an acceptable aim for religious education provided 'faith' is defined widely enough to embrace not only religious but also non-religious stances for living. For most pupils this search will no doubt be carried on in the terms of the underlying Christian presuppositions about nature, man and culture long current in our society. This need not amount to indoctrination. The process is open if Christianity is seen alongside other religions and 'non-religions' and if it is presented, not as an unquestionable package of beliefs and values, but as the basis for dialogue.

## LEARNING ABOUT CHRISTIANITY

It has been said that 'the Churches are now rather the subjects than the sponsors of study' (see Chapter 7). We need to consider ways of studying Christianity which lead to insight, appreciation and understanding.

The Phenomenology of Religion may be able to help us here. In Chapter 1 Ninian Smart's analysis of the elements or dimensions making up a religion identifies the following aspects: the doctrinal, mythological, ethical, ritual, experiential and social (see also Smart 1968). This analysis is helpful in exhibiting something of the logic of a religion's structure and also in providing guidelines for an enquiry. It reminds us that to gain a well-rounded picture of a religion — one that corresponds as closely as possible to what exists — we ought to take account of all these different aspects. The various dimensions do not, however, exist in isolation. They are part of an intricate pattern of interconnections which together form an organic whole.

Any study of Christianity as a religion must do justice to these complexities and subtleties. Phenomenology suggests that this study should be descriptive in showing what is, and evocative in its attempt to enter into the world of the Christian. In addition, the phenomenologist's concern with typology suggests one line of approach in which certain Christian practices, understandings and interpretations may be set alongside those of other religious and non-religious belief systems.

*Descriptive*

Learning about Christianity will involve the acquisition of accurate factual information. This is a prerequisite to the development of understanding and insight. The study is descriptive in that it will attempt to indicate what actually is. An awareness of the multi-dimensional character of the Christian religion will help towards the presentation of an overall picture. Smart's analysis is suggestive of possible lines of approach and is a useful check-list for the teacher designing a curriculum. For example, the ritual dimension may suggest studies of the varieties of worship within the Christian tradition, or the significance of the Eucharist, or the place of meditation, or the symbolism of Church buildings and furniture, or the place of music and hymn singing. On the other hand it is important to see how the influence of the vital central elements within Christianity reverberates, as it were, throughout the many aspects of the religion. This is particularly so in the case of the Bible and the person of Christ.

A criticism often levelled at the older syllabuses is that they were overloaded with biblical material. Granted the central position of the Bible in the life of the Church, the need to understand and be familiar with this body of literature is unquestioned. The danger is that the Bible story and its leading ideas are not seen in their proper setting, exercising a normative function in the development of Christian doctrine and an inspirational role in the life of the believer.

The Bible has been and is the basic text for the formulation of doctrine and it is richly influential in the development of ethical principles. It is read within the context of worship, it is studied by small groups and it figures prominently in the individual's devotional life. Questions as to its historicity and provenance in a Judaeo-Christian milieu are important, but these ought not to overshadow questions about its status and function within the life of the believing community. Neither this community at worship, nor the Bible study group at its meeting, nor the Christian at his devotions is primarily concerned with disputes about the inspiration and authority of the Bible. Whether or not these have been finally settled the Bible's 'ring of truth' is recognised at an experiential level. An awareness of the multi-dimensional character of Christianity allows us to see more fully the place the Bible occupies in the life of the Church.

The same is true of the study of the person of Christ. The Jesus of Nazareth and the Christ of the early Church have for long been studied in school and rightly so, for Christianity traces its origins to the Jesus who lived and died in the first century. The Church, however, has a wider and more topical interest than that provided by the study of an historical character. For the believer the Jesus of Nazareth became and is the risen Christ. There is a continuity in the life of the Church between the man portrayed in the Gospels and the one worshipped Sunday by Sunday, in whose name prayers are made, whose presence is experienced by the individual and community, whose spirit inspires faith, encourages moral endeavour and gives value to suffering. Questions about the person and work of Christ have not been finally settled but they ought not, in any study, to overshadow the significance of the believer's affirmation, 'Christ is risen.'

The study of other world religions may provide a helpful analogy here. In the Muslim religion, for example, the Qur'an plays at least as important a part as the Bible does in Christianity. Yet learning about Islam comprises far more than the study of a text. Learning about Christianity should be learning not just about historical origins and distinctive doctrines. It should embrace the way in which Christianity manifests itself today; its impact upon the individual Christian; its ethical demands, and the quality of life within a worshipping, believing, caring community.

This would begin to take account of the many ways in which Christianity expresses itself within the unity provided by acceptance of the ancient creeds, the Bible and the uniqueness of Christ. These are apparent in the organisation and structure of different denominations, in the varieties of worship, whether liturgical or free, in the patterns of ministry, whether priestly or lay. Christianity is sometimes presented as if it were a uniform, monolithic structure of belief and practice. At first sight it may appear a less exciting area of study than, say, some of the Eastern religions whose strangeness and, perhaps, exotic quality lends enchantment.

Yet there are types of Christianity which may be unfamiliar, even exotic; for example, the Orthodox Church in parts of eastern Europe, the Roman Catholic Church in southern Italy, Pentecostalism in the United States. Examples can also be found among the English Churches. At the same time there is to be found within Christianity's devotional and mystical traditions an emotional appeal and a sense of spiritual power at least as strong as that of the Eastern religions.

To outward appearances the Church may seem a static, unchanging organisation. Yet within Christianity there is a dynamic which expresses itself in tension and conflict and sometimes creative growth. Theology is far from being just a static process of passing on received doctrines. The ways in which the central doctrines are expressed (for instance the idea of a transcendent God or the divinity of Christ) are constantly under review. The uneasy position of the Church in a pluralistic society is at the present time a challenge to theology. How is the Church to understand itself and its beliefs vis-à-vis the other great world religions and in the face of atheistic and other non-religious ideologies? These inner tensions may provide starting-points for study at the later stage of schooling. The inner dynamism manifests itself in other ways too. There are experiments in forms of worship, in greater lay participation, in community living, in greater openness, in caring personal relationships.

A study of Christianity should be descriptive in the sense that it indicates and tries to understand what exists, in all its variety, as well as attempting to lay bare the fundamentally unifying elements.

*Evocative*

A study which concentrates upon external appearances and attempts an objective appreciation may not do full justice to a religion such as Christianity. We need to 'get inside', to see things as the Christian sees them, and to become, in some sense, a participant as distinct from an observer. The slogan here is 'religious education must transcend the informative' (Smart 1968).

This involves a presentation of the faith as it appears to the Christian and is practised by him. What is the meaning and value to him of the many-sided aspects of his religion? His description of a Church as 'the house of God' denotes something of the significance to him of that building and all its associations. Can we see something of the meaning to the believer of participation in the Mass or Eucharist or Lord's Supper? What value does he put upon his devotional life and upon the Bible in the nurture of his faith? How does he face up to the ethical demands implicit in his beliefs, especially if these conflict with widely held moral standards? What is the meaning to the believer of statements like 'I have been saved,' or 'my sins have been forgiven,' or 'I felt guided to take that course of action'?

Christianity, if taken seriously, engages a person at every level of his being, the affective as well as the intellectual. A study should try to gain an insight into the feelings and intentions of the participants. All this demands a high degree of imaginative identification. To what extent are pupils able to adopt the role of 'observing participant'? Is this level of identification possible without the believer's commitments being endorsed by the student? At the level of professional anthropology and psychiatric practice the answer to this type of question may well be in the affirmative. For the untrained layman, let alone the pupil, it is a much more open question. Yet the attempt ought to be made. The analogy of the film, play or novel in which we enter into another's situation and see life through his eyes without endorsing all his commitments and particular life style is helpful here. Teachers encourage their pupils 'to step into other people's shoes' especially as part of creative expression in poetry, prose, art, drama and movement.

Complete success is probably impossible but inasmuch as a study of Christianity fails to evoke something of the feelings, the intentions and indeed the whole flavour of being a Christian, to that extent the real quality and character of the religion is being misrepresented.

Contact with the Church is essential. This may take the form of visits to Church buildings preferably when worship is taking place. There is a place for dialogue with Christians both clergy and lay. Christian staff and pupils have a part to play here. Certain literature, drama, music, art and architecture can convey something of the feel and creative power of the Christian faith, when description alone leaves one cold.

*Comparative*

In a pluralistic society different religions and ideologies claim attention. There are many features of different religions which, in outward form if not in inner meaning and intention, are similar. The sacred place, the scriptures and worship, provide possible starting points. There is prayer, meditation, sacrament, sacrifice, feast and festivals, dietary laws and fasts, pilgrimage and holy relic. There are the rites of passage associated with birth, initiation, marriage and death. Then there are different belief and value systems having distinctive answers to ultimate questions. What is man? Why do we suffer? What happens after death? Is there any design in the universe or any purpose in living? These are perennial human questions to which religions and non-religions give answers.

In this type of approach Christian beliefs and practice, Christian interpretation of experience and Christian answers to ultimate questions can be explored alongside those of other religions and non-religions.

## THE STUDY OF CHRISTIANITY AS PART OF A PROGRAMME FOR RELIGIOUS EDUCATION

*Aims and objectives*

It has been suggested that an understanding of the place and significance of religion in human life is an acceptable aim for religious education. This aim needs to be broken down, both in terms of aims realisable by the end of schooling (or beyond) and in terms of objectives bearing upon decisions about content and method. The Schools Council Working Paper 36 summarises some of the long term aims: ' . . . religious education seeks to promote awareness of religious issues, and of the contribution of religion to human culture in general; it seeks to promote understanding of religious beliefs' and practices, it also aims to awaken recognition of the challenge and practical consequences of religious belief' (*Schools Council 1971*). Learning about Christianity, or some aspect of it, would be one way in which aims such as these might be realised. The aim of promoting an awareness of the contribution of religion to human culture may be taken as an example. This might be broken down into such objectives for particular courses as promoting understanding and awareness of the influence of the 'non-conformist conscience' in local and national life, of the place of the Parish Church in the life of local communities, of the role of the Church in marking important events in an individual's progress through life, or of the celebration of Christian festivals and accompanying social customs. It might lead to an exploration of the relationship between a capitalist society and the Protestant ethic.

The study of Christianity will itself have certain objectives. These can clearly be related to the aims already mentioned, many of which depend upon a knowledge and understanding of a particular religion or religions. The objectives are (a) to promote an awareness and understanding of Christianity in its doctrinal, mythological, ethical, ritual, experiential and social aspects, and (b) to promote an awareness of and insight into the feelings and intentions of the Christian believer.

For example, the place of worship in the life of the Church might form the basis of a study. Objectives here would include an exploration of the significance of the Church building, its shape and design, an understanding of the importance of the furniture (pulpit, altar, font etcetera), of the relationship of priest or minister to the worshippers, and of the use made of music, the Bible, the sermon, prayer and so on. Such a study would also attempt to uncover something of the intentions and beliefs of the worshippers and of the feelings evoked by worship. At the heart of Christian worship is a belief in a transcendent and awe-inspiring Being. The worshippers intend to express the worth and value to them of this Being. Focus upon this transcendent Other induces feeling of awe and dependence, gratitude and joy, and, possibly, ecstasy.

There are certain skills, sensitivities and capacities which need to be developed in order to achieve aims of the sort mentioned above. Learning about Christianity will require observing, classifying, abstracting and conceptualising. It will also involve feeling and imagination.

There is the capacity to enter into the experience of others. This is important if a pupil is to gain any insight into the inner world of the Christian. Any attempt to portray Christianity from the point of view of the Christian and how it seems to him presupposes this imaginative empathy. It will be developed, in the hands of the sensitive teacher, as the child begins to identify with the characters and the situations in the stories he reads and as he explores the world of others through drama, movement, art and creative writing.

The Christian faith not only involves assent to doctrines and beliefs but also excites an emotional response. (A neglected question in looking at patterns of religious commitment in our society is the one that asks what it is that people are looking for and expecting from their Church allegiance and practice.) Children need to appreciate the place and importance of feeling in human experience. They are encouraged in the techniques of empirical verification: observation, measurement and classification. Less frequently do we explore with them experiences which elude this type of verification. For example, there is the sense of joy in living and of security in love and comradeship, the satisfaction of courage and facing hardship, the feelings of fear and sorrow, hate and disgust, the urges to create and to destroy, the desire to establish an authentic identity. Somehow this side of experience needs its validation too. Children can be helped to appreciate the importance of the emotions and the place of fantasy in coming to terms with experience. This may be as they enter the world of the story (or of drama, dance or role-play) identify with the characters and project their questionings and anxieties.

Allied to this is an awareness of the importance of the myth. It will be a great gain if the myth can be rescued from the popular notion of being an untrue story worthy of little attention (see Chapter 6). An understanding of myth as neutral in terms of empirical truth or falsehood, as helping men come to terms with experience and as alive and potent in different forms in different societies, can have its beginnings as soon as the question 'Is it true?' is raised. This appreciation is vital to an understanding of religion.

In this context it is perhaps more important to understand the nature of the Bible than to have a detailed knowledge of its contents. Christians see the Bible in different ways; some set great store by its historicity; others stress its mythological character; others, like C.S. Lewis, regard the story of Jesus as, in some sense, The Myth incarnate. A scheme of study which includes the Bible in a mythological dimension may be regarded with suspicion. Yet to discern the difference between statements like 'Jesus died' and 'Jesus died for our sins' is all part of the process of distinguishing between historical statements and affirmations of belief.

This in turn is related to the appreciation of symbolism. Understanding the place and function of the symbol in language and in non-discursive forms of communication is another of the skills needed for an appreciation of the complex phenomena of a religion. Ability to handle the biblical metaphor, symbol and parable requires an insight into the symbolic character of language. For example, a pupil's understanding of St John's Gospel, studied perhaps towards the end of the secondary school, will be enriched when he is sensitive to the imaginative world of the Gospel and the way in which it draws upon symbols of universal appeal: light and dark, death and life, bread and water, birth and rebirth. In the same way, to be alive to the power of the image and symbol in music and drama, art and architecture will deepen insight into the importance of the buildings, the rituals and the other symbols of the Christian faith.

*The capacities, interests and concerns of the pupil*
Religious education is a continuing and also a developing process. Problems in selecting content are at their most acute in the early years. The introduction of doctrine and theology in the formal sense of passing on a body of teaching are inappropriate at this stage. R. Goldman and others have indicated that the ability to conceptualise necessary to handle this material comes fairly late in a child's development (Goldman 1964 and 1965).

The previous section has pointed to certain areas of experience where early foundations are important for a later understanding of Christianity. These include exploring the many dimensions of language, appreciating the experience of others, feeling after understanding through creative activity, grappling for the first time with ultimate questions, seeing something of the 'mystery' of our existence and of patterns of interdependence within the natural order. What is attempted in the early years should not only be a preparation for later fuller understanding but should also be valid in its own right for children of a certain age, capacity and experience.

Christianity is not just a body of teaching expressed in difficult concepts. As a way of life touching the whole of experience there are different aspects that it may be possible to explore in the primary school. These include festivals (especially Christmas), rituals (such as baptisms and weddings), Church buildings in the locality, and some of the activities of the Church members in the local community. Some Bible stories may have a place too, not so much as carriers of ethical or doctrinal teaching as in provoking the imagination (see Cook 1969).

The immediate social setting has an important bearing upon decisions about content. (The presence of immigrants in an infant school might make it appropriate to touch upon aspects of say Hinduism or Sikhism.) The childrens' contact with local forms of Christianity will differ from area to area. This may be as a result of family occasions such as baptisms or weddings, or through membership of a Sunday School or Church-based Cub or Brownie pack.

Later, in the secondary school, the problem is less the one of avoiding the introduction of difficult concepts and more the one of making courses that are relevant to real-life problems and concerns of the pupils. H. Loukes (1961), K. Hyde (1965), E. Cox (1967) and others have shown the importance to adolescents of existential questions. The traditional Christian terminology may seem irrelevant. It is all the more important, therefore, that the study of Christianity through the school should show it to be a religion that touches upon human experience and is not divorced from it; that it attempts to make sense of all the facts of that experience (some brutal) and that it suggests a way of life at once earthy yet having a transcendent quality.

*Outline of a study: Christianity in Britain today*
This outline can be adapted for different ages in the secondary school range. It might form part of an integrated studies course looking at the environment or a religious education project studying religion in the locality. It might

be developed as a CSE project. An active, discovery-method type of approach is suggested to allow the pupils to come into contact with local examples of religious belief and practice.

Some of its objectives would be:

(i) To be able to identify some of the Christian denominations found in Britain today and to understand something of their role in the community and in the lives of their members.

(ii) To be able to compare and contrast some of the beliefs and practices of different denominations and to sense something of what they mean to those who hold and practise them.

(iii) To recognise that members of a denomination are united by commitment to a system of beliefs and ethical principles, and that the life of the community is nurtured through individual and group rituals and other practices.

(iv) To discover some of the main aspects of the life of a believing community and how to acquire, classify and present information about these.

(v) To see the unity amidst diversity among Christian denominations.

(vi) To develop an 'open' and sympathetic attitude towards the religious beliefs and practices of others.

What follows is an outline of how this study might be organised:

1 *Introduction* This aims to show how widespread Christian belief and practice is in Britain today and how it impinges upon national, local and individual life. Audio-visual aids would be helpful here. A questionnaire would be useful, too, to discover the extent of the pupils' knowledge of local Christian groups, and the depth of their understanding of worship and religion generally.

2 *A visit to a Church* At this point it is anticipated that the class will be divided into smaller groups each of which will study a particular denomination. The groups will prepare for the visit by discussing the function of religious buildings and noting things to look out for, such as the shape of the building and the position and use of furniture. During the visit the group will meet a leader of the Church who can point out significant features and answer questions. The visit

can be followed by discussion, the recording of impressions and the preparation of reports, plans, diagrams, etc.

*3   Seeing people at worship* A second visit will be made while a service of worship is in progress. This will necessarily be in out-of-school hours but it is important that·worship should be seen in its normal setting. Again, arrangements with the leader of the denomination will have been made in advance. Preparation in the classroom will explore the meaning of worship, the importance of the community setting, the place of symbolism, and the variety of the forms of worship. Follow-up might take the form of discussion, comparing notes, recording impressions (perhaps in poetry, art, drama as well as in prose) and endeavouring to sense the impact of the worship upon the participants.

*4   An interview* The leader of each denomination, perhaps accompanied by a lay member, will be invited to visit the school to meet the group. Pupils will be able to ask questions still in their minds following the visits. They will also be able to find out more about the denomination: how and why people become members or leaders; the organisation of the group, its important meetings, and day-to-day concerns; the wider interests of the group in inter-church contacts, local social concerns and in the world at large.

*5   Further investigation* In order to gain a more complete picture of the particular denomination being studied, pupils will be encouraged to find out more about its leaders, ceremonies, festivals, use of the Bible, national organisation etcetera. This work can be pursued between the visits and other activities.

*6   Conclusions* The different groups will have much to share. This can be done by verbal reports, displays of pictures and plans, written work and recordings. It might be approached topically by considering buildings, worship, the place of the Bible, patterns of leadership, social concerns and so on. An exploration of the unity and diversity among the Christian denominations would be appropriate here. (This outline draws upon material developed by Heather Moore and Julian Frost in conjunction with the Schools Council Project on Religious Education in Secondary Schools, Moore and Frost 1975.)

## References

E. Cook (1969) *The Ordinary and the Fabulous* CUP.

E. Cox (1967) *Sixth Form Religion* SCM Press.

Bishop of Durham, ed. (1970) *The Fourth R* The National Society and SPCK.

R.J. Goldman (1964) *Religious Thinking from Childhood to Adolescence* Routledge.

(1965) *Readiness for Religion* Routledge.

P.H. Hirst (1965) 'Liberal Education and the Nature of Knowledge', in R.D. Archambault, ed. *Philosophical Analysis and Education* Routledge.

K.E. Hyde (1965) *Religious Learning in Adolescence* Oliver and Boyd.

H. Loukes (1961) *Teenage Religion* SCM Press.

H. Moore and J. Frost (1975) 'Religion in Britain Today', a teaching unit in *Journeys into Religion* Hart-Davis Educational.

P. Phenix (1964) *Realms of Meaning* McGraw-Hill.

Schools Council (1971) *Religious Education in Secondary Schools* Evans/Methuen.

N. Smart (1968) *Secular Education and the Logic of Religion* Faber.

# 16 The Bible in religious education

EDWIN COX

There has been no published research on the proportion of time taken up in religious education in British schools by Bible study. One has the impression that even in this educationally-open, thematic-centred, child-related, multi-religious, subject-integrating age, study of the Christian scriptures occupies the major portion of the lessons. Even the modern Agreed Syllabuses abound with references to it. Teachers who construct themes feel that their confection will not rise to the occasion without some scriptural leaven. Pupils sometimes protest that the lesson is not 'religious' without Bible allusions. There is a residual feeling that these are what guarantee the authenticity of religious education.

This raises the questions of what place Bible study should take in learning about religions at the moment, and how that study should be planned. To answer these questions one needs to consider the manner in which the concept of religious education has changed in the past twenty years; the different position and esteem that the Bible is accorded in our culture; the complex nature of the Bible literature itself and the manner in which the young (and the not so young) are liable to misinterpret it; and the fact that those who accept it as 'authoritative scripture' — which includes most of those who teach it in schools — claim that it gives a knowledge of ultimate reality, whereas those who think otherwise do not accept its theological statements as sufficiently proveable to be regarded as knowledge. Before one can offer practical advice to teachers on how to use the Bible in their work, one needs, therefore, to consider the role of the Bible in our present culture and the manner in which our contemporaries understand it and react to its statements.

*The place of the Bible in present culture*
Though the Bible still has a prominent place in current

religious education, not all teachers use it with the confidence that their predecessors did fifty years ago, and not all pupils accord it the respectful response that is envisaged. The reason is that the Bible — or any 'sacred' literature for that matter — is granted an authority by those in the faith system which has produced it, but not by those outside it. The Bible is revered as 'sacred' by Christians, but not by Muslims; the Qur'an is 'sacred' to the Muslims, but not to the Christians or the Hindus; and to the man who rejects religion no 'sacred' book appears worthy of special reverence. Whether or not any particular writing is regarded as a source of religious knowledge or a reliable guide to morals, depends on the readers having certain beliefs about its nature. To those possessing these beliefs it will have a unique authority; to those who lack the necessary beliefs it is just another book.

There appears to have been a time, not so long ago, when the majority of Englishmen and English school pupils had such beliefs about the Bible. They could regard it, in words used in the 1953 Coronation service, as 'the most valuable thing that this world affords' containing 'Wisdom', 'the royal Law' and 'the lively Oracles of God' (Coronation 1953). Consequently it could be used as an authoritative and final arbiter in theological and moral disputes. In its pages were certainty, because it was being used in a predominantly Christian context where almost everyone was willing to accept that that was its nature and to use it in that way. That is why RE syllabuses used it extensively as the source of religious knowledge.

That situation no longer pertains. Many question or have abandoned the Christian beliefs they once held; a new generation has emerged in which great numbers have never held those beliefs; immigration and travel have brought us into contact with other religions, adherents of which can be found living among us in significant numbers. The religious climate has changed from Christian to pluralistic, and such a change cannot help but modify the manner in which the Bible is regarded. Though it remains an oracular source of reference to those who have remained in the Christian milieu, it does not exercise the same claim on others. Its use in religious education is correspondingly modified. From being the unique source book, it becomes one of the aids to understanding how the Christian section of the population believe and behave, and its statements are true, not because they come from the Bible, but insofar as they seem verified by experience.

The difference between the Christian and the non-Christian response to the Bible is more than intellectual, and in discussing the position now accorded it we must take into account the decline in attendance at public worship. The effect of hearing the Bible read frequently and ceremonially in an emotionally charged setting is to enhance its prestige. Further, by such use it acquired to itself associations. Other things that are said in the services, and emotions that are associated with church attendance, become attached to it. The result is that, for the church-goer, Bible reading evokes ideas and convictions which are not immediately derived from the passage that is being studied. It has overtones, as it were, which add a richness to the reading but which an objective intellectual analysis cannot justify. When public worship was an almost universal activity, the Bible spoke in this way to the majority, and to use those overtones in religious education was possible, and did not generally seem either undesirable or doctrinally aggressive. Now that the greater number of pupils rarely, if at all, hear the Bible read ceremoniously in public worship in church (the reading in school assembly does not seem to have the same prestige) it is not a book held in esteem, with multifarious religious associations, but a strange literature which they never encounter out of school and which adults for the most part ignore. It will not, therefore, speak to the whole class in the way that it did formerly, and teachers have to take into account that the Bible will speak to, and be understood by, pupils who are active Christians in a way that will be incomprehensible to the others. It is perhaps the mistake of syllabus makers and many religious education teachers to assume that all pupils respond to Bible study as though they were convinced church-goers.

## Children's understanding of the Bible

One of the difficulties of the use of the Bible in school lessons is that children are not able easily to discern the type of literature that it contains. It comes from an age when the method of expressing perceived truth differed from that employed since men engaged in attempts at systematic scientific investigation and at the impersonal, accurate recording of history. Opinion today tends to regard the objective and impersonal description of things and events as reliable truth, and imaginative attempts to express value or meaning as in some way inferior and over-individual. Indeed such expressions of what men perceive as 'truth' are usually regarded as appropriate for 'entertainment' rather than as reputable expressions of reality.

The Bible writers, however, belonged to an age when the literal expression of scientific and historical events was not widely practised. They saw nothing misleading in expressing truth in the form of a parable or enshrining their ideas in a story. Sometimes the story could be an historical one because that seemed to them to express what they had in mind. At other times they adapted their description of history to bring out the meaning to which they wished to draw attention. At other times, again, they invented stories that served their purpose. The result is a collection of history, semi-history and imaginative literature. The point to notice is that they were primarily concerned to communicate an idea which seemed to them to be true, and they were not concerned with the historical and scientific accuracy of the story in which it was enshrined: the truth they tried to tell did not depend on that accuracy. They were producing fable, metaphor, parable and allegory, rather than factual and historical statements.

Unless this allusive character of a great deal of the Bible literature is recognised there is a danger that it will be misunderstood by being interpreted over-literally. The prestige that is accorded to the Bible in the Christian culture encourages such misinterpretation. Whereas, for example, the fables of Aesop are recognised as fables and not regarded as historical accounts (one does not enquire into the sex of the fox that said the grapes were sour, or debate whether it spoke English, Greek or a special vulpine language) the belief that the Bible is the repository of some particularly valuable truth causes some to insist that it must be true in all aspects, containing accurate history and accurate science as well as responsible theology. Examples of this are afforded by

Bishop Usher, who took the Bible to contain sufficient historiography to enable him to work out the chronology of world history, and those who believe that the Genesis accounts of creation give a truer picture of the emergence of the cosmos than astronomical physics and geology. The total effect of this mistaking of the nature of the Bible material is to make many of its readers think that it is a source of reference on matters with which its writers were not primarily concerned, and ignore the type of truth which they were trying to express. That is perhaps why, in our scientifically and historically orientated culture, those who are not professional Bible students tend to regard the scriptures either with irrational fervour or with puzzled scepticism.

If adults misunderstand the Bible in this way, children are likely to do so *a fortiori*. For, as the well-known researchers of Piaget and Goldman have discovered, they tend to think literally and concretely up to the mental age of twelve or thirteen years. They are incapable of understanding fully stories that are metaphorical and allegorical, and interpret them in a concretistic and literal way. Furthermore, younger children have difficulty in recognising that truth may be expressed other than in factual statement. The type of pictorial and allusive literature which is found in much of the Bible therefore escapes them, and they understand it as a collection of statements of events that all actually happened. When, in early adolescence, those statements seem to conflict with their experience of how things work in practice, and with what they are learning in other school subjects, a conflict arises which they often resolve by rejecting the Bible as unworthy of serious thought — hence the angry scorn that teachers not infrequently encounter in older pupils when they attempt to implement the Bible study prescribed by the syllabus.

The educational implications of this would seem twofold. Firstly, it is doubtful whether an unselective diet of Bible stories is appropriate in the junior school. If it is to be included, a much greater screening of material, and selection according to the maturity of understanding involved, needs to be attempted than has been the case up to the present. Secondly, some attempt needs to be made to explain to them in early adolescence the way in which the Bible writers saw the world, how they thought, how they enshrined their thoughts in imaginative and metaphorical stories, and what they are trying to say through those stories.

### The problem of 'revealed truth' and 'inspiration'

One of the chief difficulties of using any 'sacred' literature in a school classroom is occasioned by its claim to bring a special kind of knowledge through inspiration. All such writings, whether it be the Bible, the Qur'an, the Bhagavadgita, the Pali Pitakas, or the book of Mormon, are regarded by some religious groups as revealing, through prophecy, avatar or incarnation, a special sort of knowledge of gods or morals, which man either could not obtain by any other method, or could not obtain for a very long time. It is this element of oracle or inspired knowledge that causes these books to be called 'sacred' and studied as such. Two things need, however, to be noted in this connection.

The first is that this 'knowledge', for the most part, differs from discovered knowledge in that it cannot be verified by the processes we normally employ to check on what we think we know. There are means of checking the knowledge that 'this packet contains sugar and weighs one pound' which do not apply to such statements as 'God forgives sinners' or 'Allah is compassionate'. The guarantee of revealed 'knowledge' is not that it can be verified (except by living for a longish time in the light of it and finding that life satisfying) but that it is 'revealed' or 'inspired'. To accept it, therefore, one needs to make prior acts of faith that knowledge can come by inspiration, and that the inspiration behind any particular sacred book is genuine.

The second point to note follows from that. In a religiously pluralistic society any sacred book will find some who are able to make those prior acts of faith, and to whom its statements will be 'knowledge', and others who cannot make the acts of faith, to whom its statements are merely beliefs, aspirations, theories, superstitions or moonshine. The 'knowledge' that Christians find in the Bible will not necessarily look like knowledge to Humanists, materialists or to those who embrace other religious systems.

The situation, however, is not quite so clear-cut as this

would seem to suggest. For one thing there are often common elements in different sacred writings, and for another this knowledge can, as mentioned above, be verified to a limited extent by practical experience over a period of time. If a religious person decides to make an act of faith that what his scriptures say is true, and to act as though it is true, and finds that his life is resultantly ordered, intelligible and satisfying, he may reasonably conclude that his faith is justified and his belief, for him, is true. At this point some conclude that the inspiration which has brought the knowledge is genuine, while those more rationally minded admit that they have come on some knowledge of life, but reject that it was revealed, claiming that theories of revelation and inspiration are merely metaphorical ways of describing what has in fact been discovered by trial and error. The latter is a not uncommon attitude in England at present, where many will accept the wisdom of the Christian ethic as expressed in the Decalogue and the Sermon on the Mount for its practical value but have at least strong doubts as to whether the Commandments were revealed to Moses, or Jesus was the incarnation of God.

The debate about whether religious education is a reasonable, and even necessary, educational activity or whether it is questionable indocrination largely arises from the manner in which this revealed 'knowledge' is used in schools. Teachers of the subject are mostly Christians, and to them this 'knowledge' seems sufficiently certain for them to pass it on to their pupils as such. Christian pupils agree with them and accept it happily. Non-Christian pupils however, do not see it in that light, and the teacher appears to be trying to condition them to accept as truths what are in fact a series of beliefs. School pupils do not express this feeling in so many words; instead they withdraw their attention and hold both the teacher and his subject in scarcely veiled scorn. Outside the classroom, those who regard the revealed 'knowledge' as not only unverified but even as untrue and misleading, have joined with educational philosophers, who wish to bring clarity to our thinking about education, in pointing out the indoctrinatory nature of religious education lessons which deal uncritically with ideas derived from 'inspired' literature.

Since such belief-based 'knowledge' is of the very essence

of most of the major world religions, to suggest that it should not be used at all in schools would make a serious study of religion, as we now understand it, impossible. How then can the teacher use it and escape the charge of indoctrination? Perhaps the primary requisite is for the teacher to understand the difficulties, and to recognise the special status of revealed 'knowledge'. If it is borne in mind that this 'knowledge' is not universally verified and accepted in the way that the information transmitted in empirical subjects is, but that it is belief-based and will look like knowledge only to those who have the basic belief, it is possible to undertake the following activities without infringing students' intellectual freedom:

1 Teaching that people exist who hold that certain books are 'inspired' and bring information which those people regard as true knowledge; that is, teaching about the phenomenon of inspiration and its expression in sacred literature.

2 The imparting of information about the major systems of 'revealed knowledge' and the religious practices, liturgical and ethical, that follow from them; for example, teaching that this is what the Christians say is revealed to them in their inspired Bible, and this is how they respond to it in their worship and in their treatment of other people and of things; this is what the Hindus believe is revealed through their prophets and writings and how they respond to it. In the lower stages of schooling this is merely descriptive of what men do in fact believe without any suggestion that the pupils ought to believe it too.

3 In the higher forms it may be possible to discuss the truth or falsehood of revealed knowledge, and of how far the revelations of the various religions are seen to be true to experience. In these forms it may, in addition, be possible to discuss the phenomenon of revelation, the experience which leads men to think they have intuited truth, and the manner in which they have written about it.

4 Showing something of the effect of religious beliefs on those who hold them.

To apply this more directly to the subject of this chapter, what is involved for the use of the Bible in schools? It means that teachers must beware of expecting all their pupils to react to the knowledge which Jews and Christians believe is revealed in their scriptures as though it were self-obviously true, recognised as such by all right-minded and generous-minded people, and that the Bible can be used as an unquestionable arbiter in all theological, metaphysical and ethical disputes. Some pupils will not be able to respond to it in this way, and their incapacity is not necessarily due to imperception or perverseness. To insist that they should, generates ill-will and a suspicion of fanaticism. It is possible, however, to try to help pupils understand that certain people believe that certain definite ideas are revealed in the Bible and try to live in the light of them. Further, one can invite the pupils to consider how far they themselves feel inclined to accept those beliefs, which could involve asking them to try out the beliefs in practice to see if they are verified by experience, provided it is made clear that they are free to accept or reject as soon as the experiment has been conducted long enough for a sincere decision to be made. There is still a taint of indoctrination if the teacher says in effect 'Try these beliefs, and if you find you can accept them, well and good. If you can't I shall suspect you of illogical thinking, and urge you to go on experimenting till you can.' Openness on this matter must be genuine and not a temporary expedient.

Since this approach to the study of the Bible demands a certain maturity, perhaps we should here bear in mind Goldman's caveat that 'the recommendation may have to be faced that very little Biblical material is suitable before Secondary Schooling' (Goldman 1964). Further, even in secondary schooling, the study will be more objective than has been envisaged up to the present by the majority of syllabuses and teachers. There are, however, two problems worth noting, one concerning the material and the other concerning the teacher.

First, it is difficult to see how it is possible to prevent younger children coming into contact with Bible material and misunderstanding it. For one thing telling Bible stories, or stories based on Biblical material, has occupied such a considerable part of primary school religious education, that if one takes it away, the teacher is left with little to do. For another thing, in Christian areas some of these stories are so much a part of the folk culture that children are going to hear about them, and would be deprived of some cultural development if they did not. For instance, it is inconceivable that a Christmas should pass without a child hearing somewhere some part of the Bible stories concerning the birth of Jesus. Furthermore children generally react happily to what they hear, are unaware of the difficulties that adults experience about religious stories, and seem to find some meaning in them which is satisfactory. Watching a primary school Nativity play, with its literalistic interpretation of Bible metaphors, its anthropomorphisms, winged angels and all, often brings the uncomfortable realization that the actors are sincerely involved and finding meaning in material that is highly questionable if taken to be statement of fact.

Young children will, then, encounter Bible material and appear to find in it a significance that is appropriate to their understanding. There are two possible attitudes to this. Either we decide that this is conditioning them before they are able to resist and liable to cause them difficulties in thinking freely about religion when they come to adolescence, in which case we try to shield them from contact with all Bible stories and omit them from school lessons. Or we can take the view that children may hear these stories, enjoy them and possibly, in some respects, mis-understand them, and no harm results provided they are helped in early adolescence, when they are able to be critical, to reconsider their Bible knowledge and achieve an adult understanding of it. This will necessitate including in the religious education of lower secondary school pupils a study of the nature of the many types of literature found in the Bible.

The second problem is that, even when they recognise that the revelation of the Bible is a special sort of belief-based knowledge, teachers often present it as though it were part of the corpus of universally accepted fact. Some do this because they think that this is what is expected in religious education and that they will meet with disapproval if they do otherwise. Others do so because the profundity of their convictions unconsciously influences the way they talk. The ideas that they ascribe to Bible revelation are so much a part of their mental furniture that they make doctrinal statements without realising that they are doing so, and in consequence indoctrinate by accident. For instance, a primary school teacher, when telling a Bible story, can, easily and without dogmatic intention, say 'God spoke to Moses' or 'Jesus knew God didn't want him to conquer the world by fighting'. He may on reflection realise that such statements need qualification, and that he is using metaphor in an over-literal way, but there is not always time for such reflection in the hurly-burly of the classroom. Further, since such expressions are part of his normal religious conversation, he may not so reflect. In this way, telling Bible stories may involve unrecognised indoctrination.

### The attitude of the teacher

It will be appreciated from what has been written immediately above that the manner in which the Bible is used in schools depends greatly on the attitude of the teacher to it. On the whole teachers of religious education in Britain are Christians, and many have chosen to teach the subject because they are Christians. The Bible has for them a prestige and authority, a rich set of religious associations, and includes an account of the revelation of certain doctrines which they believe to be true and normative of conduct. It is difficult for them to be objective about it or to realise that it does not have the same value for all their contemporaries, or all their pupils. There are three practical policies they may pursue in their Bible lessons.

First, they may attempt to propagate their own view of the Bible, insisting that this is how it should be regarded, and that no other response to it is reasonable. This will evoke a favourable response from pupils who share this view, but a different response from those who do not.

Secondly, they may try to evade this difficulty by using the Bible as a convenient row of pegs on which to hang moral and humanitarian teachings which seem self-evidently valid in the prevailing culture. For instance, the better known parables of Jesus such as Good Samaritan or Prodigal Son are more frequently used in schools as examples of inter-racial fraternity and family affection than studied in order to discover what Jesus was trying to say through them.

Thirdly, they may see Bible study not as an end in itself and as the chief substance of religious education, but as part of a wider strategy of the subject. If religious education is viewed, not as making children religious in a particular way, nor as imparting revealed knowledge of a type which other school subjects cannot handle, but as making pupils informed and intelligent about religion and its effect on individuals and on culture, teaching about the Bible will form a natural part of a reasonable educational activity. Christians use the Bible in a particular way in their devotions and their public worship; they derive from it certain doctrines which moderate their behaviour and their attitudes. Biblical ideas and Christian attitudes dominated western culture in the days when Europe was rightly called 'Christendom' and much of that influence survives. If one is to be educated about religion and its contribution to existing culture, one needs to know about the place of the Bible in Christian thought, and its indirect effect on western civilization. This implies a fairly intensive study of its contents and the way they are understood.

To teach about the Bible in this way demands a particular attitude on the part of the teacher. He must present it, not as the truth that is plain and cannot be questioned, but as a book which some people use in a unique way and in which they, but not others, find a truth that they believe. This requires some objectivity on the part of the teacher, and those who are personally and passionately committed to the Bible, and immediately influenced by it, find this difficult. Yet in the present sceptical age, with its plurality of religious beliefs, all of which are questioned, any other approach to Bible study in schools can hardly be justified on educational grounds.

*A practical strategy*

Teachers' reaction to the foregoing will probably be 'All right, tell us how to do it.' It is not possible in the scope of one chapter to answer this request in detail. In any case, a teacher's lesson planning will depend on his view of his obligations, his conception of the subject, the syllabus he is required to teach, the beliefs of his pupils, their age, their previous learning, and many other variables. Detailed advice that would apply at all times is a fictional notion. The teacher must work out his own tactics. This chapter has attempted to discuss the situation in which those tactics are used and the principles on which they should be based. It is possible, however, to summarise what has been written in the form of a general strategy of Bible teaching.

(a)  In infant schools, stories from the Bible may be told for their value as entertaining stories. Children will enjoy them as they do their fairy stories, without expecting them to have profound metaphysical significance. They will, however, ask 'Is it true?' and in view of later study, it may not be possible to say, as one might of fairy stories 'No it's only a tale.' For that reason it may be wise to avoid stories that involve doctrinal content, such as tales of miracles and theophanies. There are other stories available, such as the longer Gospel parables, tales of kindliness, such as Joseph's treatment of his brothers (Genesis 45) and David's treatment of Mephibosheth (II Samuel 19) and accounts of heroism, such as Paul's courage during the shipwreck at Melitá (Acts 27).

(b)  In the junior school there is an argument for doing less scripture study, since it is in the concrete thinking stage that children seem to acquire the ideas of the Bible that cause them difficulty at a later stage. They are not able to understand the complex nature of the Bible literature, and they respond to what they read literally. If given a diet of miracle stories and interpreted history, they will tend to regard the Bible as a book of history and science which, in the light of later experience, will appear untrustworthy. There are many other things that can reasonably occupy religious education at this stage, such as the phenomenological investigation of different religions and their practices, so that sacred literature could take minimum place in the syllabus during these years.

(c)  In the lower secondary school or upper middle school, when pupils can bring it to greater understanding, the Bible may be studied in a fresh light. This is a critical age, for it is here that many are rejecting the Bible as 'kids' stuff' and 'unbelievable'. If they are to be helped to think about its statements and stories in more adult and sympathetic fashion, they need to be shown what sort of literature it is. A study of how the ancient writers thought, and the literary conventions they employed, seems indicated. Further some knowledge of the diversity of Bible material could be acquired. If at this stage of their development they can be brought to appreciate that the Bible is a collection of history, myth, allegory, fable and parable that expresses the religious awareness of the Hebrew people and the early Christians and their evaluation of the meaning of experience, then the way is opened to discussion of the accuracy of that awareness and the wisdom of that evaluation. In brief, a good deal of time needs to be given in early adolescence to the origin and nature of Bible literature rather than to its content.

(d)  In the upper secondary school, provided stage (c) above has been successful, the way should be open for a reasoned discussion of the Christian regard for the Bible as a source of enlightenment about the nature of experience and about moral choice. In view of the religiously open nature of our present culture, perhaps this should raise questions of why certain religious bodies use the Bible as they do, and whether or not their claims about it can be sympathetically understood, if not necessarily shared by all.

This strategy is a long term one. As in other subjects of study, children need to grow and mature in their understanding of the Bible, if they are to be educated rather than superstitious about it. In spite of pious statements to the contrary, it is not the sort of book all pupils can profit from fully at all stages of schooling. A developed taxonomy of religious education would include some such long-term strategy for dealing with a book as religiously influential as the Bible (as it would include a policy for study of the sacred literature of other religions). Whether the one outlined here is the right one, cannot be decided until it is tried.

**References**

*Coronation of Her Majesty Queen Elizabeth II* (1953) Novello and   Co.
R.J. Goldman (1964) *Religious Thinking from Childhood to Adolescence*
   Routledge.

# 17 Recent trends in Christian theology

PATRICK MILLER

*Theology as a form of design*

A common taunt about the so-called New Theology is that the best is not new and the worst is not 'theology'. As the latter criticism would be the more destructive, were it to be found true, it is worth asking at the outset what is meant by 'doing theology'. To an outside observer it can sometimes appear a curious study, as obscure as ergonomics or as futile as phrenology. Yet in fact it is a very human exercise which is both fairly straightforward and to some purpose.

Theology is a pattern-making activity, a form of design. And theologians, by use of words and ideas rather than paint or musical notation, attempt to design patterns from the miscellaneous incidents which constitute a person's total experience; to give sense and direction to the multifarious impressions he receives from being alive. Theology, therefore has fairly been described as 'reflection on the problems of human existence' (Tillich 1953).

There are of course a number of other studies that engage the attention of theologians, which have little to do with creating a design and which are nevertheless spoken of as 'doing theology'. For example, theologians can be found busily analysing the beliefs of different religions, making a critique of other theological 'patterns'; they may be studying Hebrew, textual criticism, religious art or music, the influence of the monasteries, or a thousand other excellent descriptive or historical topics. But none of this is strictly speaking 'doing theology'; it is making a study of religious phenomena – a very different matter. Such descriptive religious studies relate to 'doing theology' as the history of art does to painting. They are in a way parasitic. Hegel once used a harsh analogy for such theologians, using an image appropriate to the golden age of capital investment. 'Were the knowledge of religion historical only,' he wrote, 'we should have to regard theologians as resembling the bank clerk who enters in his ledger large sums of money belonging to other people, yet acquires little of his own' (quoted in Mackintosh 1937).

When theology is done badly, it can be no more than a popular parade of anecdotes, making patterns from commonplace observations, or framing the partial impressions of one individual. In such cases the design has become self-indulgent doodling.

Theology can be distinguished from other pattern-making activities in several respects. In the first place by its inclusiveness. Theological designs, to be satisfactory, should not be selective. They should include the full panorama; views of success and pleasure, not merely of failure or pain, scenes of youthfulness and festivity as well as old age or isolation, of African and Oriental culture as well as European or Semitic. Theology, like the religion it articulates, should be a man's 'total reaction upon life' (James 1902).

Secondly, theology is distinguishable from other pattern-weaving by its level of interest. Literally the word means 'God-talk', which, whatever logical problems this raises, must mean that it is talk about what is 'real' for that person, and has final authority for him. This then becomes the perspective from which he draws his design of the world he sees. The design will inevitably bear marks of wholeness, purpose or perfection about it. 'The object of theology is what concerns us ultimately,' wrote Tillich (quoted in MacQuarrie 1967), which if it is not to be a tautology must refer partly to the attitude of the theologian, the level of interest properly shown by him. William James, once wrote of religion 'there must be something solemn, serious, and tender about any attitude which we denominate religious. If glad it must not grin or snicker; if sad, it must not scream or curse' (James 1902). I would take it that the same applies to theology and is the reason why, when it is being true to itself, theology will always be listened to; why, in fact, it is too serious a matter — as it is said — to be left to the theologians.

### 'An arbitrary system of grunts and squeals'
Then theology is marked by being a peculiarly verbal form of articulation. Where others frame their patterns through

dance, colour or harmony, theologians deal in words, ideas and images. Theology cannot rest content with an attitude of 'ultimate concern', even if it is possible to argue that religion can. Theology must articulate that belief as clearly as possible. Although religion is both more elusive and more colourful than theology, and a person's belief is wider than his ability to express it, nevertheless without 'God-*talk*' there can be no theology.

This need to articulate is the Achilles heel of theology. Words are symbols and it is tragically easy to forget how fragile and approximate they are. However scientific our use of words, it is worth remembering Chesterton's florid and spectacular passage when he wrote

> whenever a man says to another, 'prove your case; defend your faith', he is assuming the infallibility of language: that is to say, he is assuming that a man has a word for every reality in earth, or heaven, or hell. He knows that there are in the world tints more bewildering, more numberless and more nameless than the colours of an autumn forest . . . yet he seriously believes that these things can every one of them, in all their tones and semitones, in all their blends and unions, be accurately represented by an arbitrary system of grunts and squeals. He believes that an ordinary civilized stockbroker can really produce out of his own inside, noises which denote all mysteries of memory and all the agonies of desire . . . for the truth is, that language is not a scientific thing at all, but wholly an artistic thing, a thing invented by hunters, and killers, and such artists, long before science was dreamed of (quoted in Mascall 1957).

When this if forgotten, theology ceases to be design and becomes technical drawing. We may even try to speak of it as a science. Theologians become cartographers, drawing maps supposedly to scale on the evidence of surveyors' sightings. Men burn and shoot to defend the precision of their 'grunts and squeals'. However, in spite of this danger of a verbal fundamentalism, theology must make the attempt to articulate belief. Macquarrie quotes W.M. Urban: 'when in order to grasp reality we abandon linguistic forms the reality like quicksilver slips through our fingers' (Urban 1939).

## 1962—3 and 'sharpened awareness'

The year 1962/3 is a convenient starting point to speak of recent theology. It was the year of the Cuban crisis, the Beatles in America, Colonel Glenn on the moon. It was also a year in which occurred some remarkable theological events. 1960, it should first be explained, was the unsung centenary of *Essays and Reviews*, a publication which occasioned such a storm of abuse and protest in Victorian England that two contributors were brought to trial, the Archbishop of Canterbury received 137,000 lay signatures in gratitude, and 11,000 clergy signatures in defence of the true faith, while Samuel Wilberforce declared roundly that such writers could not 'with moral honesty maintain their posts as clergymen of the established church' (Chadwick 1966). In retrospect the beliefs seem harmless enough. Jowett, the master of Balliol, argued that the Bible should be 'interpreted as any other book'. But if anything earned the collection of essays the reputation of being 'new', it was that all the contributors accepted the underlying ideas of evolution and the scientific method as a proper approach to Christian evidences.

As a result the hundred years since 1860 have seen an unprecedented amount of digging, recording, observing, interpreting and applying. Documents and texts were compared, Jewish and early Christian history was recombed. We have had varieties of religious experience analysed, other cultures and religious beliefs recorded, the psychology of belief scrutinised. These studies inevitably followed from the 'new' attention given to the inductive method and to data and evidence in Christian belief.

In a sense there has been nothing comparable to this nineteenth-century revolution of method. Yet in 1962/3 there appeared, quite independently as it happened, some publications which justify our speaking at the very least of a new impetus. As the centenary approached, a collection of essays was planned. *Soundings*, edited by A. Vidler, came out in the autumn of 1962. The following year saw a series of lectures entitled *Objections to Christian Belief* (Vidler 1963) which was attended by some 1,500 undergraduates on each occasion. *Honest to God* (Robinson 1963) was published, and reached sales of half a million within the year. Other books by radicals were Paul Van Buren's *The Secular Meaning of the Gospel* (1963), and *God is No More* by Werner and Lotte Pelz (1963). In the Roman Catholic world, 1962 marked the opening of the Second Vatican Council and only the year previously the cold war had thawed sufficiently to allow the Russian Orthodox Church to join the World Council of Churches. A book by Losskey (1963) marked a fresh approach from an Eastern Orthodox writer to the theology of God.

Some would say that Vatican II will be seen to have had the greatest impact. Certainly it is as if pent-up academic energies have been released without the fear of imprimatur. And there has been unfettered discussion on such subjects as whether or not the Church is essential to a Christian, on whether different theologies can be tolerated without compromise, and on what is the meaning of continuity in doctrine. And in the sphere of ecumenical affairs it has had an immense and irreversible effect. As far as creative theological design is concerned, it is too early to judge. In the Protestant, English-speaking world however, it was *Soundings* which set the agenda for the next decade. In itself an unassuming volume, it made no great cosmic claims. The flyleaf quotation was 'Man hath but a shallow sound, and a short reach, and dealeth onely by probabilities and likeyhoods' (Miles Smith, Bishop of Gloucester 1612–24), and the first essay concludes with 'the starting-point for natural theology is not argument but sharpened awareness. For the moment it is better for us that the arguments have fallen to pieces' (Root 1962).

The essays were on subjects we were to hear a great deal more about in the following years; 'The uneasy truce between science and theology' (Habgood), 'Theology and self-awareness' (Williams), 'The relation between Christianity and the other great religions' (Smart), 'Towards a Christology for today' (Montefiore), 'The grounds of Christian moral judgments' (Woods). Above all the essays on natural theology and 'the idea of the transcendent' (Woods) set, as far as the subject matter was concerned, the main trend in subsequent Christian theology. In all a new impetus was given to the studies of theologians, and a new cast of mind, recognisable in the readiness to listen and to learn from other disciplines.

By comparison with the relatively timid orthodoxy of the forties and fifties, in England at least, this represented a major shift of emphasis, seen perhaps most clearly in the following four ways:

*1  A new agenda* This was not only wider in its interest, but gave first priority once again to what must surely be the central part of any theological design – belief in God. 'Christian theology without metaphysics (that is, for our purposes, natural theology) is an illusion. However much some theologians may wish to avoid the issue by speaking of revelation there comes a point when the question can no longer be evaded: Why believe in God at all?' (Vidler 1962). Six years and reams of radicalism later, by which time the major thrust in Protestant theology of English-speaking countries had been in the sphere of natural theology, Gilkey could still say 'questions of the reality of God and the possibility of language about him are still our most pressing current theological problems, prior to all other theological issues' (Gilkey 1969). And in 1971 'the problem before us is the problem of God,' wrote Kee, by which time it looked as if the only 'solution' was going to be by elimination.

There are a hundred ways in which this question can be ducked – and we shall look at some of them – but since 1963 it is doubtful if ever again sidesteps or feints will deceive any opponent. Attention can only be diverted successfully to the secondary questions (of the church, biblical criticism, Christian discipline, and so on) either in an Age of Faith (say sixteenth-century Europe) when belief in God seems generally accepted, or in an age of theological complacency (post-war England) when belief in God is thought to be assured. Perhaps the most outstanding trend in recent Christian writing has been to place religious language, the objections to belief, God talk, and such topics, in the centre of the stage.

*2  A new purpose* A dialogue had been deliberately opened with non-theists and other world religions, which continued throughout the sixties. In 1955 a sharp debate had been engendered in academic circles by *New Essays in Philosophical Theology* (Flew and MacIntyre 1955) in which an attempt was made to face the profoundly critical spirit of

Oxford's analytical school of philosophy. What happened in the post-1963 scene was that, as Pendennis of the *Observer* wrote, '*Honest to God* has taken theology right out of its old academic seclusion' (quoted in Robinson and Edwards 1963). This too was the explicit purpose of *Objections to Christian Belief* (Vidler 1963), a recognition that difficulties from science, psychology, morality, history were felt by the mass of people and not just by dons, and that while they could be faced without incoherence, they could not be answered glibly. In a similar vein, David Jenkins in *Living with Questions* (1969) was critical of any theologian who has not sensed the argument from atheism, the logical notion of self-contradiction in the idea of God's existence. In other words, we can see a deliberate revival of apologetics without arrogance, of putting the Christian case before sceptical opposition, but in a new spirit of openness to the force of alternative points of view.

3  *A new cast of mind* It was apparent from Harry Williams' essay on 'Theology and Self-awareness' that we were beginning to see a far greater readiness to learn from other disciplines. The words and phrases of repeated theological argument had become as lifeless as the valley of dry bones. It was clear now, however, that younger theologians would enrich the discussion with illustrations, language and thought-forms from psychology, sociology, science, philosophical analysis, all of which were in the next decade accepted as having a great deal to say in the construction of any theological 'design'.

In a recent paper Macquarrie recognised this trait as one of the virtues in modern theology, calling it a 'new humility' It was, he said, a far cry from the 'Syllabus of Errors' of 1864; Protestants had moved a considerable distance from the arid bibliolatry of the nineteenth century and the rejection of evolution. Similarly the new cast of mind was especially noticeable in Pope John XXIII's leadership and in the relationship with other churches since Vatican II.

4  *A new location* A useful analogy is to think of traditional theology as a rainbow, with its colours and pattern clearest where they are furthest from the ground, but faint and indistinguishable where they touch down. Traditional theologians looked at the unchanging revelation,

high in the sky, and deduced what Christians ought to believe and do. An increasing number of writers in the eighteenth and nineteenth centuries looked to the 'evidences' on the ground, accepting that observation was as important as logical consistency with 'revealed truth'. It is as if the empirical method directs our attention to the two ends of the rainbow, to find the evidence for belief on the one hand, and to apply it to behaviour and changing circumstance on the other.

One of the most important tasks of recent theology has been to try to locate the transcendent, to discover data for belief (or at least areas where belief will be evoked and standpoints from which it will seem reasonable) beginning, in John Robinson's phrase, 'from below' (Robinson 1967). Then again we have seen numerous attempts to apply belief to politics, education, personal morality, revolution, violence. This is the 'so what?' end of the rainbow. The effect of these two concerns is to raise again the doctrine of man. The new theology has shown us a fresh evaluation of man, not necessarily more optimistic but certainly more realistic and caring.

In all this it is hard to discern any clear pattern. The spate of new theological publications continues unchecked and it is impossible to review the whole scene in a single chapter. Moreover, so strong has been the impetus given to individual experiment, that many of the writers quoted here will have already revised their opinions. In particular, Harvey Cox, Alistair Kee, Paul Van Buren would no longer wish to be identified with or shackled by their earlier books. Nevertheless at the time these spoke forcibly to the main items in the theological agenda and the teacher of RE would profit from following the major debates of the past decade. Three tolerably distinct groups may be distinguished.

## (i) The doers-without

There is a large group of 'theologians' not engaged in 'doing theology' in the sense in which it has been taken here. They are not, that is to say, creating any design. Perhaps this is because they prefer to interpret the patterns of the past, on the grounds that they have been done well enough already. Eric Mascall seems to do this in *Words and Images* (1957).

For him the traditional categories are still an adequate articulation of belief. We have also seen continued efforts by biblical literalists to perpetuate the established securities of the past. Neither of these approaches seems to be a recent trend, as such, in Christian theology, but on the contrary a repetition of former theologies. For many Protestants, the debate on 'why believe in God at all?' was postponed while the ground of the sacred/secular dispute was ploughed over repeatedly. The majority of writers reject Otto's claim that the holy is a unique datum of experience, something wholly other, discernible by human beings because in addition to sense experience, we all possess an innate religious conscious-ness. Against this, many recent writers (following Bonhoeffer's lead) have argued that 'there is no way, ontological, cultural or psychological, to locate a part of the self or a part of human experience that needs God. There is no God-shaped blank within man' (Bonhoeffer 1959). Or again, 'no special places, times, persons or communities are more representative of the One than any others are. No sacred graves or temples, no hallowed kings or priests, no festival days, no chosen communities are particularly rep-resentative of him in whom all things live and move and have their being' (Niebuhr 1961). In J.G. Davies' view 'a theology which does not take the exit from the sacral universe seriously would itself be less than serious. It would be . . . to fail to read the signs of the times and to perpetuate an archaic religion which is already becoming less and less relevant to more and more people' (Davies 1973).

There have been other forms of postponement. For years the air rang loud with the debate on Christianity without religion (initiated by Bonhoeffer) or on the defects of the Church, or on the question whether the Church is any longer necessary for a Christian. Perhaps the most interesting examples of this debate, because the most surprising, are to be found among Roman Catholic writers. It would be fairer to say that for these, the subject is rather an essential ground-clearing than an evasion of the central issues. Hans Kung, for instance, has long contended that 'insofar as the body of the Church is divine and *human*, the human and all too human elements, actual sin and evil, can insinuate themselves into her, though without ever being able to overmaster her. This applies to ecclesiastical institutions and ordinances as well' (Kung 1961). An adequate concept of the Church will include, he argues, both 'what the Church receives from above, from God's sanctifying grace ... and what the very same Church receives and absorbs from below through her sinful members'. Such a statement in the year of the second Vatican Council clearly raised the most controversial question, whether it might not therefore be reasonable to expect that the Church would err, not only in the behaviour of its individuals, but also in its encyclicals and pronouncements, that is to say in its mind as well as in its body.

McBrien pressed this matter further. By sharply distinguishing between the Kingdom of God and the Church, his book *Do We Need the Church?* led to the conclusion that it is the former that men really need. Certainly the Church is both a 'sign of the present Kingdom', in its Eucharistic life and by demonstrating the solidarity and fellowship of life in Christ, and also 'a sign of the future Kingdom', by refusing to embrace without qualification the standards and values of the world. Nevertheless, he writes, 'not all men are called to membership of the Christian community.' Moreover there is 'no specifically ecclesiastical way of caring for orphans, aged or sick ... The Church best serves not by competing or duplicating services offered but by donating its resources for their initial and continuing success.'

In the sixties there were attempts to divert interest from the question of 'why believe in God at all?' by theologies of hope, or celebration, or by the kind of Christology that appeared from time to time in the 'Death of God' school. When Hamilton, Altizer or Dorothee Solle wrote as if it were possible to avoid the centrepiece of the design, and concentrate rather on Jesus Christ, they naturally laid themselves open to the taunt that what they taught was, 'while there is no God, Jesus is his only Son'. It is hard to consider this theology.

More blatant examples of evasion can be seen in the concerns of some Protestant writers on the continent. Many write as if the reality of God is assured and the interests of the previous decade continued. This seems to be the case with Ebeling's work on preaching, as of Otto, Pannenberg and Kaseman on existentialism, hermeneutics and history.

We now reach the main division among modern theological writers. It is between (a) the translators (or reformers) and (b) the doers-without (or real radicals). The translators are recasting the mould, reshaping the original substance. They agree with much of the diagnosis of the classical Christian understanding of God and certainly of its expression, but believe that the language can be reformed and that process theology, or theology of the future, or of presence, or existentialism can be a better method of articulating the original beliefs about God, preserving his transcendence and immanence in balance.

The doers-without, including writers such as Werner and Lotte Pelz, Paul Van Buren (but despite their apparent position probably not the Death of God theologians) hold that attempts to reform miss the point and are muddle-headed. These real radicals agree with atheists and conservative critics when they claim that reformers are in fact heretics, that they have broken the essential continuity with the past. Reformers are giving new names like process, depth, future hope, or whatever, only to appear relevant and keep the dialogue open. This, claim the doers-without is cowardice. It is better to be tough-minded and admit you have broken with the original teaching. This naturally raises the prior question as to how we could possibly know when a particular theology stands in an acceptable line of development from the past, and when it breaks continuity so clearly that it would make a nonsense to call it 'Christian' theology. Vidler once wrote

> There are those who hold that the work of translation must never lose sight of what they believe to be the original traditional or objective substance of the gospel which affirms that a transcendent God has acted decisively in history, above all in the life, death and resurrection of Jesus . . . God was in Christ reconciling the world unto himself. Translate, reinterpret, demythologize or remythologize as much as you like, provided you can still say that (Vidler 1965).

More recently K. Rahner has argued that there can be a plurality of valid theologies, which while clearly not contradictory, are certainly different and which need not be synthesized. He would hold that there is not simply one theology which stands in continuity with the received original tradition. It is possible to have variety without compromise or deviation (Rahner 1969). This debate in the Roman Church is still unresolved and promises to be particularly fruitful.

Parallel to this, amongst Protestants, is a recent book by Maurice Wiles (1974) in which he argues that there can be no fixed criteria for determining what should and should not be acceptable. Unpredictability is the hallmark of creative theology. The element of continuing identity, he writes, would 'have to be looked for in the sources to which reference is made, the kinds of concern which direct that reference and the general pattern or character of the affirmation.' There can therefore be no blueprint to which we can refer in order to predict the future development of theology.

## (ii) The translators

Some of the most useful points of departure for the RE teacher can often be found in the new perspective with which traditional 'theological' problems are being considered. For example, there is the recent work on Christology by John Knox, *The Humanity and Divinity of Christ* (1967) or John Robinson, *The Human Face of God* (1973). Alternatively a most valuable treatment of the problem of evil is seen in John Hick's *Evil and the God of Love* (1966). But the clearest examples of 'translation' are still to be found in the central issue of belief in God (for example Baker 1970 or Davies 1973). It is still hard to better, in small compass, earlier treatment of this subject in, for instance, Bonhoeffer's *Letters and Papers from Prison* (1959) or in Tillich's *The Shaking of the Foundations* (especially the sermon on 'The Depth of Existence') (1962), or more substantially, John Baillie's *Our Knowledge of God* (1939). But translation began in earnest in the academic papers following on John Wisdom's essay on 'Gods' (1960) and later from the stir made by Braithwaite's *An Empiricist's View of the Nature of*

*Religious Belief* (1955).

However, perhaps the clearest, and certainly the most notorious, examples of retranslation can be found in, *Honest to God* (1963) or better still in *Exploration into God* (1967). In these, John Robinson sees the task of new theology to find a new projection by which we may understand the original belief in God. For him the image of a Super Person distracts from the really real. By turning people's eyes upwards or outwards to a Being for whose existence the evidence is to say the least doubtful we are prevented from focussing our attention on the 'beyond in the midst'. The defect of the old supranaturalistic projection is that it has never really succeeded in putting God at the centre. 'One of the central and distinctive features of the Christian Gospel is the utterly intimate, personal relationship which is summed up in Jesus' word *Abba* (Father or Daddy). It is this relationship at the heart of the universe at the very core of reality, for which Christian theology has to find expression' (Robinson 1967).

Another person trying to rearrange the old patterns to form a new design is Schubert Ogden, one of the principal exponents of what is known as Process theology. Ogden strongly dissociates himself from the Death of God school and writes, like Robinson, 'We are justified not in rejecting God as such, but in casting aside the supernaturalist' c conception of his reality which is in fact untenable, given our typical experience and thought as secular men.' He then goes on to argue that there is 'an original confidence in the meaning and worth of life' which is the place to find belief in God. 'I hold that the primary use or function of "God" is to refer to the objective ground in reality itself of our ineradicable confidence in the final worth of our existence' (Ogden 1967).

It is only fair to point out that many critics would see in this a theological sleight of hand. As a poetic description of the human condition they have some sympathy with it, but when the pronoun 'he' is introduced to refer to what is sensed as an underlying 'grace' or 'worth' in life they claim some verbal trick has been played. By all means use this language to describe your 'design', if you are of an existentialist frame of mind, but as A. Kee writes, 'why any theologian should try or even want to entitle this cosmic chop-suey, "God", is beyond my understanding' (Kee 1971).

J. MacQuarrie falls under the same axe. Using much of the language of Tillich, he argues 'If we are still seeking to make sense of life and to bring order into existence so that its potentialities can come to fulfilment, we have frankly to acknowledge that we must look for support beyond humanity itself, pervaded as this is with disorder.' And so he presses for a faith in 'the wider being', or 'a depth beyond both man and nature.' 'Human existence can make sense if this wider being supports and supplements the meagre heritage of our finite being as we strive to fulfil potentialities of our being' (MacQuarrie 1971).

Harvey Cox is a writer of a very different stamp. A prophet crying out in the modern secular city wilderness, he has little time for existentialism, or traditional religious ideas. The old tribal society has vanished, he observes, as has the later town culture. Today we have technopolis the super city of automation which succeeded it, mass communication, mobility and anonymity. There is no room for obsolete mysteries of religion with its ideas of God as Father, or even Supreme Being. We must talk this world language. New expressions for our faith must be invented. We should eliminate the word 'God', sure in the belief that a new name will be found and a new religion lived.

One of the most influential and constructive encounters with positivism and analytical philosophy can be found in *Religious Language* by I.T. Ramsey (1957). He relates our God-talk to other ordinary experiences. He calls them moments of discernment, of disclosure, of commitment, and argues that there are many occasions which defy logical analysis, moments when 'the penny drops' and a new realization breaks through. These are the places where we should locate the transcendent.

The death of God theologians, such as W. Hamilton, T. Altizer and D. Solle, form a particularly interesting group of reformists, though they would no doubt call themselves the 'doers-without'. In their view Robinson was right to reject objectified theism but entirely wrong to suppose that his own non-objectified theism was any better. They deny the basic religious assumption (especially of the existentialists) that 'without God life is an outrageous terror', or that there is a God-shaped blank within man. Theological work is more likely to come from worldly contexts than ecclesiastical ones, from participation in the Negro revolution than from ecumenical committees. Altizer's vision is of a man willing to undergo the discipline of darkness. He speaks of waiting, a new epiphany in the darkness. At some points this theology is reformist, 'a profane destiny may yet provide a way to return to the God who is all in all, not by returning to a moment in the past, but by meeting an epiphany of the past in the present.' 'The theologian must exist outside of the Church; he can neither proclaim the Word, celebrate the sacraments, nor rejoice in the presence of the Holy Spirit. Before contemporary theology can become itself it must first exist in silence' (Altizer and Hamilton 1966).

At other points however it seems more radical, genuinely 'doing without' God. 'The radical Christian proclaims that God has actually died in Christ, that this death is both an historical and cosmic event, and as such, it is a final and irrevocable event, which cannot be reversed by a subsequent religious or cosmic movement'.

Again, 'This group persists, in the face of both bewilderment and fury, in calling itself Christian. It persists in making use of the phrase "death of God" in spite of its rhetorical colour, partly because it is a phrase that cannot be adapted to traditional use by the theologians today.' Perhaps the most unequivocal statement, which taken by itself would certainly place the group amongst the 'doers-without' is Altizer's 'The dead God is not the God of idolatry, or false piety, or "religion", but rather the God of the historic Christian Church, and beyond the Church, of Christendom at large' (Altizer 1967).

### (iii) Non-theistic designs

As Vidler once wrote, 'on the other hand there is a divergent way of conceiving what needs to be done. There are those who would say that it is a mistake to insist that the Gospel has an objective substance that must somehow be translated afresh. Christianity is not a system of doctrine with an unchanging core, nor does it imply or depend on any theory of the nature of the universe, nor even on belief in a transcendent God. It can in fact, some go so far as to say, now dispense with the God concept altogether.'

Paul Van Buren, like Braithwaite a decade before him, translates all God-language into ethics, pointing to Jesus as the way of standing before our neighbour. 'The empiricist in us finds the heart of the difficulty not in what is said about God, but in the very talking about God at all. We do not know what God is, and we cannot understand how the word "God" is being used' (Van Buren 1963).

This is, or appears to be, the final capitulation. It was because he thought that Robinson was making this kind of reduction, that one of his most powerful critics wrote, after *Honest to God*, 'what is striking about Dr Robinson's book is first and foremost that he is an atheist' (quoted in Robinson 1967). Robinson strongly denies this charge and answers it in the debate. Buren, however, does not. 'Statements of faith are to be interpreted, by means of the modified verification principle, as statements which express, describe, or commend a particular way of seeing the world, other men, and oneself, and the way of life appropriate to such a perspective.' This seems to be the final reductionist position.

The 'doers-without' group should be extended to include explicitly non-theistic designers. A. Kee is one such (Kee 1971). He claims that his position 'does not include a supernatural being, but it deals with the dimensions of reality previously "answered" by the God-solution. It is not a positive position, nor is it a reduction.' It is escalation. 'Theology must not simply concern itself with man; it must not be reduced to ethics, not even a Jesus-ethic. It is inevitable that a secular interpretation of theology will be largely taken up with what it says about man, but if it warrants the name of theology it will involve larger issues too' (Kee 1971). This is why he calls it escalation.

It is writing of this kind that gave rise to one of the recurring disputes of the past decade, on whether an explicit use of the word 'God' is necessary to 'doing theology'. There is a design. It seems to be total and of ultimate concern to the writer. But the vital name is missing. Is it theology? 'A religion without God,' wrote Comte, 'My God, what a religion' (quoted in Robinson 1963a). Ogden has made his point of view clear: 'However absurd talking about God might be, it could never be so obviously absurd as talking of Christian faith without God' (Ogden 1967). Macquarrie has the same difficulty with Van Buren and the Death of God theologians. 'One would hesitate to give the name of "theology" to an enterprise which has rejected theology's key word "God" ' (MacQuarrie 1967).

However, what seems to be emerging after the debates of the past ten years is that the word itself may not be so crucial. Robinson himself, accused of being an atheist, quoted with approval, in defence, the RC philosopher Leslie Dewart: 'Precisely as a name, God's name matters little. It is not truly a Holy Name, and we may please ourselves whether we retain it or not. It is our own invention, not God's, and what we have invented we may improve upon' (Dewart 1967).

### The greatest leap in the dark

If we accept that theology is articulating a total design, a reality which determines a man's life, then it may be of no consequence that the name 'God' has been dropped. On the one hand apparently negative atheist positions may turn out to be theology. 'God is dead' means one thing to Nietzsche, for whom he was never alive but was just a cultural habit, now past, and it means quite another to Altizer for whom God died in becoming man; he became hidden, really incarnate in fact. The first is clear atheism, but the second, however much it may be criticised as theology, is still theology.

But of course, on the other hand, apparently positive positions may turn out to be non-theology, to break that essential continuity with the past. When Tillich speaks of 'ultimate concern,' the difficulty is that the concern can so easily be a trivial one. If a man is ultimately concerned about his career, or a woman with the appearance of her home, are we to say that these are theological pursuits? And to distinguish a legitimate 'ultimate concern' from a trivial one requires a standard other than that of ultimate concern itself. The concern must, as Kierkegaard put it, preserve the 'infinite, qualitative distinction' between earth and heaven (quoted in Barth 1933).

Perhaps what emerges most clearly of all is that it may be a rather profitless exercise trying to distinguish one inclusive and final design from another. Of all the lines that can be drawn in society, the most. important in this context is perhaps between those who are able or inclined to see some pattern amongst the fragments, and those who are disinclined, or unable to do so, and for whom the search is fanciful. The difference between them is complex. It is not due to stupidity, wilfulness, nor even on all occasions to an ignorance of logic (which of course is one of the reasons why it is proper to speak of theological belief rather than theological observation). Amongst the pattern makers there are, needless to say, some wide and irreconcilable disagreements. But in the present climate, it is probably more useful to see these as in the nature of internal disputes and family squabbles, rather than widely diverging philosophical positions. The greatest psychological, or logical, leap in the dark is to frame any pattern at all.

# References

T.J. Altizer and W. Hamilton (1966) *Radical Theology and the Death of God* Pelican.

T.J. Altizer (1967) *The Gospel of Christian Atheism* Collins.

J. Baillie (1939) *Our Knowledge of God* OUP.

J. Baker (1970) *The Foolishness of God* Darton, Longman and Todd.

K. Barth (1933) *The Epistle to the Romans* trans. E. Hoskyns, OUP.

D. Bonhoeffer (1959) *Letters and Papers from Prison* Fontana.

J. Bowden and J. Richmond (1967) *A Reader in Contemporary Theology* SCM Press.

R.B. Braithwaite (1955) *An Empiricist's View of the Nature of Religious Belief* CUP.

F. Brown (1971) *Faith without Religion* SCM Press.

P. Van Buren (1963) *The Secular Meaning of the Gospel* Pelican.

O. Chadwick (1966) *The Victorian Church* vol.2 A. and C. Black.

H. Cox (1968) *The Secular City* Pelican.

J.G. Davies (1973) *Every Day God* SCM Press.

L. Dewart (1967) *The Future of Belief* Burns Oates.

A. Flew and D. MacIntyre, eds. (1955) *New Essays in Philosophical Theology* SCM Press.

L. Gilkey (1969) *Naming the Whirlwind: the renewal of God language* SCM Press.

J. Hick (1966) *Evil and the God of Love* Macmillan.

W. James (1902) *The Varieties of Religious Experience* Fontana edition 1960.

D.T. Jenkins (1962) *Beyond Religion* SCM Press.

D. Jenkins (1969) *Living with Questions* SCM Press.

A. Kee (1971) *The Way of Transcendence* Pelican.

J. Knox (1967) *The Humanity and Divinity of Christ* CUP.

H. Kung (1961) *The Council and Reunion* Sheed & Ward.

V. Losskey (1963) *The Vision of God* Faith Press.

L. McBrien (1969) *Do we Need the Church?* Collins.

A. Macintyre (1963) 'God and the theologians' in *The Honest to God Debate* SCM Press.

H.R. Mackintosh (1937) *Types of Modern Theology* Nisbet.

J. MacQuarrie (1960) *An Existentialist Theology* SCM Press.
(1967) *God-Talk* SCM Press.
(1967) *Principles of Christian Theology* SCM Press.

J. MacQuarrie (1971) *Twentieth Century Religious Thought* SCM Press.

E.L. Mascall (1957) *Words and Images* Longman.

J. Moltmann (1967) *Theology of Hope* SCM Press.

H.R. Niebuhr (1961) *Radical Monotheism and Western culture* Faber.

S. Ogden (1967) *The Reality of God and other Essays* SCM Press.

W. and L. Pelz (1963) *God is no More* Pelican.

N. Pittenger (1967) *God in Process* Penguin.

K. Rahner (1969) 'Pluralism in Theology and the Unity of the Church's profession of faith' in *Concilium* vol.6 no.5.

I.T. Ramsey (1957) *Religious Language* SCM Press.

J.A.T. Robinson (1963) *Honest to God* SCM Press.

J.A.T. Robinson and D.L. Edwards (1963) *The Honest to God Debate* SCM Press.

J.A.T. Robinson (1967) *Exploration into God* SCM Press.
(1973) *The Human Face of God* SCM Press.

H.E. Root (1962) 'Beginning all over again' in *Soundings* CUP.

P. Tillich (1953) *Systematic Theology* vol.1 Nisbet.
(1962) 'The Depth of Existence' in *The Shaking of the Foundations* Pelican.

W.M. Urban (1939) *Language and Reality* Allen & Unwin.

A.R. Vidler, ed. (1962) *Soundings* CUP.
(1963) *Objections to Christian Belief* Constable.

A. Vidler (1965) *Twentieth Century Defenders of the Faith* Religious Book Club, SCM Press.

M. Wiles (1974) *The Remaking of Christian Doctrine* SCM Press.

J. Wisdom (1960) 'Gods' in *Logic and Language* First Series Blackwell.

# FURTHER READING
# NOTES ON THE CONTRIBUTORS
# ACKNOWLEDGEMENTS

# Further reading

Since 1965 there have been literally hundreds of books published on this subject. This in itself is something new, an indication that there is a widespread feeling that change is due. This volume is an attempt to bring that change into perspective. Readers may like to follow up some of the chapters by looking at books mentioned in the text, expecially some of the most recent:

J. Holm (1975) *Teaching Religion in Schools* OUP.
D. Horder ed. (1975) *Journeys into Religion* teaching units and introductory handbook, Hart-Davis Educational.
J. Hull (1975) *School Worship: An Obituary* SCM Press.
R. Rummery (1974) *Catechesis and Religious Education in a Pluralist Society* E.J. Dwyer, Sydney.
E. Sharpe (1975) *Comparative Religion: A History* Duckworth.
N. Smart (1974) *The Phenomenon of Religion* Macmillan.

Readers may also like to know of a useful companion volume for students:

E. Lord and C. Bailey (1973) *A Reader in Religious and Moral Education* SCM Press.

# Notes on the contributors

Colin Alves, M.A. Director, National Society RE Centre, St Gabriel's College, London. Author of *Religion and the Secondary School* (1968) SCM Press. Reviews Editor, *Learning for Living* (1968–1974) SCM Press. Chairman, Schools Council RE Subject Committee.

Michael C. Brown, M.A., B.D., Ph.D. Senior Lecturer, City of Newcastle College of Education. Author of *The Logic of Religious Education in Integrated Studies* (1973) Ph.D. thesis, University of Lancaster.

C. Edwin Cox, B.D., M.Th. Senior Lecturer in Education, University of London Institute of Education. Author of *Changing Aims in Religious Education* (1966) Routledge, *Sixth Form Religion* (1967) SCM Press.

Julian Frost, M.A. Teacher, Hurst Junior School, Bexley, Kent. Senior Project Officer, Schools Council Project on Religious Education in Primary Schools, University of Lancaster.

Brian E. Gates, M.A., S.T.M. Principal Lecturer in Religion, University of London Goldsmith's College.

Peter Gedge, M.A. Head of Religious Studies Department, S Martin's College of Education, Lancaster.

Jean Holm, B.A. Head of Religious Studies Department, Homerton College, Cambridge. Author of *Teaching Religion in School* (1975) OUP. Joint author of *Phoenix – A Religious Education Study Series* (1964–1965) Schofield & Sims.

Donald Horder, B.D. Deputy Director, Schools Council Projects on Religious Education, 1969–1973 and 1973–1976. Editor of *The Christian Education Handbooks* (1954–1962) Independent Press, *Religious Education in Secondary Schools* (1971) Evans/Methuen.

John M. Hull, M.A., B.Ed., Ph.D. Lecturer in Religious Education, University of Birmingham School of Education. Author of *Hellenistic Magic and the Synoptic Tradition* (1974) SCM Press, *Sense and Nonsense about God* (1974) SCM Press, *School Worship: an Obituary*

(1975) SCM Press. Editor of *Learning for Living* Christian Education Movement.

Kenneth E. Hyde, B.D., Ph.D. Staff Inspector for Religious Education, Inner London Education Authority. Author of *Religious Learning in Adolescence* (1965) Oliver & Boyd, *Religion and Slow Learners* (1969) SCM Press.

O. Raymond Johnston, M.A., Dip.Th. Formerly Lecturer in Education, University of Newcastle-upon-Tyne. Author of *Religion in our Schools* (1968) Hodder, *School Worship* (1973) Newcastle-upon-Tyne Education Committee. Director of Nationwide Festival of Light.

Patrick F. Miller, M.A. Director of Social Studies, Queen Mary's College, Basingstoke, Hants. Author of *Creeds and Controversies* (1969) EUP.

David Naylor, M.A. Advisor for Religious Education, Hampshire.

Richard M. Rummery, M.A., M.Ed., Ph.D. Staff member, Catholic College of Advanced Education, Castle Hill, New South Wales. Author of *Catechesis and Religious Education in a Pluralist Society* (1974) E.J. Dwyer, Sydney and Hong Kong. Editor of the catechetical review, *Our Apostolate*.

Eric J. Sharpe, M.A., Teol.D. Senior Lecturer in Religious Studies, University of Lancaster. Author of *Comparative Religion: A History* (1975) Duckworth/Scribner's. Secretary, International Association for the History of Religions.

R. Ninian Smart, M.A., B.,Phil., D.H.L. Professor and Head of Religious Studies Department, University of Lancaster. Author of *The Teacher and Christian Belief* (1964) James Clarke, *Secular Education and the Logic of Religion* (1968) Faber, *The Religious Experience of Mankind* (1971) Collins. Director, Schools Council Projects on Religious Education, 1969–1973 and 1973–1976.

Peter Woodward, B.A., B.D. Inspector for Religious Education, City of Birmingham Education Committee. Secretary, Shap Working Party on World Religions in Education. Editor of *World Religions: Aids for Teachers* Community Relations Commission.

# Acknowledgements

The Publisher's thanks are due to the following copyright owners who have kindly given us permission to use their material: Mrs Clare Winnicott and the Hogarth Press for an extract from *Therapeutic Consultations in Child Psychiatry* by D.W. Winnicott; Pergamon Press for an extract from *The Masks of Hate* by David Holbrook; the McGraw-Hill Book Company for an extract from *Realms of Meaning* by P.H. Phenix; William Collins for two extracts from *Christian Reflections* by C.S. Lewis; the Merrill Press for an extract from an article by Jerome Bruner in *Sources for the Intellectual Foundations of Modern Education,* edited by W.E. Drake; and the Bodley Head for an extract from *Orthodoxy* by G.K. Chesterton.